The European Community
in World Affairs
Economic Power and Political Influence

The European Community

in World Affairs

WERNER J. FELD

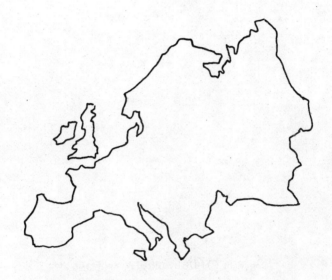

Economic Power
and
Political Influence

Printed in the United States of America

Library of Congress Cataloging in Publication Data

Feld, Werner J.
    The European community in world affairs.

    Bibliography: p. 76- 76444
    Includes index.
    1. European Economic Community. 2. European
Economic Community countries—Commercial policy.
I. Title.
HC241.2.F43   382'.9142   75-44209
ISBN 0-88284-040-1
ISBN 0-88284-037-1 pbk.

ACKNOWLEDGMENTS

Although the responsibility for the genesis and writing of this book are my own, I must share the credit for the actual existence of the work with many others. First, I must thank my students, who over the years have provided me with new vision and fresh perspectives with which to view our world. Second, many of my colleagues have commented on various parts of the work and I appreciate their help. I expressly want to thank Robert Jordan of the United Nations Institute, James Kuhlman of the University of South Carolina, and Robert Pfaltzgraf of the Foreign Policy Research Institute, all of whom read the manuscript and provided me with invaluable criticism. A special note of thanks is for Janet Davis of the University of New Orleans for typing the manuscript so carefully. And finally, I want to thank Irene Rubinson of Alfred who guided the work through its various production stages and John Stout, my editor.

CONTENTS

Preface

PREFACE

The purpose of this book is to examine and to analyze the impact and effects that a new economic colossus, the European Community (EC), has had and is likely to have on the world's economic and political relations. Clearly, the Community, which has grown from a limited experiment in regional integration into a major world power, has affected every nation of the globe either economically or politically. We will not limit our examination to the specific provisions contained in the three treaties underlying the EC for the conduct of external relations. In order to get a total picture of the Community's involvement in the international arena, we will also turn our attention to matters for which the EC organs have only peripheral responsibilities according to the treaties but which in the course of the Community's evolution have become foci of increasing global interest. Moreover, we will analyze the efforts made outside these treaties to coordinate the foreign policies of the member states and attempt to evaluate the effectiveness of these arrangements. Examples are the monetary policies of the Community and its member governments and their worldwide implications, the possible role of Euratom in the solution of the energy problem faced by the member states, and the issues associated with concerns of European security and with East–West negotiations in which the questions of transnational trade may engage the Community institutions in a meaningful role.

To fully understand the Community's impact on the current world pattern of economic and political power and influence, the book will briefly focus on the nature of the EC and then examine its competences for "foreign policy" making. This will be followed by a detailed analysis of the structures and procedures for external policy formulation and a discussion of some of the problems stemming from the complexities and the often very severe and conflicting pressures inherent in the EC decision-making processes. Here we will also examine the ad hoc frameworks created for the coordination of the member governments' foreign policies outside the Community system. Since it has become amply clear that the enlargement of the Community in 1973 has had and continues to have far-reaching implications for international interactions, chapter 3 will trace briefly the history of the efforts of Britain and other countries to join the Community and analyze the politics of enlargement from both inside and outside the Community. This will be followed by a chapter on the Community's association policy, which is of prime importance to the Third World and raises a number of questions. Is the EC policy designed primarily to aid the developing countries associated with the Community by providing better opportunities for their exports and financial assistance, or is this policy an instrument for expanding political influence? Will the end product of this policy be a division of the world in competing trading blocs or will the special trade preferences between the association partners be dismantled later to place all developing countries of the world on the same level of treatment? The next three chapters will focus on other aspects of the evolution of EC trade policies toward the industrially developed and developing countries of the Third World. This will give us an opportunity to analyze the transatlantic trade problems that have been a major source of the malaise and frictions that have developed over the last few years between the United States and the EC, and to which certain aspects of the EC association policy have contributed. We will also examine the Community's difficulties in controlling the trade relations with Communist countries and the efforts to develop uniform policies toward the Third World.

We have already mentioned the need to take a close look at the international monetary policies pursued by the EC members and it is in chapter 8 that we will deal with this issue. This chapter will also address itself to the energy problem that confronts the EC countries, including the part that Euratom plays in this crucial matter. Finally, it will focus on selected strategic problems of Community members such as a European nuclear force and the coordination of weapons procurement among the member states.

In the last chapter we will examine how far the aspirations of the EC member states to "speak with one voice" have been realized. This will involve an evaluation of the impact the Community has had on world affairs and of the effect that pressures emanating from the international arena may have had and are likely to have on the development of the Community. Some of these pressures emanate from the operations of American multinational corporations within the Community. Have all these pressures strengthened tendencies in Western Europe to move the Community toward a closer-knit political union or has the pursuit of conflicting foreign policy goals by the individual member governments of the EC brought about a gradual disintegration of the Community edifice? The danger of the partition of the world into competing blocs and the position of the United States in this situation will also be discussed. The chapter closes with an examination of the relations between the Community and the United States and the policies that need to be pursued by both to ensure a harmonious transatlantic relationship.

The
European
Community
in World Affairs

Economic Power and Political Influence

1

The European Community

An Emergent Power In World Politics?

Source: The European Community Information Service, Washington, D.C.

During the "Fanfare to Europe" celebrating Great Britain's entry into the European Community at the beginning of 1973, Prime Minister Edward Heath suggested that to be heard in the world, "Western Europe must speak with a single voice."[1] This statement was not original but had been expressed earlier by other leading statesmen of Western Europe. Since the enlargement of the Community from six to nine member states,[2] the cry for a single voice has been raised again from time to time, especially when outside powers, such as the United States, have engaged in policies thought to be harmful to the Community. Examples are the devaluation of the dollar in 1971 and 1973, which was eveatully seen as a threat to the exports of the member states, and the 1973 embargo on agricultural commodities needed badly by West European farmers.[3]

It has been argued that when faced with external pressures, the solidarity of the Community increases, and the potential for unification rises.[4] Without doubt, during the initial stages of the Community in the early 1950s the Soviet threat against Western Europe was an important factor bringing the original six members of the Community together and providing the essential trigger for the establishment of the European Coal and Steel Community (ECSC). However, the oil embargo imposed by the Arab oil-producing countries in the fall of 1973, which seriously threatened the economies of the Community member states, did not bring forth a uniform response to this threat, nor did it strengthen the solidarity among the Community members. On the contrary, the name of the game was "every man for himself." The result was that the larger Community countries, led by France and followed by Germany, Great Britain, and Italy, selfishly rushed their foreign ministers to the Middle East in order to obtain the best possible bilateral agreements, bartering the delivery of oil against shipment of arms and other goods from the individual countries. The poor Dutch, labeled "enemies" by

3

the Arab oil producers, were left in the lurch. Perhaps the most deplorable spectacle was the insistence of an "uninvited" delegation of Arab foreign ministers of the oil-producing countries that they be heard at the Summit Meeting of the Heads of State and of Government of the Community countries in Copenhagen in December 1973. It turned this meeting, designed to promote the unification process within the Community, into a circus in which the major actors were the Arab foreign ministers and not the chiefs of the Community Governments.[5]

Despite the oil fiasco the Community members had begun to speak with a single voice in some instances during 1973. This was done not only in economic affairs but even in security matters—the preparatory European Security Conference in Helsinki is an example. Nevertheless, it has become patently clear that the desire to speak with a single voice is an aspiration for the future rather than a reality. It is a vague aspiration, not a deeply held commitment. Nor can this aspiration be founded on the legal framework underlying the Community, that is, the Treaties of Paris and Rome.[6] But its realization would have to be based on a complex and often difficult coordination of the foreign policies of the nine member states.

In fact, the competences for the conduct of external relations that the Community treaties have assigned to the EC institutions, especially the Commission and the Council of Ministers, are relatively limited in scope and are primarily significant for trade matters and the affiliation of nonmember states. Yet to assure the full authority of the EC organs to carry out even these limited assignments has been a very laborious task and has necessitated a long struggle by the Commission, legally the main executive and administrative body. As we will see, this struggle continues as powerful political and bureaucratic forces in the member states persist in holding onto at least some of the traditional national prerogatives in the field of foreign trade policy. Nevertheless, the authority of the EC organs to conduct external relations has been fleshed out gradually, and with the enlargement of the Community from six to nine members in 1973 its impact on the international scene has expanded accordingly. And while this impact is foremost in the economic sphere, the line between international economics and politics has become increasingly blurred over the years and therefore the pertinent actions of the EC organs are likely to have political effects as well.

THE POWER OF THE ENLARGED COMMUNITY

In 1973 the geopolitical map of Western Europe was changed drastically. The six founding countries of the Community—France, Germany, Italy, Belgium, the Netherlands, and Luxembourg— were joined by three new members—the United Kingdom, Ireland, and Denmark. To this imposing and powerful nucleus were linked through free trade agreements seven other European countries—Austria, Finland, Iceland, Norway, Portugal, Sweden, and Switzerland—all either full or associated members of the European Free Trade Association (EFTA), which had been founded in 1959 under the leadership of Great Britain but now has almost lost its raison d'être.[7] Five more European countries —Greece, Turkey, Spain, Cyprus, and Malta—have been tied since 1961 to the Community through various kinds of special affiliation accords providing for preferential treatment for trade between these countries and the EC and other advantages for the affiliates. Some of these countries such as Greece and perhaps Spain may join the Community as full members, although this is not expected until the 1980s or later. Finally, a network of preferential trade agreements has been erected covering most countries bordering the Mediterranean and a large number of African countries below the Sahara. Originally most of these agreements were with colonies of the six founding countries of the EC, but they have been gradually expanded to include the Commonwealth areas of Africa, the Caribbean, and the western Pacific as well. Some of these agreements bestow not only preferences for exports of the developing countries, but also so-called reverse preferences for goods shipped by the member states of the EC to these countries.

Table 1.1 compares major elements of world power among the six founding countries of the EC, the nine present members, the United States, and the Soviet Union, and provides an

Table 1.1
Europe in the World Balance (1973)

	The Six[a]	The Nine	United States	Soviet Union
Population (millions)	196	260	210	249
GNP (1972) ($ billion)	721	902	1150	410.5[a]
Percent of world exports	29.8[b]	37.2[b]	11.9[b]	3.6
Percent of world imports	27.4[b]	35.6[b]	12.9[b]	3.7
Percent vote in IMF	17.7	29.1	21.5	not eligible
Public development aid ($ billion)	1.9	2.6	3.1	0.2-0.4 (est.)
Gold, SDRs, convertible currency reserves	37.9	43.9	13.19	n.a.
Defense expenditures, est. ($ billion)	26.3	34.3	80.0	39.8 (48.2 Warsaw Pact)
Regular armed forces	n.a.	2,075,000	3,160,000	3,305,000 (4,275,000 Warsaw Pact)

Source: *Vision,* no. 8/ 9 (July–August 1971): 38; Statistical Office of the European Communities, *Basic Statistics of the Community* (1974), pp. 73, 116; OECD, *Development Assistance* (1969 Review), p. 48; U.N. Statistical Office, *Yearbook of International Trade Statistics* (1973); U.S. Department of Commerce, *Survey of Current Business.*

a. Estimated net material product 1971.
b. Excludes trade with Communist countries in Asia.

impressive picture of the changing distribution of power in the international arena and of the new pattern of international transactions emerging as a consequence of the Community's enlargement. The first striking feature of this comparison is the rise in economic power that the enlarged Community has gained. With respect to population, Gross National Product (GNP), the share in world trade, and voting in the International Monetary Fund (IMF), the enlargement suggests increases ranging from 30 to 65 percent for the Community of Nine. In terms of population, the Nine exceeds the United States and the Soviet Union. However, the American GNP continues to be ahead of that of the Nine by a large margin. As far as world trade and commerce, the Nine will account for more than one-third of world exports and imports; even excluding intra-Community trade, their share exceeds that of the United States. The economic power of the Nine is also reflected in its voting strength in the IMF, which surpasses that of the United States by nearly 8 percent. With respect to gold, SDRs (Special Drawing Rights), and convertible currency reserves we should note that the Nine possessed over three times as much as the reserves available to the United States by the end of 1971, although this ratio appears to have improved since then in favor of the latter.

In terms of security politics, the Nine, however, must continue to look to the United States as the chief defender of the free world. Defense expenditures of the United States are more than twice as large as those of the Nine, and the number of military forces is more than 50 percent larger than that maintained by the enlarged Community. But the need for their own defenses may in fact not be very urgent for the Nine since the rough nuclear balance existing between the Soviet Union and the United States and the continued superiority of both countries vis-à-vis the Peoples' Republic of China are likely to assure peace in the forseeable future, just as this balance has been the chief guarantor of peaceful relations between the two superpowers in the past. Moreover, since the end of World War II the protection of Western Europe has been an essential part of American strategic security interests and the West European countries benefited automatically from the American defense umbrella without having to put up the full cost of their own defense.[8] However, the strategic dependence of the United States upon European real estate and manpower may have been lessened by the initial success of the Strategic Arms Limitations Talks (SALT) in 1972, the continuance of these bilateral negotiations with the Soviet Union, the enhanced flexibility of American strategic foreign policy as the result of President Nixon's visits to Moscow and Peking, and the clear interests of the Soviet Union and China to expand economic relations with the United States. Future successes in the European Security Conference negotiations in Helsinki and Geneva may also contribute to lowering the European and American concerns with military-strategic matters.[9] It is uncertain at this time whether such an event would justify the perception of a reduced Soviet threat to Western Europe, military or political,[10] but it cannot be stressed enough that the strong military posture of the United States and NATO has been a major incentive for the Soviet Union to move from lip service to "European security" to actual negotiations, especially with respect to the mutual and balanced reduction of military forces in West and East Europe. Nevertheless, under the present conditions for the reasons outlined above, the economic factor is likely to loom very large in international politics, and therefore the growing economic power of the enlarged Community may well emerge as a main element for changes in the international system, political changes that are likely to favor the position of the Nine at the expense of the United States.

THE REACH BEYOND
THE COMMUNITY BOUNDARIES

One of these changes is the alteration of the world trade patterns caused by the free trade agreements of the Community with the remaining EFTA countries and the numerous preferential accords in the fringe areas of Europe, the Mediterranean, and Africa. The elimination or the reduction of tariffs and other barriers to the flow of trade cannot but have beneficial effects on exports and imports between the Community and its affiliates, and at the same time lead to diversions of trade adversely affecting nonaffiliated third countries. While in some cases the monetary value of these diversions may not be very significant, the total impact on third countries can be considerable. If we combine the European Community of the Six and all the countries with which it had preferential agreements (including associations) by the end of 1972, more than $13.4 billion (1974 figures) of U.S. exports were subject to some kind of discrimination in favor of EC suppliers and producers. These exports constituted 16 percent of total U.S. exports. If we add to this area the three new EC member states, the EFTA countries with which free trade agreements have been concluded, and the Commonwealth countries in Africa and the Caribbean that were promised associated status should they so desire, the value of American exports subject to discrimination would rise to nearly $24 billion (1974 figures). This amounts to nearly 28 percent of total U.S. exports.[11] While the trade figures by the time that all these free trade areas and affiliates have become fully operative are likely to be higher, the percentages are apt to remain the same. These percentage figures present a dramatic illustration of the dilemma the nonmember countries of the world face as the result of the growing economic influence that the enlarged Community will be able to exert on world affairs.

This influence also has political implications, which need to be noted. Despite occasional complaints by the affiliated developing countries that one feature or another of the affiliation agreements is unsatisfactory, the governments of these countries are pleased with the benefits they receive from the Community, which in most cases include monetary grants from the European Development Fund (EDF) for specific projects. As a result, an increasingly close relationship has evolved between many developing countries and the Community, which in turn has produced a very subtle climate of political dependency. Foreign aid grants from the EDF, reinforced by national aid measures of the member governments of the Community, as well as specific trade benefits can always be used to extract in a very unobtrusive manner occasional political concessions from the affiliates. The stage is thus set for the creation of an expanding and

9

deepening sphere of political influence in the Mediterranean and Africa, areas of growing strategic importance in the world. At the same time, the shining image that the United States used to project toward the developing countries of the world as the result of the large amounts of foreign aid given previously has been tarnished by the reduction of funds voted in Congress. As a consequence, American foreign aid, which, as Table 1.1 shows, was already in 1970 nearly matched in magnitude by the public development aid of the Nine despite the much larger GNP of the United States, won't be able to contribute to halting the bandwagon effect generated by the expanding economic power of the Community in the minds of many governmental leaders in the Third World.

The political potential of the monetary prowess of the Nine to influence world politics, although not always easily discernible for the average citizen, is nevertheless considerable. President Nixon's initial plans for drastic changes in the international monetary and trade fields announced on August 15, 1971, involving the imposition of a 10 percent surcharge on imports into the United States and forcing the revaluation of other currencies without actual devaluation of the dollar, had to be abandoned or modified at least in part by the unified pressure of the Community member governments.[12] In the elaboration of a new global monetary system, the Community governments will play an influential role that will restrict American options in a field that had been an area of clear U.S. dominance since 1945. Although the Community objective of returning to a fixed exchange rate system with only very narrow fluctuations has not yet been achieved, and IMF decisions in September 1975 have greatly diminished the role of gold so cherished by the French, the monetary power of the enlarged Community will nevertheless increasingly affect the global arena.

THE NATURE OF THE COMMUNITY

Before entering into a detailed examination of the international policies and activities of the EC, it may be useful for the full comprehension of its growing power to make a few observations about the nature of the Community. In terms of political science and international law, the ECSC, EEC, and Euratom, making up the Community, are international inter-governmental organizations (IGOs) that were created by the founding six member governments to attain certain goals such as continuous and balanced economic expansion and accelerated rise in the standard of living in the member states, and which now operate under the unified management of one Commission and one Council of Ministers with the primarily consultative assistance of the European Parliament and the Economic and Social Council.[13] Functionally, the Common Market may be viewed as an incipient political system through which the re-sources and energies of a regional society are mobilized for the pursuit of these goals and which possesses the necessary mecha-nism to process the wants and demands of this society into appropriate decisions and policies.[14] For the achievement of these purposes the organs of the Community, especially the Commission and the Council of Ministers, have been endowed by the EC Treaties with a number of powers usually exercised only by the governments of sovereign states. These powers are frequently referred to as "supranational" and suggest a volun-tary limitation of the normal sovereignty possessed by the member states. Some of these powers lie in the field of foreign economic policy and permit the Community organs to define and shape the trade and other economic relations between the EC and nonmember states. Considering the fact that trade with nonmember states accounts for approximately 60 percent of the total export trade of the member states—in other words, it is larger than intra-Community trade—the magnitude of the responsibility and authority assigned by the EC Treaties to the Community organs in the area of foreign economic policy becomes evident.

The decision-making process involved in the formulation and implementation of economic policy for the relations with third countries is clear-cut and relatively simple on paper, but it is highly complex in practice. The main official actors in this pro-cess on the "European" level are the Commission and the Coun-cil of Ministers, chief organs of the Community; however, an institution barely mentioned in the EC Treaties, the Committee of Permanent Representatives, consisting of the ambassadors of the nine member states supported by their not inconsiderable staffs, also plays a very significant part. Minor roles are played by other organs of the Community such as the European Parliament and the Economic and Social Committee. Since the formulation of foreign economic policy often involves the accommodation and arbitration of conflicting private economic interests, important national interest groups in the member states affected by the decisions of the official actors are eager to participate in the decision-making process. Although there is much argument about the influence that interest groups have on the formulation of a state's foreign policy, it is safe to assume that in the realm of economic policy such groups are more influential than in the determination of national security policy involving vital state interests. Thus national economic interest groups in the member states and the umbrella organizations they have formed on the "European" level must be regarded as unofficial actors who seek to make their influence felt in the shaping of Community policy toward nonmember countries.

THE MEANING OF
COMMUNITY "FOREIGN POLICY" MAKING

We would like to close this chapter with some comments about the capacity of the Community to engage in "foreign" relations as derived from the legal nature of the EC. The member states have conferred legal status upon the ECSC, the EEC, and Euratom, and as a consequence each of these entities possesses legal capacity to act in its own name under international law on the international plane. While we therefore can say that the Community as a collective body can exercise legal rights and assume legal obligations in the international arena, does this mean that this capacity equals that of a nation-state, recognized as the predominant unit under international law?

The state is a creation of man just as IGOs are. Through centuries of custom and usage certain rights and duties have been ascribed to states so consistently that they are considered as flowing from the very definition of statehood. States are thus capable of concluding international agreements, can send and receive diplomatic missions, are able to bring claims before international tribunals, and can be held liable for their acts under international law. IGOs are much more recent in origin; yet since the beginning of the twentieth century they have acted increasingly as entities in carrying on international relations, separate and distinct from the states that are their members. In this capacity they have met in a satisfactory manner the needs of the international community. However, since IGOs are not entities identical to states and since they vary in function and purpose, the extent of their international legal personality must be determined in each case by an analysis of their individual functions, purposes, and powers.[15] As a consequence, the extent of the competences the Community as a legal entity possesses for its relations with nonmember states is determined both by the express provisions in the EC Treaties and by the concrete purposes and functions assigned to the three individual communities. Care must be taken, however, that powers that might be inferred from this evaluation of purposes and functions are not contradicted by explicit treaty clauses. In practice, moreover, the exercise of formal powers may be partially or completely obstructed by hostile political actions or attitudes of one or several member governments.

The Court of Justice of the European Communities has expressed itself on this subject in a landmark decision in 1971.[16] The Court stated:

> To determine in a particular case the Community's authority to enter into international agreements, one must have regard to the whole scheme of the Treaty no less than to its specific provisions. Such authority may arise not only from an explicit grant by the Treaty but may equally flow from other provisions of the Treaty and from steps taken, within the framework of those provisions, by the Community institutions.

> Each time the Community, with a view to implementing a common policy, envisaged by the Treaty, lays down common rules, the member-States no longer have the right, acting individually or even collectively, to contract obligations towards non-member States affecting those rules.

13

Where the Community has authority to negotiate and conclude a treaty in pursuance of a common Community policy, this excludes the possibility of a concurrent authority on the part of member-States, since any initiative taken outside the framework of the common institutions would be incompatible with the unity of the Common Market and the uniform application of Community law.[17]

If the Community were to move from its present organizational status as a unique supranational IGO to a genuine federal system, something to which many supporters of European unification aspire, foreign policy making as well as defense matters would have to come under the exclusive control of the central government.[18] However, as we have already suggested, the formulation and execution of foreign policy are traditionally the most jealously guarded spheres of national sovereignty. Therefore, the bold but necessary step of the drafters of the Community Treaties to transfer certain, though rather limited, foreign policy making powers from the national governments to the Community organs has understandably created tensions and stress in the Community system. Conflicts are likely to arise when, in the view of member governments, the attainment of broad, important policy goals requires the use of economic foreign policy instruments such as trade or commercial agreements to offer or induce special concessions, and the availability of such instruments is found to be restricted by the obligatory transfer of certain segments of foreign policy making to the Community. Conflicts may also be generated by the difficulty of drawing a clear line between the area of economic policy and national security policy. Finally, if one considers that the establishment of the three Communities was in itself a manifestation of the foreign policies of the member governments in the pursuit of prominent, long-range national goals, one can readily realize the complexity of the interaction and coordination between the foreign policies of the member states and the development of a distinct economic "foreign" policy of the Community as a separate organization. To sort out these complexities and discuss the competing structures for the Community's foreign policy is the topic of the next chapter.

NOTES

1. *The Times* (London), January 3, 1973.

2. France, Germany, Great Britain, Italy, Belgium, Denmark, Ireland, the Netherlands, and Luxembourg. In fact, in a technical sense, there is not one, but three European Communities—the European Coal and Steel Community (ECSC), created by the Treaty of Paris in 1951 and entering into force in 1952; and the European Economic Community (EEC) and European Atomic Energy Community (Euratom), set up by the Treaties of Rome in 1957 and becoming operational in 1958. However, for convenient shorthand, it is appropriate to refer to only the European Community (EC), which has become common usage.

3. See *International Herald Tribune,* July 17, 1973, pp. 3, 4; and *L'Independant* (Perpignan, France), July 13, 1973, p. 1. It is somewhat ironic that it was President Pompidou who urged the first official U.S. dollar devaluation in December 1971 on a seemingly reluctant President Nixon. The Community leaders also accepted the second devaluation in February 1973 as proper, but then especially France began to see the continuing slide of the dollar as a purposeful U.S. policy to aid U.S. exports.

4. For example, see Gerhard Mally, *The European Community in Perspective: The New Europe, the United States and the World* (Lexington, Mass.: Heath, 1973), pp. 51-68.

5. See *Agence Europe Bulletin,* December 19, 1973; January 11, 17/18, 1974 for details.

6. See footnote 2.

7. For more details see Michael Curtis, *Western European Integration* (New York: Harper & Row, 1965), pp. 238-247.

8. For the intriguing relationship between benefactors and beneficiaries of military defense see John Gerard Ruggie, "Collective Goods and Future International Collaboration," *American Political Science Review* 66, no. 3 (September 1972): 874-893.

9. Without doubt these negotiations will drag on for years just as it took four years to reach the first successes in the SALT talks. At the same time, the reduced dependence of the United States on European real estate and manpower for its security may spur the EC member states to greater cooperative efforts for a purely European defense capability. This will be discussed in more detail in chapter 8.

10. Former Prime Minister Heath seemed to express such doubts during a television interview in the United States on February 4. See *International Herald Tribune,* February 5, 1973, p. 3.

11. OECD, *Statistics for Foreign Trade* (May 1975).

12. Cf. Harald B. Malmgren, *International Economic Peacekeeping in Phase II* (New York: Quadrangle, 1972), pp. 1-15, 230-234.

13. The Commission consists of thirteen members of whom no more than three can be of the same nationality. Once appointed, they become independent of the member states and are to represent only the Community interest. Since July 1, 1967, the Commission is not only the executive body of the EEC, but also of the European Coal and Steel Community (ECSC), and the European Atomic Energy Community (Euratom). Prior to that date each Community had its own executive body.

The Council is composed of one minister from each of the member governments; depending on the subject matter to be discussed, the minister attending a meeting may be the foreign minister, the minister of agriculture, the minister of economics, or any other minister who might be concerned with the matter under consideration. The Council has a dual function: It represents the national interests of the member states, but it also functions to advance the interest of the Community as a unit.

14. These concepts are those of David Easton as formulated in *A Systems Analysis of Political Life* (New York: Wiley, 1965), p. 153, where a political system is defined as "a set of interactions through which valued things are authoritatively allocated for a society." See also pp. 57-69, 158-229.

15. For a brief discussion of various legal theories regarding the external powers of the international organizations, a highly controversial area, see Werner Feld, "The Competences of the European Communities for the Conduct of External Relations," *Texas Law Review* 43, no. 6 (July 1965): 891-926. See also the profound analysis of Pierre Pescatore, "Les Relations extérieures des Communautés Européennes," *Recueil des Cours de l'Academie de Droit International,* 103 (1961): 5-244.

16. Re—The European Road Transport Agreement: *EC Commission* v. *EC Council* (Case 22/70) in *Common Market Law Reports* (1971, Part 50), pp. 335 ff.

17. Ibid., p. 335.

18. Cf. K. C. Wheare, *Federal Government,* 4th ed. (New York: Oxford University Press, 1964), pp. 169-208, who considers the exercise of exclusive foreign policy and defense functions by the central government as one of the main characteristics of a true federal system.

2

The Competences, Structures, and Procedures for External Policy Formulation and Implementation

The specific competences for the conduct of external relations inserted into the three Community Treaties are unevenly distributed. In view of the important role that trade plays between the Community and nonmember states, and considering the EEC Treaty's long-range goal of integrating the economics of the member states, the most significant competences are found in the EEC Treaty. Especially in the field of commercial policy the authority assigned to the Community organs by this treaty is relatively broad. Also strongly affecting the international trade relations of the EC is the capability of Community institutions to negotiate association agreements with third countries. The competences for such agreements are contained in both the EEC and Euratom Treaties, but it has been particularly under the EEC Treaty that these provisions have assumed their far-reaching significance.

In contrast to the EEC Treaty, the organs of the Coal and Steel Community have not been granted any significanct authority by the ECSC Treaty to formulate and execute a common commercial policy toward nonmember countries. As a result of this divergence between the two treaties, the important economic sector of coal and steel is excluded from the common policies that may be developed by the EEC organs. However, a strong obligation for the coordination of this sector with other external economic policies exists by virtue of the very fact that the member states have concluded the later EEC Treaty and have inserted into this treaty the responsibility and authority of the Community organs to develop a common commercial policy. We should note that the merger of the High Authority, the executive organ of the ECSC, and the EEC and Euratom Commissions into a unified Commission on July 1, 1967,[1] has not changed this situation because this body must operate under the rules of the treaty that applies to the subject matter under consideration. Only a fusion of the three Communities through appropriate changes in the underlying treaties will fully solve the problem. Fusion is not anticipated in the foreseeable future.

Before discussing in greater length the competences for external relations stipulated in the EEC Treaty, some comments must be made about the "foreign policy" powers in the Euratom Treaty. These powers primarily serve the purpose of supporting the research and technological missions of the Euratom organization and therefore are rather limited. They are designed to help in the solution of problems confronting Euratom in the utilization and development of nuclear energy. For this reason the framers of the Euratom Treaty declared in article 2(h) that the Community shall "establish with other countries and with international organizations any contacts likely to promote progress in the peaceful uses of nuclear energy."[2]

In order to enable the Community to coordinate its external relations and to formulate and execute a common policy in the peaceful use of nuclear energy, article 106 requires those member states that had concluded agreements with third countries for cooperation in the nuclear field prior to the entry into force of the Euratom Treaty to enter into necessary negotiations with these countries for the purpose of transferring to the Community, "as far as possible," the rights and obligations arising from these agreements. It should be noted that the member states have not complied with the procedures prescribed by article 106 and that a number of individual nuclear energy agreements with third countries continue to exist.[3]

With regard to new agreements by the member states, the Euratom Treaty also imposes certain restrictions upon the freedom of action of the member governments in order to ensure a uniform Community policy. Euratom article 103 requires the member states to submit to the Commission the draft of any agreement that they intend to conclude with a third country, an international organization, or a national of a third country, if such an agreement concerns to any extent the field of application of the Euratom Treaty. In the event that the draft of such an agreement contains clauses that might impede the application of the treaty, the Commission may raise objections to the conclusion of the contemplated agreement. In that case, the member state concerned has a choice. It can either attempt to remove the objections of the Commission, or it can petition the Court of the European Communities for a ruling on the compatability of the proposed draft with the provisions of the Euratom Treaty. If the advisory opinion of the court is negative, the state cannot conclude the agreement unless it has been modified in accordance with the opinion rendered by the court.[4]

The injunctions on the treaty-making power of the member states contained in articles 106 and 103 point up the importance of bestowing upon the Community the power[5] of concluding agreements with third countries, international organizations, and a national of a third country "within the limits of its competence." In view of the highly technical and specialized nature of the Euratom Treaty, only a relatively small segment of the economic life in the member states is affected by the treaty-making power of the Euratom Community organs. Specifically, under the Euratom Treaty the European Community can conclude agreements for the purpose of exchanging scientific or industrial information on nuclear matters.[6] It can enter into agreements with third countries, international organizations, and nationals of a third country regarding their participation in the financing and management of joint enterprises in the field of nuclear energy.[7] The Community, through its supply agency established under the Treaty, has the exclusive right of concluding conventions that have as their principal object the importation of fissionable materials and appropriate ores from outside the territory of the member states. Finally, it can make agreements concerning measures of safety and security with respect to fissionable materials and nuclear fuels.[8]

THE COMMON COMMERCIAL POLICY

The main clause providing the Community institutions with the authority to engage in foreign economic policy is article 113 of the EEC Treaty. It stipulates that after the transitional period (1958–69) had expired, a common commercial policy toward third countries based on uniform principles was to be instituted "particularly in regard to tariff amendments, the conclusion of tariff or trade agreements, the alignment of measures of liberalization, export policy and protective commercial measures including measures to be taken in cases of dumping and subsidies." The enumeration of activities in article 113 is not exhaustive. Therefore, measures such as the regulation of export and import prices, the establishment of import and export quotas, the stipulation of conditions for export transactions, the issuance of currency regulations for commercial transaction with nonmember states, matters concerned with tourist trade, and perhaps others also seem to fall under the competence of the Community organs. Not covered, however, are such matters as exchange rates for the currencies of the member states, balance of payments problems, and policies regarding economic trends, because special provisions of the EC Treaties govern these subjects.

Prior to the expiration of the transitional period, the Community organs possessed only a limited competence in the field of external commercial policy. Article 111 of the EEC Treaty required the member states to coordinate their commercial relations with nonmember countries so that proper conditions could be created for the future implementation of a common policy for external trade. Specifically, the member states were obligated to adjust their tariff agreements with nonmember countries in order not to delay the institution of a common external tariff for the Community at a later date. Coordination by the member states was also required for the reduction and abolition of quantitative restrictions on trade with nonmember countries. Uniform lists of liberalization applying not only to the import and export of goods but also to the transfer of payments were to be drawn up by the member states. Finally, in order to prevent distortion of competition between enterprises in the member states, the EEC Treaty specifies in article 112 that before the end of the transitional period the member states were to progressively harmonize their subsidy measures for exports to nonmember countries.

It was anticipated by the treaty framers that the implementation of the common commercial policy toward third countries could at times cause economic difficulties for the Common Market members when disparities in the execution of commercial policy measures by the various member governments arose or diversions of trade were produced. If such difficulties should appear in the economy of one or more member states, the Commission may, according to article 115, recommend methods whereby the other states provide the necessary cooperative assistance. In the event that these methods fail to remedy the problem, the Commission may authorize the states involved to take specified protective measures such as temporary changes in tariff rates or interim restrictions of imports. The member states have made extensive use of these protection measures, especially with respect to products coming from countries with very low wages or state-operated foreign trade, the usual method in Communist states.

Another unfortunate consequence of the implementation of the Community commercial policy might be difficulties in a member state's balance of payments. If such difficulties are likely to prejudice the functioning of the Common Market or the progressive establishment of the common commercial policy, article 108 requires the Community organs to organize "mutual assistance" operations in the form of concerted action in international organizations, the provision of limited credits, or special trade measures.

THE COMMON EXTERNAL TARIFF (CET)

An essential ingredient for the creation of a customs union, upon which the Community is based, is the erection of a common external tariff toward the outside world. As Leon Lindberg observes, "it is the fundamental instrument of trade and external policies of the Community."[9] The basic means for reconciling the relatively high tariffs of France and Italy with those of the low-tariff countries, Germany and the Benelux states, was the utilization of the arithmetical average of the duties applied in the four customs territories within the Community. The duties to be taken into account for calculating this average were in general those applied by the member states on January 1, 1957. This method of ascertaining the CET conformed to the requirement of the General Agreement on Tariffs and Trade (GATT) that the level of this tariff be no higher than the "general incidence" of the national tariffs of the member states. Meeting this requirement was essential for the Community to obtain the necessary exemption from the application of the most-favored-nation clause, a basic GATT principle, which imposes on each GATT member country the obligation of extending to other members the lowest tariff extended to any third country.

Several exceptions to the basic method of computing the CET are found in a number of lists appended to the EEC Treaty.[10] In addition, the Council of Ministers is authorized to set tariff quotas at reduced rates of duty or duty free for individual member states, when the Commission finds that certain supplies traditionally imported from nonmember states are short in the Community. However, such quotas can be granted only if there is no damage to the interests of the other states.

The original schedule specified by the treaty for the introduction of the CET set January 1, 1962, the end of the first stage of the transition period, as the target date for the completion of the tariff. But the CET was 97 percent completed nearly two years before this date when in March 1960 agreement was reached in the Council on most tariff items.

The completion of the CET did not signify that its duties were to apply immediately for all imports into the Community; rather the CET was to be used as a guideline toward which the four individual tariffs were to be either lowered or increased in three stages beginning on January 1, 1962. By the end of the transition period in 1970, the CET was to be applied exclusively. If member states met with special difficulties in implementing the CET according to schedule, they could be authorized by the Commission to postpone for a limited time the raising or lowering of duties.

Several reasons, such as charges of protectionism and discrimination against the Community's tariff policy and the prospect of a speeded-up reduction of internal tariffs within the Community, induced the Community authorities to begin the progressive adjustments of the four individual tariff schedules toward the CET in January 1961, a year earlier than that specified in the EEC Treaty. The second alignment was made two and a half years ahead of schedule, on July 1, 1963, and the full implementation of the CET took place on July 1, 1968, the date when all internal tariffs were eliminated.

TREATY-MAKING POWER

Probably the strongest reason for approximating the international legal personality of an IGO such as the EEC to that of a sovereign state is the capacity of that organization to conclude treaties with nonmember states and other international organizations. The treaty-making power, in turn, is one of the most important instruments for the implementation of foreign policy. Several provisions of the EEC Treaty (among them the authority for the negotiation and conclusion of agreements to implement the common commercial policy) explicitly bestow treaty-making powers on the Community organizations.

The negotiations for a tariff agreement with nonmember states are conducted by the Commission, which requires an authorization or mandate from the Council to begin negotiations. The Commission may submit recommendations regarding the opening and substance of negotiations, but the Council can also act on its own and ask the Commission to commence the negotiation of an agreement. The Commission is not legally obligated to comply with such a request, but for political reasons the Commission may be well advised to follow the wishes of the Council.

In the conduct of the negotiations, the Commission must follow the directives issued by the Council and consult with a special Committee appointed by the Council, called "Committee 113," because its employment is stipulated in article 113 of the EEC Treaty.[11] This Committee is composed of national officials of the member states who, depending on the nature of the particular negotiations, may come from the foreign, economic, or agricultural ministries. The Commission is not required to seek the consent of this Committee for specific actions in the negotiations; all it needs to do is to establish rapport with the Committee in order to enable that body to perform its supervising and possible influencing function for the Council. In practice, however, the members of the Committee are quite influential and often are bound by and carry out specific instructions of their governments.

The agreements negotiated by the Commission are concluded by the Council on behalf of the Community, for which a qualified majority vote is sufficient.[12] Properly concluded agreements with third countries bind not only the EEC as an intergovernmental organization, but also the member states. In other words, for the member states the effect is the same as if they themselves had concluded the agreement with the third countries.[13]

The exact scope of the treaty-making power of the Community organizations is not specified in the EEC Treaty but since this authority is contained in the same provisions that apply to the development of a common commercial policy, the assumption seems to be justified that all matters falling within the scope of the common policy may also be the proper subjects for bilateral or multilateral commercial agreements between the EC and nonmember states. Thus these agreements may include the fixing of quotas, trade liberalization matters, the determination of measures to be taken in cases of dumping or subsidies, the issuance of currency regulations for commercial transactions with nonmember states, and possibly also guidance for tourist trade. Some observers, however, consider this interpretation of the Community's treaty-making powers too broad. They hold that it is primarily the principles of policy that are under the control of the Community organs and that, as a consequence, the conclusion of any concrete and detailed agreements remains in the hands of the member states. Although this interpretation appears to contravene the spirit and purpose of the EEC Treaty, it may well be preferred by the member governments.[14]

ASSOCIATION AGREEMENTS

In terms of impact on international politics, perhaps the most significant treaty-making power of the Community is the ability to enter into agreements of association with nonmember states, "unions" of such states, and international organizations. Article 238 of the EEC Treaty, authorizing the creation of associations, stipulates only that they must embody "reciprocal rights and obligations, joint actions and special procedures." There are no geographic limitations for associate countries; in other words, they may be located anywhere in the world. For agreements leading to an association the Council of Ministers must act unanimously at all times, that is, both during and after the transitional period. As in the case of tariff and commercial agreements the Commission conducts the negotiations for an association; in the performance of this task it must follow the directives of the Council and consult with Committee 113. Prior to the conclusion of the agreement, the Council is obligated to consult the European Parliament, but the advice of the Parliament is not binding.[15]

In the most general terms the objective of an association agreement is the creation of a relationship exceeding that which can be attained by the conclusion of a tariff or commercial accord, but falling short of full membership. Although the Treaty does not furnish a definition of the objectives, certain possibilities come to mind. For an association with the Community that is based on the concept of a customs union, a first objective might be the extension of this union to include the associated state or states. For European countries wishing to join the Community as full members, but unable to fulfill the economic conditions for accession, the establishment of a customs union by the association agreement may serve a secondary purpose—preparation for full membership. Another objective of an association with the Community may be the creation of a free trade area, in which case the customs duties between the Community and the associated country will be abolished but no common external tariff will be established. Under the provisions of GATT both customs unions and free trade areas may qualify under certain conditions for exemptions from the terms of the most-favored-nation clause. Long-range objectives of all association agreements may be the raising of living standards and economic levels in the associated countries.[16]

27

In its reference to the embodiment of "joint actions and procedures" in an association agreement, the EEC Treaty recognizes the need for institutions and well-defined methods to operate the associations between the Community and the associated countries. An institutional structure is essential if the often far-reaching activities that the association agreements specify are to be carried out properly. Moreover, the institutional framework is one of the distinguishing features that differentiates an association agreement from a mere tariff, trade, or commercial agreement.

The central institution of all association agreements concluded so far is the Council of Association. It is the top-level forum for consultation and decision making for the association partners, although the specific competences vary from agreement to agreement. All the EEC associations also have an Association Committee, which takes care of all routine matters for the Council. Since the Council meets only infrequently, the Association Committee supplies the continuity necessary for the smooth operation of the association arrangement. When preparing the work of the Council sessions, the details of many important decisions are hammered out in these Committees. Additional institutions are parliamentary association bodies consisting of equal numbers of delegates from the European Parliament and from the parliaments of the associated states, and adjudicational groups—either a special arbitration tribunal or the Court of the European Communities—to settle disputes between the association partners.

Since the association agreements are based on international law treaties concluded by equal partners, the principles of bilateralism and parity must characterize the institutional structure and must be controlling elements in the administration of the associations. At the same time, since the EC as a legal unit is now, and may be in the future, a partner in several associations, the autonomy of the Community decision-making process must be safeguarded in the same way as a sovereign government would want to retain its freedom of action in arriving at decisions. Thus it seems that the associated countries can not demand to participate in the internal decision-making process of the Community organs on matters affecting the association; rather, their participation must be confined to the decision making in the institutions especially constituted for the operation of the association. Otherwise, the Community's freedom of action would be considerably impeded since a relatively large number of countries have joined the Community under various association agreements. By not limiting the decision making power of the associated countries, association could become tantamount to full membership.

ADMISSION TO FULL MEMBERSHIP

Admission to Community membership may also constitute an important subject of Community foreign policy. According to article 23 of the EEC Treaty[17] any European state may apply for membership in the Community, but the term "European state" is not to be construed in too narrow a geographic sense. As a consequence, Turkey is considered to be a European state, although the greater part of its territory is located in Asia. On the other hand, Israel cannot be regarded as European because it lacks any geographic connection with Europe, although much of its population has European roots.

To ensure the smooth adjustment of the new member state into the existing Community system, important economic and essential political conditions must be met by the applicant country. First, the level of economic development in the prospective member state must be roughly equal to that of the current Community members. Otherwise, the broad, economic equilibrium necessary for continued successful economic integration might be upset and serious problems encountered eventually by the Community as a whole. The lower level of economic development in Italy has cast repeated shadows over the Community's operations. Secondly, the political system in the applicant state has to be congenial to that prevailing in the Community. This means that applicant countries must be committed in a broad sense to democratic ideals and that their governments follow practices that are ultimately responsive to the wishes of their populations. It implies periodic elections and shifts in governments and their policies in accordance with the wishes of the people as expressed by their votes.

The procedure for accession requires that an application be addressed to the Council, which is to act by unanimous vote after obtaining the opinion of the Commission. No consultation of the European Parliament is necessary, but the Council and Commission can avail themselves of such consultation if they deem it advisable. On the basis of a favorable decision by the Council, negotiations between the member states and the applicant are to be conducted to determine the conditions of admission and the necessary adaptation of the Treaty to the new situation. For example, the distribution of weighted votes among the member states in the Council of Ministers has to be altered to reflect the increased membership. Similar changes must also be made for the European Parliament, the Economic and Social Committee, the annual contribution to the Community budget, the Social Fund, and the European Investment Bank.[18] The size of the Commission, the Parliament, the Court of Justice, and other collective bodies has to be considered. Such changes were made when Great Britain, Ireland, and Denmark joined the Community as full members. Since the resulting agreement alters the existing Treaty, it requires ratification by all the contracting states in accordance with their respective constitutional rules.[19]

In contrast to association, admission to membership carries with it by definition the assumption of rights and obligations equal to those of the original member states. Nevertheless, it is conceivable that for a limited period the admission agreement may permit a differential treatment for the new member in order to ensure an orderly transition in such critical fields as agriculture and the adjustment of various industries to the common external tariff. However, the eventual full assumption of treaty rights and obligations is imperative and it is for this reason that a neutral state such as Austria has been reluctant to petition for admission and has preferred to seek associate status in order to ensure its continued neutrality.

RELATIONS WITH INTERNATIONAL
INTERGOVERNMENTAL ORGANIZATIONS

During the last few decades international intergovernmental organizations have assumed an increasing importance on the world scene. For the foreign policy of a state, participation as a member of major global or regional IGOs has become an essential instrument of policy; in some cases merely to be an observer is regarded as being of considerable significance. The Community, itself a collective IGO, also requires a variety of contacts with other IGOs in order to safeguard and promote its interests. Hence the EC Treaties contain explicit provisions with respect to Community relations with those IGOs with which cooperation is likely to be profitable.

The most specific of the provisions, article 229 of the EEC Treaty,[20] stipulates that the Commission is responsible for ensuring all "suitable" contacts with the organs of the United Nations, its specialized agencies, and with GATT. Beyond that, the Commission also has the task of engaging in "appropriate" contacts with other IGOs.

"Suitable" contacts are those involving the exchange of information or the dispatch of observers; they are concerned primarily with technical matters. The term "appropriate" contact appears to suggest that it must be useful for the Community. Obviously, organizations of an economic nature fall into this category, but, beyond that, it is not inconceivable that relations with organizations of a general political character may also be beneficial.

While the Commission is obligated to assume contacts with international organizations, other Community organs are not excluded from maintaining, within the context of their functions, whatever contacts may be appropriate. For example, the Court of Justice of the Communities may have connections with the International Court of Justice at the Hague; and the European Parliament may have a special liaison arrangement with the Assembly of the Western European Union. Moreover, even though the Commission has the responsibility for contacts with international organizations, the Council has a voice in determining the advisability, procedure, and nature of such links.[21]

Two IGOs have been given special treatment by the EEC Treaty. These are, understandably, the Council of Europe and the Organization for Economic Cooperation and Development (OECD), formerly the Organization for European Economic Cooperation (OEEC). According to articles 230 and 231 in the EEC Treaty,[22] the Community as a whole, not just the Commission, must establish close collaboration and cooperation with the two organizations. This seems to indicate that the relationship with these organizations is considered to be on a broader basis than that with the United Nations, its specialized agencies, or any other international organization. However, beginning in 1974 the Community began to play a more significant role in U.N. affairs when the General Assembly approved U.N. observer status for the EC. Indeed, during the Seventh U.N. General Assembly Special Session to examine practical approaches to economic aid for the developing countries, the Community representatives assumed a leadership position for the Nine. They put forward common positions for the member states throughout the discussions, even sometimes on questions outside the Community's field of competence.[23] After observer status was received, the Community made a special contribution of $150 million to the U.N. Special Fund for developing countries hardest hit by rising food and oil prices.

The Commission's task of establishing suitable or appropriate contacts with other international organizations has been interpreted as including the authority to conclude agreements of a technical or administrative nature, either with the organization as a whole or with one of its organs. Most arrangements provide for exchange of information, reciprocal authorization for observers to attend the respective meetings of the parties to the arrangement, and the creation of joint working groups of experts to study certain technical matters.[24]

Beyond this limited authority of the Commission, the Community can also conclude formal agreements involving action by the Council and following the usual procedures for the exercise of the Community's treaty-making power. Moreover, the member states themselves, without action of the Community organs, may arrange for participation of Community institutions in the activities of international organizations. An example is the participation of the EEC Commission in the work of the OECD, which is regulated by the Convention establishing the OECD, signed in Paris in December 1960 and by Supplementary Protocol No. 1 attached to this Convention. Only the member states, not the Council of Ministers representing the Common Market, are signatories to this Convention.

Finally, according to article 238 of the EEC Treaty, the Community organs can also conclude agreements with IGOs and "unions of states." The term "union of states" refers to multilateral conventions such as GATT or economic and customs unions that may represent a close tie between a number of countries without taking the shape of formal organizations.

The general obligation of the member states to act in concert with each other and with the EC organs and to refrain from measures likely to jeopardize the attainment of the treaty objectives is given special impetus by treaty provisions governing the actions of the member states in IGOs of an economic nature. According to article 116 of the EEC Treaty the member governments can proceed in matters of particular interest to the functioning of the Common Market only by concerted and uniform action. As a consequence, the member governments are deprived of their freedom of action in economic IGOs insofar as such actions may affect the unified market operations of the Community.

How is such common action to be organized? A delegate of one of the member governments may be requested to act as spokesman for the Nine. Usually this delegate would come from the country that occupies the chair in the Council of Ministers, but in exceptional cases where the interests of one member state are particularly affected, a delegate from that state may be selected to act as spokesman for the whole group. Another possibility is the selection of a Commission member to act as spokesman for the member governments.

It should be emphasized that although the EC may establish and maintain a variety of relations with other international organizations, it does not become a member of these organizations nor does it act for the collectivity of the member states. Rather, the governments of the member states retain their positions in these organizations but their activities require close coordination and cooperation.

Table 2.1
Community External Relations Structure

Commission of the European Communities

Directorate General I (External Affairs)	Directorate General VIII (Development and Cooperation)
Directorate A — Internal Organizations	*Directorate A* — General Affairs and Primary Products
Directorate B — North America, Australia, New Zealand, South Africa; Commercial questions with respect to Agriculture; Protocol; External Offices	*Directorate B* — Trade and Development
Directorate C — Latin America, Asia, UN (except UNCTAD)	*Directorate C* — European Development Fund (EDF) Programs and Projects
Directorate D — Middle and Far East, External Economic Policy	*Directorate D* — EDF Technical Operations
Directorate E — Countries with Planned Economies (mostly Communist)	
Directorate F — Northern, Central, and Southern Europe	

Source: Bulletin of the European Communities, Special Supplement "Directory of the Commission of the European Communities," January 1974.

Clearly it is representation and cooperation in the councils, committees, and working groups of the OECD and GATT from which the Common Market, as a primarily economic organization, draws the greatest benefit. However, the Commission has also participated in the work of Council of Europe committees aiming at the elaboration of a European Social Charter and a European Consular Convention, reflecting its general interest in European unification. In addition, the Community has sent representatives to almost every meeting held by an intergovernmental organization anywhere in the world. Thus it has not only participated in European organizations, but also in meetings of the OAS, the Organization of African Unity, and many other international organizations. These widespread activities not only demonstrate that Community interests are worldwide, but they also suggest that the Commission considers such participation an excellent way to advance the organization's international image and stature.

THE ORGANIZATIONAL FRAMEWORK FOR EXTERNAL POLICY OPERATIONS

The proposals for the formulation of the Community's external policy are worked up in Directorate-General I, which has been given the main responsibility for the conduct of external relations. Other foreign policy proposals come from Directorate-General VIII, concerned primarily with relations to developing countries.[25] (The organizational structure of the two Directorates-General is shown in Table 2.1.) The personnel of Directorate-General I also maintain the daily contacts with the members of the various diplomatic missions accredited to the Community. These contacts provide much of the information needed to formulate and implement policy. The Council of Ministers must be kept apprised of all important communications by third country diplomats. More than ninety diplomatic missions from nonmember countries have been established in Brussels, attesting to the importance attributed by the majority of the countries of the world to the activities of the Community.

35

There has been considerable argument as to whether the Community has the power to establish diplomatic missions in third countries. The principle of such right has been accepted by both the Council of Ministers (as early as 1960) and the European Parliament. In a resolution adopted November 19, 1960, the Parliament declared that "the European Communities by virtue of their international legal personality enjoy the active and passive right of legation," and in view of this it advocated the establishment of permanent missions in London and Washington.[26] In practice, however, the Community has not made use of its active right of legation except in Great Britain, where the ECSC had a representative with ambassadorial rank from 1956 until the end of 1972, when Britain became a member.[27] In 1971 an ambassador of the Community was appointed in Washington. The slow evolution of the active right of legation was due primarily to the determined opposition of General Charles de Gaulle. It took two years after de Gaulle's resignation as president before the French government consented to an extension of this right. We should note that the ambassador in Washington represents only the Community Commission, not the member states as a collective unit. In order to provide him and his staff with the traditional diplomatic immunity and privileges usually accorded to diplomatic personnel of nation states, a special law had to be introduced and passed by Congress.[28] In 1975 ambassadorial appointments that followed generally the procedural lines worked out in Washington were made in Japan and Canada.

ACCREDITATION PROCEDURES

Although the active right of legation has been beclouded by conflicting arguments, no basic objection was raised to the passive right, as evidenced by the accreditation of ninety-one diplomatic missions of nonmember countries.[29] Requests to establish a mission to the EEC and proposals for prospective chiefs of mission are approved or disapproved by joint decision of the Council and Commission. Up to the end of 1965, a chief of mission ready to present his letter of credence was officially received by the president of the Commission, then Dr. Walter Hallstein, with all the pomp and formality one would expect during a reception by the head of a sovereign state.[30] After the presentation of the credentials and the reception, the Council was informed and the new chief of mission paid a courtesy visit to the president of the Council.

Opposed to strengthening in any way the political powers of the Community's central organs, de Gaulle became increasingly irritated over the diplomatic reception practices of Dr. Hallstein, which appeared to cast him in the role of a "chief of state." When the Luxembourg Conference of the Foreign Ministers of the Member States (January 1966) settled the crisis provoked by France's six-month boycott of Common Market proceedings —a crisis that had its real roots in France's opposition to any expansion of Common Market authority and in her fear of losing national prerogatives—the French government insisted that the methods of accreditation be changed to give the Council of Ministers an equal share in the proceedings. As a consequence, letters of credence must now be addressed separately to the Commission and the Council, and ambassadors are to be received separately by the presidents of the two institutions. Furthermore, the former ceremonial formalities have been eliminated.[31]

DIPLOMATIC RELATIONS
WITH COMMUNIST COUNTRIES

Although the vast majority of the non-Communist developed and developing countries have accredited individual diplomats or full diplomatic missions to the EEC, ECSC, and Euratom, evidencing thereby diplomatic recognition of these organizations, the Communist countries, following the leadership of the Soviet Union, have largely withheld formal recognition. The reason for this attitude goes back to 1948, when the Soviet Union refused to participate in the Marshall Plan and prevented the East European countries from availing themselves of its benefits. Since then the Communists have attacked every aspect of every step that the West European countries have taken toward economic integration and perhaps political unity. The OEEC, the European Payments Union, NATO, and the ECSC were assailed as manifestations of American imperialism, as conspiracies of the big monopolies against the smaller producers and farmers, as the efforts of the capitalists to more effectively exploit the working class, and as aggressive organizations directed against the socialist countries.

Prior to and for some time after its establishment, the Common Market was subject to attacks similar to those hurled against the other European organizations. It was branded as another attempt of capitalism to save itself from inevitable decay and as a fraud perpetrated on the developing countries. However, in 1959 Soviet attitudes toward the Common Market changed; it became recognized as an economic and political reality, although gloomy predictions about the sharpening conflicts among the capitalist countries continued. During the 22nd Congress of the Soviet Communist Party in 1962, Nikita Khrushchev embarked on a sharply worded tirade against the EEC; yet at the same time, following the theme of peaceful coexistence, the Soviet government initiated a trade offensive aimed at the conclusion of more and broader bilateral trade agreements with the West.[32] Despite the desire for greater commerce with the EC countries, the Soviet Minister for Trade refused in 1963 to accept a document containing EEC offers for trade concessions delivered by the Dutch ambassador in Moscow, because he represented the Community as a whole (a unit that had not been diplomatically recognized by the Soviet Union).

By 1975 the fundamental position of the Soviet government had not changed, although it could not help but acknowledge the increasing power of the EC as an "objective reality." Nevertheless, although no ambassadors have been accredited to the Community, certain trade arrangements, especially with respect to farm prices, have already been made with the Community by the Communist countries of Eastern Europe, the so-called people's democracies; and informal contacts exist between Polish, Hungarian, and even Soviet officials and the EC personnel dealing with external relations. However, with the exception of Yugoslavia, none of the people's democracies has yet established a diplomatic mission to the European Communities.[33] The long and difficult negotiations in the framework of the European Security Conference dealing with economic cooperation touched on the diplomatic recognition of the Community as well as the Council for Mutual Economic Assistance (Comecon), but no tangible results emerged.[34] We will return to this subject in a later chapter.

Following a visit to Peking in May 1975 by Christopher Soames (the Commission member responsible for external relations), the People's Republic of China expressed its intentions to establish formal diplomatic relations with the European Community.[35] In July of that year it requested the accreditation of a diplomatic mission to the EEC. Accreditation was granted a few weeks later. This made China the second country in the Communist world to take such an action, an action undoubtedly motivated, at least in part, by the continuing enmity between Peking and Moscow, and their competition for leadership in the Communist camps. It was a major breakthrough for the Community in surmounting the Iron Curtain and might put pressure on the Soviet Union to modify its position toward the EC.

PROCEDURAL DIFFICULTIES OF
THE COMMUNITY POLICY-MAKING PROCESS

In our examination of the Community competences for the conduct of external relations we have indicated the functions that the EC Treaties assign to major Community organs for the formulation of pertinent policies and decisions. On paper, the distribution of functions for this task is clear-cut; in practice, however, the decision-making process is highly complex and intricate. This characterization applies not only to the decision-making process in the area of external relations, but also to the evolvement of any kind of major Community decision. It is a process that involves multilevel interaction and interpenetration among the Community institutions, national governments and administrations, and interest groups, a relationship much more intensive and extensive than that usually prevailing between traditional IGOs and national authorities or professional interest groups. The goals pursued by national economic groups in the member countries, the domestic politics of each member state, and the interstate politics within the Community play significant roles in the making of specific EC policies.[36] Especially as far as external policies are concerned, the general foreign policy goals pursued by the member states and the pressures exerted by third countries both on the national and Community level may also materially affect the end product.

According to the ingenious arrangement devised by the treaty framers it is the Commission that is to act as the driving force of the decision-making apparatus. It is the initiator of proposals upon which the Council is called to act. As the Common Market moved through the three stages of a transitional period from 1958 to 1970, the Council was authorized increasingly to make its decisions with a qualified majority.[37] However, it cannot amend a Commission proposal except by unanimous vote. In the majority of cases the Council is not able to make a decision unless a Commission proposal has been offered, and it does not have a legal tool to force the Commission to submit a specific proposal. On the other hand, the Commission can modify, substitute, or withdraw its proposal at any point up to the last moment prior to the Council's decision unless the timetables of the treaties preclude such withdrawal. Thus the treaties have drawn a careful balance of power between the two organs, which forces them to cooperate in governing the affairs of the Community. However, in practice, as we will see, there is considerable imbalance, weighing heavily in favor of the Council.

A third organ, the Committee of Permanent Representatives (CPR) or COREPER, following the French title, has the duty of preparing the sessions and decisions of the Council (which usually meets only a few days each month) and of carrying out any tasks assigned to it by the Council. In addition, the staff of the CPR is frequently consulted informally by the Commission before it submits a formal proposal to the Council. In order to

accomplish these missions, the CPR, composed of the ambassadors from the nine member states and their staffs, totaling more
than four hundred civil servants, has established a number of
working groups, subcommittees, and special ad hoc committees
patterned after the administrative structure of the Commission.[38]
For example, one of the working groups deals with the Common Market's relations to third countries and concentrates on
questions of commercial policy and GATT problems. Another
working group is concerned with relations to other international
organizations; and two subcommittees deal with problems
arising from various associations in Europe, the Middle East,
and Africa.

Clearly, the CPR, as handmaiden of the Council, has gained
over the years in importance and influence and has materially
contributed to the shift in the balance of power from the
Commission to the Council. Prior to submitting a proposal to
the Council, the Commission engages in preliminary and informal consultations with the staff members of the CPR in
order to gain more knowledge about the views of the member
governments. Information is also sought through meetings with
national officials who possess expert knowledge on the matter
under consideration and through formal meetings or informal
contacts with national and European-level interest group associations such as UNICE, the Union of Industries in the European
Community.[39] After all the information is collected, a defini-
tive proposal is formulated by the Commissioner for External
Affairs and by collegial action of the entire Commission, which
usually meets once a week. Decisions are made by simple majority, formal votes are rare, and the Commissioners are bound
to support collective decisions.[40]

After the Council receives the Commission proposal, it is
sent to the CPR for further study, highlighting again the importance of that Committee. The president of the CPR then has
the politically salient task of determining to which working
group or subcommittee to assign the proposal for detailed
study. Since many issues may fall within the competence of
several working groups or subcommittees, and since the varying
political attitudes of the staff in the varying groupings are apt to
be reflected in their deliberations and decisions, the selection of

the working group or subcommittee may be crucial for the fate of the proposal. We should note that in the working groups and subcommittees national officials with expert knowledge participate and that in the plenary sessions of the CPR representatives of the Commission are present. Attempts are usually made to find a compromise or at least come to an understanding within the CPR as well as with the Commission on minor points. Therefore, these meetings are often difficult bargaining and negotiating sessions unless the instructions received by the chiefs of the nine delegations of the member states are so strict and explicit that no room for maneuver is available. Altiero Spinelli, one of the Commissioners, has characterized the work and nature of the CPR (COREPER) as follows:

COREPER constitutes a sort of legislative chamber for the member countries and examines, amends and approves (or disapproves with relegation to the files) a large part of the proposals for rules or directives made by the Commission. It is an accepted constitutional custom that when an agreement is reached in COREPER, the Council ratifies it without further discussion. COREPER, for its part, passes to the Council only those points on which the Permanent Representatives have not wished to reach agreement, either because the points at issue are politically too important for the level of authority granted them, or because they have been unable to reach agreement due to too many incompatible differences in their mandates.[41]

The Council and COREPER have tended to mistrust the Commission and have therefore eroded its dynamism, furthermore its own lack of a political power base has induced the Commission to accept too often a relatively subordinate role, such as that of a secretariat of COREPER.[42]

It is often politically useful for the Council, although not often required in the EC Treaties, to request the European Parliament and the Economic and Social Committee to express their opinions on a Commission proposal. Neither body enjoys much effective power in the decision-making process of the Community, but consultation of the two bodies adds to the opportunity for interaction between Community organs, national interest groups, and political parties and favorable opinion by either or both organs may in fact help the prospects of a Commission proposal for Council adoption.

In the Council sessions the Commission is normally represented and since it usually has superior knowledge about all aspects of a proposal, it has a definite advantage in the discussion. Council sessions on crucial issues are often long and arduous, involving intra-Nine bargaining and marathon negotiations. All important factors known to parliamentary democracy play a role in the working of the Council—personal relationships, corridor deals, logrolling, convenient absences, inconvenient deadlines, and simple misunderstandings. In order to obtain ultimate agreement on a difficult issue, the Commission has become very adept in acting as the final conciliator by producing a multipoint package near the end of a long, tortuous Council session. By this time all participants recognize that if an agreement is to be reached at all, it must be on the basis of this package. Of course, Council sessions do not always have this happy ending. Sometimes a proposal may be returned to the CPR for further study and possible reconciliation of conflicting opinions. The informal atmosphere, especially at lower levels of CPR, is often more conducive to the solution of problems than the more formal procedure in the Council. At other times, issues may simply have to be dropped from the Council agenda or their solutions postponed to a later date. What member governments decide to accept at any given time depends on very complex considerations, not the least of which is the pursuit of their own domestic and foreign policy goals.

THE INFLUENCE OF
ECONOMIC INTEREST GROUPS

The discussion of the Community policy-making process makes it amply clear that economic interest groups in the member states have many opportunities to express their opinions and press their demands. However, it is equally obvious that in order to be successful in eliciting favorable Community policies, these groups also require the support of both their national administrations as well as the Community institutions. It is therefore proper to speak of a two-tier foreign policy making process in the planning and formulation of Community economic policies toward third countries: policy decisions made by the member governments are essential elements in the final Community-level decisions. Thus, all factors operating in policy making on the national plane are apt to have their influence, directly or indirectly, on the ultimate Community external policy product.

It is generally recognized that there is a definite interrelationship between a state's domestic politics and the formulation of its foreign policy. The pursuit of domestic political objectives can have an important bearing upon the selection of foreign policy goals and the methods for their implementation. For this reason, when formulating foreign policy, every democratic government must pay some attention to the demands and attitudes of several types of elites, which Gabriel Almond classifies under four main headings:[43] the political elites, including the elected and highly appointed as well as the party leaders; the administrative or bureaucratic elites; the interest elites, which include the representatives of a vast number of economic, ethnic, religious, and ideological associations; and the communications elites, which are the owners, controllers, and active participants of radio, television, the press, and movies.

While acknowledging the influence of these elites, we must guard against overestimating their influence. Certainly, in the formulation of national security policy and the strictly political aspects of foreign policy, their influence is often likely to be minimal. But even in the field of economic foreign policy, where, according to one of the myths about American politics, economic interest groups are assumed to be especially successful, this claim may be at times exaggerated. There can be little doubt that congressmen are apt to take economic group pressures more seriously when it comes to the definition of economic foreign policy than national security policy, but on many occasions conflicting interests may mitigate the pressures and encourage a measure of responsibility that looks beyond the economic interests immediately affected and takes into account long-range national goals.

Similar considerations, though varying from country to country, seem to apply also to Western Europe. Professor Jean Meynaud, a very knowledgeable student of French interest group activities, states that "it is impossible to accept without serious reservations the theses which attribute to business a decisive influence upon [foreign] policy."[44] However, he recognizes that economic interest groups may be moderately effective in influencing economic foreign policies.

The numerous statements made in the publications of both national and European-level interest groups show the definite concern of these organizations with seeking favorable Community decisions in the field of external policy. However, while they do not disregard the Community institutions, it seems that most industrial and agricultural groups direct the main thrust of their lobbying efforts at their own governments because they regard the national government route as promising greater success.

Most economic interest groups in the member states also seek to enlist the assistance of political parties for the pursuit of their objectives. At a minimum, they wish to keep the channels of communication to the party organizations open. Even in the France under de Gaulle, where party officials admitted freely that the influence of their parties, including the Gaullist UDR, upon governmental policy making was small, economic groups maintained relations with the political parties. Their hope was that this would ensure the availability of the necessary contacts when the political situation in France had changed.

How effective are the approximately 250 European-level interest group confederations, located mostly in Brussels, in obtaining favorable results when presenting the demands of their constituent national groups directly to the Community institutions? The answer depends to some extent on the degree of cohesion and level of administrative capability of these organizations. The most prominent agricultural umbrella confederation, COPA (Comité des Organisations Professionelles Agricoles de la C.E.E.), leads all other organizations in efficiency. UNICE as well as other industrial and commercial umbrella organizations are less effective; and the labor organizations such as ECFTUC (European Confederation of Free Trade Unions in the Community) and others have had much less influence than their agricultural and industrial counterparts despite repeated reorganizations on the European level.[45]

There seems to be general agreement that the objectives of national economic interest groups tend to become diluted in all umbrella organizations, including COPA and UNICE, because the structuring of a united front requires the reconciliation of conflicting economic interests. This, in turn, requires bargains and compromises and seems to confirm Lindberg's observation with regard to these organizations that "Common positions are reached when interests coincide, but otherwise decision-making is of the lowest common denominator type, with final agreement rarely exceeding what the least cooperative participant is willing to grant."[46]

When economic interest groups seek to present their demands directly to the Community institutions, the most lucrative target appears to be the Commission, although success, at least on the level of the Commissioners themselves, seems to be often quite elusive. Even COPA and UNICE, organizations whose establishment was strongly encouraged by the Commission, have encountered aloof and unresponsive attitudes on the part of the Commission members. Contacts with middle- and upper-middle-rank Commission officials appear to be more fruitful. Through them it is often possible to obtain advance information on proposals planned by the Commission and to disseminate information memos that might serve to influence the individuals who were doing the "pick and shovel" preparation for the elaboration of Commission proposals.

An increasingly attractive lobbying target appears to be the CPR because it plays a crucial role in the evolution of Community policy, perhaps much more so than was previously assumed. On the other hand, despite the EEC Treaty requirement that Parliament must be consulted before an association agreement can enter into force, access to the parliamentary deputies is not regarded as remunerative. Equally unimportant appear to be approaches through the ESC. However, two other potential targets on the Community level may be more attractive for economic interest groups. They are the European Agricultural Guidance and Guarantee Fund, which is responsible *inter alia* for providing subsidies for exports of farm commodities to third countries; and the European Investment Bank, which is one of the sources for financing projects in associated countries.

It is evident from the foregoing that economic interest groups have extensive opportunities to influence the Community decision-making process, including, of course, the formulation of external Community policy. Despite the relatively low expectations that the Community institutions hold the key for ultimate success for their demands, the economic groups often seize these opportunities with skill and sometimes with great vigor. However, since national economic interest groups also use their political muscle in the member states and frequently pursue different and conflicting objectives, the already complex Community decision-making process is complicated further, and the rules of the treaties suffer additional emasculation. In this connection, we must, however, not overlook that the manifold contacts between Community civil servants and interest group representatives also provide channels through which Common Market organs may exercise some influence upon the policy formation in the capitals of the member states. Thus, it is conceivable that subtle cooperation between the Commission and some national interest groups in the pursuit of a common external policy objective may lead to the application of concerted pressure on the national governments and perhaps through them, on the Council, resulting eventually in a favorable decision. On the other hand, no matter how shrewdly interest group efforts are devised for the elicitation of favorable Community decisions in the field of external policy, overriding considerations, stemming from the pursuit of general foreign goals and from perceptions of the national interest, may prompt a member government to protect and promote the economic interests involved exclusively through national foreign policies rather than through common Community policies or, in fact, withhold all protection or promotion.

DIVERGENT NATIONAL FOREIGN POLICY GOALS
OF THE MEMBER STATES

Perhaps one of the most intriguing aspects of the formulation of Community policy toward third countries is the relationship of this process to the pursuit of major long-range foreign policy goals by the member governments. In analyzing this relationship we must keep in mind several important factors. First, the establishment of the Common Market represents in itself the realization of certain convergent economic foreign policy goals of the member governments. Second, in the field of external relations for which, according to the EC Treaties, the Community organs are competent, the Community represents a centralized effort of the member states for the formulation and implementation of certain facets of their economic foreign policies, especially commercial policy. However, economic foreign policy goals cannot always be separated neatly from foreign policy goals concerned with national security or the advancement of a country's political power in general. In fact, there is a certain degree of interdependence among the economic, political, and strategic goals of a state, and the attainment of an economic policy objective may be a means for the accomplishment of a political or strategic goal. It is also possible that the attainment of economic goals may be closely intertwined with the simultaneous acquisition of political advantages or be dependent on making certain political or strategic concessions.

Another factor strongly influencing the pursuit of economic foreign policy goals can be assertions of what member states and their governments perceive as their "national interest." Such assertions may render the formulation and execution of a coordinated commercial policy within the framework of the EC highly complicated or entirely impossible. Of course, in many cases the national interest and the foreign policy goals of the member governments are compatible and could be attained through the employment of common EC policies. In fact, the use of joint policy instruments, such as the conclusion of an association agreement, may be the only method available for attaining certain economic, political, and even strategic foreign policy goals and thereby enlarges the range of foreign policy instruments at the disposal of the member governments. However, significant divergent elements, some potential rather than actual, are also evident in the goals of all nine member states. Therefore, as we will see, it has not been and will not be unusual that a clash of wishes, will, and wiles, highly traditional in interstate relations, but dysfunctional and therefore not desirable in the framework of the Community, has impeded or obviated the formulation of common external EC policies, although theoretically the member states are not opposed to having such policies.

A third factor complicating the formulation and implementation of common policies has been the reemergence of nationalism in the member states, which has tended to accentuate what is conceived of as "national interest." Although France is the obvious case of the reemerging nationalism, flashes of strong nationalistic feelings have been observed during the last few years in all of the member states. Beliefs that each government must serve foremost the interests of its own people before worrying about the Community interest are heard frequently. Such sentiments strengthen the resolve of national governments to employ national instruments for the pursuit of their foreign policy goals rather than to submit to a joint approach under Community auspices. Since the realities of the power distribution between the central institutions and the national governments continue to strongly favor the latter, it is not surprising that the reemergence of nationalism has severely weakened the position of the Commission as the main guardian of the Community interest. Examples in later chapters describing the problems of evolving common Community policies will illustrate these conditions prevailing in the policy-making process.

Lastly, the views and attitudes of the national civil service in the member states concerned with Community affairs have a significant bearing on the effectiveness of external policy making in the EC. Sentiments of opposition against a "takeover" of their functions by Community civil servants—often called Eurocrats—may express themselves in the use of subtle means to boycott the objectives of EC Treaties to turn over gradually the formulation and direction of certain economic foreign policies to the Community organs.[47]

It is important to stress that the views and attitudes of *any* civil service play a role in shaping the policies of those who wield political power in a state. These attitudes are likely to affect working papers that may become the basis for policy decisions, and tend to influence the implementation of any instructions received. Passive resistance and a lack of enthusiasm often suffice to block a policy. A pertinent example of the influence of the bureaucracy in foreign policy was the lack of sympathy with European integration within the British Foreign Office, which probably was an important factor contributing to British reluctance prior to 1961 to join the Six in their endeavors.[48]

In what ways are the attitudes and views of the civil servants in the member states significant for the elaboration of the Community's policy toward third countries and where are they to be found? We can identify four categories of national officials who may be able to exercise influence upon the Community decision-making process.

In the first category, most removed from the center of the Community decision-making process, are certain civil servants in the economics, agriculture, and finance ministries. In many cases they deal with Community external problems because of their expertise. They are the officials concerned with the definition of domestic economic interests, their priorities, and their relationship to economic foreign policy. They frequently have close liaison with influential economic interest groups in the member states and therefore occupy a highly strategic position controlling the flow and content of interest group demands on their way to the Community institutions. Clearly, the importance that these officials may attach to particular economic interests and the protection that they might want to accord to them are likely to become crucial factors in the formulation of external Community policy.

Officials in the foreign ministries of the member states occupied with EC affairs constitute a second group of civil servants who might be influential in the formulation of Community policy toward third countries. Their task may be to evaluate proposals for a common policy in the light of national foreign policy goals and they may have to decide whether meritorious interest group objectives should be pursued through national or Community policies. For officials in the foreign ministries, dealing with Community external policy matters is regarded as a logical extension of their traditional role. They transmit instructions to their Permanent Missions in Brussels and thereby are in a key position to control the channel of communication between domestic ministries and the Community, although direct contacts between officials of functional ministries and Eurocrats have been made and in fact are increasing.[49]

A third category of national civil servants whose attitudes and views may be highly significant for the formulation of external Common Market policy is the staff in the Permanent Missions to the Community. As we have seen from the description of their functions, these officials are closely involved in every phase of the Community decision-making process.

Finally, equally involved, but on a much more sporadic basis, are the thousands of governmental experts who are called in for consultation by the Commission, the Council, and the CPR. They constitute the fourth category of national civil servants, and the importance of their views for the definition of a common external policy is obvious from the nature of their function.

With such a large number of national officials rubbing elbows with Eurocrats in the numerous working groups set up by the Commission and within the CPR, the question of gradual political socialization inclining the national civil servants involved in these activities toward pro-Community and pro-integration attitudes has been raised frequently and often answered in the affirmative. However, getting to know the Community and integration is not the same as getting to love them. While common experiences in working groups composed of Community and national civil servants may have engendered some attitude shifts among the latter, they did not unidirectionally impel integrative attitudes. In fact, a 1973 attitude survey of national officials probing into this subject reveals that their experiences were counterproductive in the case of political integration.[50] Indeed, there may be a slow renationalization in the attitudes of the Eurocracy, whose commitment as specified in the EC Treaties should be exclusively the promotion of the Community interests. Some of the ministries in the new member

51

states seem to consider Eurocrats of their nationality as agents to bargain for national advantages.[51]

ALTERNATE SOLUTIONS FOR
A COMMON EUROPEAN FOREIGN POLICY

The subtle and perhaps sometimes unconscious opposition of national civil servants to the transfer of their functions to the Community organs has contributed, at least to some degree, to the search for other means of evolving common foreign policies on the part of the EC member states. It is fair to assume that national foreign service officials were especially interested in these efforts to find special methods of foreign policy coordination since this would ensure their continued participation and influence in most phases of foreign policy making while at the same time retaining as much as possible the prerogatives of the member governments across the whole range of foreign policy formulation. In terms of bureaucratic politics it would be a convenient means to bar the "intruders" from the Community's Directorate-General I and would assure the vigorous continuance of their career patterns and in fact their survival as powerful administrators.

As a result of these efforts an alternative structure outside the Community decision-making framework as specified in the three Community Treaties was created in 1970 for coordinating the foreign policies of the Community member states. This structure has only very loose, poorly defined ties to the Community system. Its origins were in the so-called Fouchet Plans, which were elaborated in 1961 and 1962 by a committee of diplomats chaired by Christian Fouchet, then the French ambassador to Denmark. The basic idea of the Fouchet Plans—there were two somewhat different proposals made by the committee—was the creation of a Council at the level of heads of state and government, which was to meet every four months and, acting by unanimity, was to coordinate foreign and defense policy. To assist the Council and to prepare policy proposals an intergovernmental European Political Commission, perhaps in the form of a permanent secretariat, was to be established. This was to be composed of senior officials in the national foreign services and to be located in Paris.[52]

Although a chance for success seemed to exist in the early stages of the negotiations on the essentially Gaullist draft treaty for policy coordination, no synthesis between the divergent positions of France and her Common Market partners could be evolved. Therefore, the concepts of the Fouchet Plans lay dormant from 1963 to 1969, although some students of European integration felt that the ideas embodied in the two Fouchet Plans should have been given further consideration and study. After the summit meeting of the heads of states and governments of the Six held in The Hague in December 1969, efforts were again initiated to find new paths for the construction of some kind of European Union. One of these efforts was the creation of a committee composed of high foreign ministry officials of the Six under the chairmanship of Vicomte Davignon of the Belgian Foreign Ministry. This group held a number of sessions beginning in April 1970.[53] The results of the deliberations of the Davignon Committee were published on July 20, 1970, in a report of the foreign ministers of the Community member states.[54] In accordance with this report, the foreign ministers of the Six began to schedule joint meetings every six months. In important cases a conference of chiefs of state and government could also be called when crucial issues justified such a meeting.

To prepare the sessions of the foreign ministers a committee was created composed of the political directors of the Six foreign ministries, to which were added in 1973 their counterparts of the three new member states. This committee was named the Political Committee and was to meet at least four times a year, but actually has met more often. Subordinate to this committee are various working groups and groups of experts, which have the mission to investigate particular problems and recommend possible solutions. The place for the sessions of the Political Committee is rotated from one member country to the other in accordance with whatever country chairs the Community Council of Ministers, whose presidency changes every six months. In line with the rotation of this presidency, the chairmanship of the Committee also changes every six months.

The major task of the periodic sessions of foreign ministers is the consideration of important questions of foreign policy. The member governments can suggest any issue for consideration that may pertain not only to general foreign policy problems but also to such matters as monetary affairs, energy, and security. Whenever the work of the Political Committee or of the foreign ministers impinges on the competence and activities of the European Community, the Commission is requested to submit its own position on the matter under consideration and is invited to send a representative. It is interesting to note that during the discussion in the Political Committee regarding the preparatory conference on European security and cooperation in Helsinki, it was felt that this subject was likely to deal with problems affecting the activities and competences of the European Community in the international trade field. Therefore, a Community representative was invited and the President of the Commission, then Franco Malfatti, participated in some of the sessions.

The foreign policy coordination activities of the Political Committee are supplemented by periodic sessions of staff members in the embassies of the Nine, located in different capitals of the world. Such meetings had already taken place prior to the creation of this Committee when Community affairs affecting third countries needed to be discussed and coordinated, but their scope has now been expanded.[55]

To strengthen the work of the Political Committee and the foreign ministers, the establishment of a permanent secretariat has been proposed. It would be located in one of the capitals of the Nine or operate on a rotating basis in the capital of the Committee chairman. Moreover, some kind of liaison arrangements with the staff of the Permanent Representatives of the Nine located in Brussels is in the process of being established through ad hoc groups of senior civil servants of the foreign and other ministries so that matters affecting Community policies can be discussed together. So far the Permanent Missions have not played any role in the coordination activities of the Political Committee.

The emergence of the Political Committee as an important factor in the formulation of common foreign policies may pit three organizational and bureaucratic groups against each other. One group consists of the officials of the foreign ministries operating through the Political Committee and perhaps in the future through a permanent secretariat, which will be concerned with the coordination of a wide range of foreign policy issues and thereby may invade the competences of the Community. Secondly, we have the Community decision-making process with its own group of civil servants striving to produce and implement external policies in accordance with the provisions of the Community Treaties. It is noteworthy that in this process, which originally was to be dominated by the international civil service of the European Community, we find expanding control by a third group of national officials. These officials operate through the offices of the Permanent Representatives, whose increasingly influential role in the decision-making process of the Community we have discussed earlier.[56] Some of these national officials come from the foreign ministries of the member states, and others are assigned by the ministries of economics, agriculture, and finance as technical experts. These experts may be called upon to give advice not only to working groups of the CPR, but also to those of the Commission, since the major competences of the Community are concentrated on the activities with which these technical experts are concerned. Hence, these national officials play perhaps a more salient part in evolving decisions for the Community than do their colleagues of the foreign ministries. We therefore see not only a subversion of the original concepts of Community decision making in the field of foreign policy by the national officials, but we can also discern competition and interpenetration between two distinct national bureaucratic groups struggling, perhaps subtly, to extend their own competencies and those of their institutions. Indeed, as Helen Wallace reports, the endeavor of different government departments in the member states to stake out their own areas of responsibility for formulating policy has provoked tensions between foreign ministries and domestic departments, as foreign ministries have had to increase their awareness of domestic policy considerations and ministries concerned with

55

domestic problems had to involve themselves more in international negotiations. At the same time, the Permanent Missions have come to enjoy a special status and to acquire a certain solidarity with each other.[57] For the foreign ministry officials, on the other hand, the Political Committee constitutes their seat of power, which they seek to expand by including within its boundaries every type of foreign policy issue including economic matters, a range of subjects corresponding to the existing set of functional division in their ministries. The rapid expansion in the Committee's activities and increasing frequency of meetings of senior officials and ministers have produced great satisfaction and are seen as signs of effectiveness and progress. The Political Committee therefore constitutes a kind of "caucus" in which the participants "understand each other," can engage in trade-offs on policy developments that cause few surprises, and most importantly, can continue to play their traditional roles without being inundated by "innovative" proposals from the Commission experts.

Since the Political Committee is occupied with such wide-ranging issue areas in foreign policy, we might also begin to see some kind of overlap and perhaps competition between that Committee and the Permanent Representatives of the member states to NATO.[58] The Political Committee's successful elaboration of a common position in the Helsinki negotiations on European security is a good case in point. Although the bureaucratic linkages springing up among the policy makers in the Community, NATO, and the member states represent opportunities for creating a closer union among the Nine, they also are apt to produce frictions in and impediments to the formulation of external Community policy, since the competing bureaucratic groupings may well be more concerned with advancing their personal and organizational goals than promoting the fortunes of the Community and a united Europe.[59] This is the reason that the Commission, in its Report on the European Union, issued in 1975, insists on the expansion of its own foreign policy competence and asks a "potential" competence even in the defense field.[60]

NOTES

1. See footnote 13, chapter 1. The technical name of this body is the Commission of the European Communities.

2. Euratom Treaty art. 2(h). See also Euratom Treaty art. 1, which states that one of the aims of the Community is to contribute to commercial exchanges with other countries "by creation of conditions necessary for the speedy establishment and growth of nuclear industries." One of these conditions was created on January 1,1959, when a common external tariff toward nonmember states was introduced, which permitted some materials to enter the Community free of duty and subjected others only to a relatively low tariff.

3. For instance, the French agreement with Vietnam signed in 1951. The French embassy in Washington has said that this treaty is "confidential" and has not been published in any compilation of treaties. The treaty may now be obsolete.

4. The Commission has given its consent under article 103 to several agreements involving nuclear matters such as the French treaties with Yugoslavia and Brazil, signed September 30, 1957, and May 2, 1962, respectively. Again, these treaties are "confidential" and have not been published in any compilation. The Court of Justice is the adjudicatory institution in the Community framework and has been given considerable powers. See Werner Feld, *The Court of the European Communities: New Dimension in International Adjudication* (The Hague: Martinus Nijhoff, 1964).

5. Euratom Treaty art. 101(1).

6. Ibid., arts. 10, 29.

7. Ibid., arts. 46–47. See also art. 16(5).

8. Ibid., arts. 52(b), 64, 77(b).

9. Leon N. Lindberg, *The Political Dynamics of European Economic Integration* (Stanford, Calif.: Stanford University Press, 1963), p. 206. Tariffs determine the amount of monetary levies (duties) imposed by states on imported goods either for the purpose of protecting domestic industries or raising revenues or both.

10. See lists A-G and arts. 19, 20 of the EEC Treaty.

11. The Committee used to be called "Committee 111" in accordance with the number of the article governing its operation during the transitional period.

12. During the first 8 years of the transition period a unanimous vote was required for this act (art. 114). In practice a unanimous vote is still required if vital interests of a member state are involved.

13. For details see art. 228.

14. Cf. Werner Feld, *The European Common Market and the World,* (Englewood Cliffs, N.J.: Prentice-Hall, 1967), p. 13.

15. For fuller information see Werner Feld, "The Association Agreements of the European Communities: A Comparative Analysis," *International Organization* 19, no. 2 (Spring 1965): 223-249.

16. Probable objectives of association agreements concluded under the ECSC and Euratom Treaties are cooperation and consultation with third countries. These, in fact, were the objectives of the association between the ECSC and the United Kingdom, concluded in 1954. Whereas the Euratom Treaty contains provisions for association agreements identical to those in the EEC Treaty, the legal situation under the ECSC Treaty is more complex. See ibid., 224-225.

17. Similar provisions in the Euratom and ECSC Treaties are 205 and 98, respectively.

18. EEC Treaty arts. 138, 148, 194, 200, 203; Statute of the Bank art. 4. The provisions of the ECSC Treaty for accession are somewhat different from those of the EEC Treaty, whereas the Euratom Treaty provisions are identical to them. Cf. ECSC Treaty arts. 98, 100.

19. Cf. Werner Feld, "Legal Dimensions of British Entry Into the European Community," *Law and Contemporary Problems* 37, no. 2 (Spring 1972): 247-264.

20. Euratom Treaty art. 199.

21. This was explicitly specified in the Luxembourg Conference of the Foreign Ministers of the Member States held in January 1966.

22. Euratom Treaty arts. 200, 201.

23. *European Community,* no. 181 (November 1974): 22; and *Agence Europe Bulletin,* September 18, 1975.

24. For full details see Jean Raux, *Les Relations extérieures de la Communauté Economique Européenne* (Paris: Editions Cujas, 1966), pp. 119-127, who provides an excellent analysis of the Community's relations with international organizations.

25. Each Directorate-General is under the supervision of a Commission member. Since the enlargement of the Community in 1972, Christopher Soames is the Commission member responsible for Directorate-General I, and Claude Cheysson for Directorate-General VIII.

26. *Amtsblatt der Europäischen Gemeinschaften,* 1960, p. 1496/60; and EEC Commission, *Third General Report,* sec. 390. In this connection it is interesting to note that the German Bund (1815-66) possessed the active and passive right of legation simultaneously with that of the sovereign states that were members of the Bund.

27. Accreditation was to the British government, not the Court of St. James. However, with regard to all diplomatic functions, the ambassador was treated on an equal basis with colleagues accredited to the Queen.

28. H.D. 11229, S. 2700; and *Agence Europe Bulletin,* December 7, 1972.

29. Fifty-one of these missions are accredited to all three Communities, twenty-nine only to the EEC, one to the EEC and ECSC, and one to the EEC and Euratom. In all cases except that of Nationalist China, the accreditation process was accomplished without difficulties. In the case of Nationalist China the Community had given its approval to the establishment of diplomatic relations, but by the time an ambassador was to be appointed, the French government had recognized the People's Republic of China and withdrawn its recognition of the government on Taiwan. As a consequence, the French refused to give their consent to the appointment of an ambassador from the Taiwan government. Cf. Gordon L. Weil, *A Foreign Policy for Europe?* (Bruges: College of Europe, 1970), pp. 43, 44.

30. The Brussels police provided a motorcycle escort for the new ambassador and a red carpet was rolled out at the entrance of the Commission building. Formal dress (striped pants, etc.) was the order of the day and champagne toasts were given.

31. *New York Times* (International ed.), July 9-10, 1966, p. 1. The crisis was triggered by a dispute between France and her partners over the financing of the EEC agricultural policy. For a full account see John Lambert, "The Constitutional Crisis 1965-66," *Journal of Common Market Studies* 6, no. 3 (May 1966): 195-228. It is not quite certain whether the legal status of third country diplomats assigned to the European Communities equals that of their colleagues accredited to the King of Belgium. Are the diplomats accredited to the Communities assimilated to those accredited to the King or are there actually two separate diplomatic corps in Brussels, one at the Court and one at the Community? See N. March Hunnings, "The European Communities and Public International Law," in *Expansion of the European Communities* (Conference Papers III on Foreign and Regional Relations in the Community, the British Institute of International and Comparative Law, Dublin, September 1970).

32. Thirty-two theses dealing with imperialist integration in Western Europe were published by *Pravda* on August 26, 1962, of which one stated that "The extension of economic relations between States, and of peaceful cooperation is one of the most important ways of preventing war and consolidating cooperation between people." Quoted by John P. de Gara, *Trade Relations Between the Common Market and the Eastern Bloc* (Bruges: DeTempel, 1964), p. 22.

33. See Commission of the Communities, *Fourth General Report on the Activities of the Communities,* 1968, p. 389; and *Agence Europe Bulletin,* November 27/28, 1972. General Reports will henceforth be cited by report number and year.

34. See Johann Karat, "Soviet Union and the European Communities," *Aussenpolitik,* English ed. 23, no. 3 (March 1972): 299-308.

35. *European Community,* no. 187 (June 1975): 17, 18; and *Agence Europe Bulletin,* July 3, 1975.

36. See Leon Lindberg, "Decision-Making and Integration in the European Community," *International Organization* 19, no. 1 (1965): 56-80.

37. Where decisions can be made by a qualified majority, the votes of the member states are carefully counterpoised and give France, Germany, Italy and Great Britain a weight of 10, Belgium and the Netherlands a weight of 5, Denmark and Ireland a weight of 3, and Luxembourg a weight of 2. In such instances 40 favorable votes are required for a decision to be adopted. This means that the four large countries can outvote the others; on the other hand, three large countries and the votes from Belgium and the Netherlands can outvote the fourth large member state. When Council decisions are envisaged without Commission proposals, the forty necessary votes must represent at least five member states. A simple majority may be obtained by a favorable vote of five states.

38. The Permanent Missions also constitute excellent observation posts for the member governments to keep informed about the happenings in the Commission.

39. At this state it is possible in some instances that the European Parliament may also be consulted. See also Pierre Gerbert and Daniel Pepy, eds., *La décision dans les Communautées européenes,* Brussels, 1969.

40. As a link between a Commissioner and the Directorate-General and their subdivisions, each member of the Commission has a small staff, called his "cabinet."

41. Altiero Spinelli, *The European Adventure* (London: Charles Knight, 1972), pp. 32-33.

42. Ibid., p. 173.

43. Gabriel A. Almond, *The American People and Foreign Policy* (New York: Praeger, 1960), pp. 130-143. See also James N. Rosenau, *Public Opinion and Foreign Policy* (New York: Random House, 1961).

44. Jean Meynaud, *Nouvelles Études sur les groupes de pression en France* (Paris: Librarie Armand Colin, 1962), p. 391. See also pp. 392-393.

45. Cf. Marguerite Bouvard, *Labor Movements in the Common Market Countries* (New York: Praeger, 1972), pp. 96-104.

46. Leon N. Lindberg, *The Political Dynamics of European Economic Integration* op. cit., p. 99; see also pp. 333-339, and for a description of these organizations, pp. 96-105. It is not inconceivable that occasionally the consensus of a specific issue reached in an umbrella organization does

not really represent the true intent of all national groups. One or more of these groups may have only agreed to the proposed common view because they knew that their governments would in fact oppose the endorsed Commission proposals in the Council of Ministers.

47. See Werner Feld, "The National Bureaucracies of the EEC Member States and Political Integration: A Preliminary Inquiry," in Robert S. Jordan, *International Administration* (New York: Oxford University Press), pp. 218-244; and Werner Feld and John K. Wildgen, "National Administrative Elites and European Integration: Saboteurs at Work?" *Journal of Common Market Studies* 13, no. 3 (March 1975): 244-265.

48. Anthony Nutting, *Europe Will Not Wait* (London: Hollis & Carter, 1960), p. 5.

49. Cf. Helen Wallace, *National Governments and the European Communities* (London: Chatham House: PEP, 1973), pp. 42, 65-68.

50. Cf. Feld and Wildgen, op. cit., 255-256.

51. See Werner J. Feld, "Political and Administrative Concern in the Member States: What Effects on Community Policies," paper presented to the Cornell University Conference on "Domestic Politics in the European Communities," September 19-20, 1975.

52. For details see Alessandro Silj, *Europe's Political Puzzle* (Cambridge, Mass.: Harvard University Center for International Affairs, December 1967, Occassional Papers no. 17).

53. Cf. *Agence Europe Bulletin,* March 6; April 3, 15, 1970.

54. For details see "Bericht der Aussenminister der Mitgliedstaaten der Europäischen Gemeinschaften an die Staats- bzw. Regierungschefs vom 20. July 1970, betr. mögliche Fortschritte auf dem Gebiet der politischen Einigung," *Europa Archiv* 25, no. 22 (1970): D520-D524.

55. Cf. Ralf Dahrendorf, "Possibilities and Limits of a European Communities Foreign Policy," *The World Today* (April 1971): 161. The commercial councillor of the embassy of the member state that holds the presidency in the Council of Ministers of the Community at a particular time prepares a report on these meetings. These reports are addressed to the president of the Council and are also distributed to the Permanent Representatives in Brussels and a number of national governmental agencies. If no objections are raised by a member government within eight days, a copy of this report is furnished to the Commission. When Community affairs are discussed in the embassy meetings officials of the EC Information Service participate if the Service has an office in a particular capital such as Washington or Geneva. In such cases the Community officials make a direct report to the president of the Commission. Policy coordination meetings have also been held in the United Nations to assure the maximum cohesion in voting and policy positions of the member

states. The influence of the Commission staff in these meetings may well have been increased when the EC was granted official observer status by the U.N. (Cf. *Agence Europe Bulletin,* September 18, 1975). An interesting study made by Leon Hurwitz regarding voting cohesion by the member states in 518 roll call votes in the General Assembly from 1948 to 1973 shows the following results. The variations in cohesion levels are wide: The Netherlands and Luxembourg have the highest level (92 in a 0–100 scale), France-Italy the lowest level (72 in the same scale), the original EEC members have a cohesion level of 84, and the three new EC members about 80. (See Leon Hurwitz, "The EEC in the United Nations: The Voting Behavior of Eight Countries, 1948–1973," Prepared for delivery at the 1974 Annual Meeting of the American Political Science Association, Chicago, Illinois, August 29–September 2. Copyright, 1974, The American Political Science Association.)

56. See pp. 40–42.

57. Wallace, op. cit., p. 84.

58. For a discussion of selected aspects of the EC–NATO relationship, see chapter 8, pp. 295–304.

59. Cf. *Agence Europe Bulletin,* November 8, 1971. Bureaucratic infighting takes place also between the Community departments DG I and DG VIII. Because of the conclusion of the Lomé Convention in 1975 (see ch. 7) and the increasing harmonization of member state policies toward the Third World, the influence and prestige of DG VIII has risen at the expense of DG I, traditionally the "prestige" Directorate-General. Skillful bureaucratic leadership by the Commission member in charge of DG VIII and paranoia of national foreign service officers vis-a-vis DG I personnel accounting for some hostility toward them may also have played a significant role in this development.

60. See ibid., June 27, 1975.

3

The Enlargement of the Community:

Process and Problems

To fully appreciate the role of the European Community in world affairs requires as the first task the discussion of the international ramifications of the Community's enlargement from six to nine members. The ramifications are enormous and their impact has not been clearly anticipated by the outside powers and perhaps not even by the old and new member states. Although the United States has always been anxious to see Great Britain a member of the Community and enthusiastically supported the enlargement policies from 1961 to 1972—an enthusiasm perhaps somewhat diminished toward the end of the period in spite of official rhetoric—the reactions of American policy makers after the expansion of membership suggested apprehension regarding the effects enlargement might have on the United States and other third countries. Clearly, the potential impact of the emerging economic giant in Western Europe on international relations had not been foreseen fully.

The relationship between Great Britain and the Six with respect to the economic and perhaps the political integration of Europe dates back to 1951. At that time the British government was invited to become a charter member of the ECSC, but the invitation was turned down; although in December 1954 Britain joined the Coal and Steel Community as an associate member.[1] The British also refused to participate in the establishment of the European Defense Community (EDC) in 1952, when the treaty for the creation of a European Army was signed by the Six. (The French Parliament rejected its ratification two years later and as a consequence the EDC did not become a reality.) Again in 1955 and 1956 Britain was asked to join in the negotiations of the Six for the establishment of the EEC and Euratom and the British government at first seemed to show some genuine interest in the new enterprise. However, motivated in part by the fear that participation in the planned customs union would harm the relations between the United Kingdom and the

65

Commonwealth countries, and apprehensive about the supranational aspects of the proposed treaties, the British again declined the invitation,[2] and thereby spurned the overtures of the
Six for a joint European venture for the second time within
five years.

In July 1956 the British government suggested during a
meeting of the Council of the Organization for European Economic Cooperation (OEEC) the appointment of a working
party to study the possibility of establishing a free trade area
comprising all the OEEC countries and including the Common
Market as one of its members.[3] Although skepticism and reservations about such a plan were voiced in the prospective Common Market countries, the OEEC Council passed a resolution
early in 1957 to enter into negotiations for the creation of a
European Free Trade Area that would associate, on a multilateral basis, the Common Market with other member countries
of the OEEC.

The negotiations, carried on for nearly a year and a half,
were not successful. The position of the French government,
which insisted on a common external tariff, a common commercial policy toward third countries including the Commonwealth, and the harmonization of social policies for the whole
trade area, could not be reconciled with the much more limited
objectives of the British government. In view of the collapse of
the plans for a free trade area encompassing all of Western
Europe, Greece and Turkey requested association with the
Common Market in June and July 1959, respectively. These
actions were one of the motivations for Britain to seek the
establishment of a free trade area with the Scandinavian countries, Austria, Switzerland, and Portugal. In November 1959 a
convention establishing the European Free Trade Association
was signed in Stockholm. It called for a gradual elimination of
internal tariffs on industrial products but, in contrast to the
EEC Treaty, no provisions were made for a common agricultural policy, although a number of bilateral and multilateral trade
agreements have led to a greater interchange of agricultural
goods between the EFTA members. Despite objections from the
Soviet Union, Finland became an associate member of EFTA in
March 1961 and Iceland did the same in 1967.

EFTA AND THE EEC

As soon as EFTA was established, apprehension about the unfortunate consequences of a Western Europe divided into two trade blocs prompted a number of proposals aiming at the construction of a bridge between EFTA and the Common Market. The Consultative Assembly of the Council of Europe in the fall of 1960 unanimously adopted a resolution recommending a multilateral association between the countries of the two trading blocs. Another idea came from Alwin Muenchmeyer, then president of the Diet of German Chambers of Industry and Commerce, who proposed that the EEC, as a unit, become a member of EFTA. In this way it would be possible to maintain the institutional unity of the Common Market, whereas in the case of an association the EEC "would be dissolved like a piece of sugar in a cup of tea."[4] A third concept was advanced early in 1961 by Professor Alfred Mueller-Armack, a high-ranking official of the German Ministry of Economics, who advocated the establishment of an all-European modified customs union without political character. His scheme was a cross between a free trade area and a customs union in which EFTA and the EEC would remain separate organizations but would effect a large degree of harmonization in their tariffs toward third countries.

None of these efforts succeeded in constructing the bridge between EFTA and the Common Market. The basic reason for this failure was that both trading blocs were seeking a different kind of unity in Europe and insisted on using different approaches to attain their objectives. The EEC laid out a fairly detailed master plan in advance, including the guidelines for solving (under the auspices of comprehensive Community institutions) such delicate problems as antitrust regulations, tax policy, and government subsidies. EFTA was started with a much less detailed plan, a minimum of institutions, and reliance on the member governments to work out details cooperatively as they were encountered. Moreover, Switzerland and Sweden objected to the comprehensive arrangements of the EEC Treaty as a violation of their traditional neutrality; and Austria was fearful that her unilateral declaration of neutrality given in

67

exchange for the 1955 peace treaty with the Soviet Union would bar it from becoming a full member of the EEC. Finally, and most important, Great Britain was reluctant to give up sovereignty to supranational institutions.

International power considerations also militated against the bridge-building process between EFTA and the EEC. France had been hostile to the expanded association even before de Gaulle came to power because of the lingering suspicion that Britain was seeking to reduce France's leadership role on the Continent. German Chancellor Konrad Adenauer was not willing to sacrifice his most important objective, French–German partnership, for possible trade gains and better relations with Britain. And Great Britain was intent on retaining its friendly ties with the Commonwealth countries, ties that might be impaired by a close association with the Common Market.

THE FIRST BRITISH APPLICATION
FOR EEC MEMBERSHIP

To the surprise of many on both sides of the Atlantic, the British government announced on July 31, 1961, that it would seek to open negotiations with the EC member states with a view to becoming a full member of the Common Market. According to Prime Minister Macmillan's statement in the House of Commons on August 2, the reasons for the decision to join the Common Market were primarily political: Britain would be affected by whatever happened on the Continent; there would be no security in isolation; she would have to play her role and use her influence for the free development of life and thought in Europe; and she had to take her place in the vanguard of the movement toward the greater unity of the free world. In the official communication of the British government to the acting president of the Council of Ministers requesting access to the Common Market, the Prime Minister asked that in the forthcoming negotiations Britain's special relations to the Commonwealth and the other EFTA countries be taken into account, and that the essential interests of British agriculture be considered.[5]

Economic reasons also played a part in motivating the British decision to seek membership in the Common Market. In the spring of 1961 Britain was in the throes of a serious balance-of-payments crisis. While exports to the Commonwealth countries accounted for slightly over half of total United Kingdom exports in 1951, they had fallen by 1961 to only a little over 33 percent. On the other hand, EFTA was only a moderate success as a trading group and the United Kingdom registered the lowest percentage of total exports going to the EFTA partners, namely 12 percent in 1962.[6]

For Denmark, which in 1961 also applied for membership in the EEC—in fact, one day after Britain—economic considerations were the crucial factor for making the request for negotiations. In 1960 more than 40 percent of Danish agricultural exports went to the Common Market countries, this constituting nearly 30 percent of her total exports. Danish agricultural exports such as beef, pork, bacon, butter, cheese, and eggs would be affected by the Community's evolving agricultural protectionism, and, therefore, Danish farm imports, especially in the important German market, were likely to be displaced by French or Dutch goods. Admission to the EEC, therefore, would be an important safeguard for the economic health of Danish agriculture. Similar considerations induced Ireland in 1961 and Norway in April 1962 to follow Denmark's lead and also to apply to the Common Market for admission.

The prospect of increased economic benefits would most likely also have prompted the three neutral EFTA countries—Sweden, Switzerland, and Austria—to request admission to the Common Market if they had not feared that full membership might endanger their neutral status. All three countries would have opted, if possible, for an extended free trade area between the two trade blocs, but since the chances for such a development in 1961 were practically nonexistent, they considered association with the EEC as the second best solution to their problems and requested the initiation of negotiations for this purpose in December 1961. Following the example of the neutral states, Portugal also requested the Community in the spring of 1962 to open negotiations on either an association or perhaps even full membership.

69

THE NEGOTIATIONS WITH BRITAIN

It would exceed the scope of this volume to discuss in detail the drawn-out negotiations for British accession to the Common Market. The first set of negotiations lasted from November 1961 until the fateful day of January 29, 1963, when the Belgian Deputy Foreign Minister, Henry Fayat, informed the British representatives that negotiations had to be broken off because of disagreement among the Six caused by de Gaulle's veto of British membership. Several excellent accounts from official and unofficial sources are available relating the details of these negotiations.[7] We will focus only on those aspects of the negotiations that are of particular significance for the understanding of the Community's external policy.

The negotiations were carried on at three levels. At the top level were the foreign or economics ministers of the Six and the Lord Privy Seal for Britain, then Edward Heath, supported on occasion by the Secretary of State for Commonwealth Relations and the Minister for Agriculture. They met about once a month, usually for two days, until the summer of 1962, when the number of meetings increased. At the level below the ministers, the Permanent Representatives of the member states and the British ambassador in Paris, Sir Pierson Dixon, conducted the negotiations in Brussels as deputies for the ministers, meeting nearly every week. On a third level, various expert working parties dealt with different problems, mainly of a technical nature. In addition to the formal multilateral negotiations, a large number of bilateral contacts were maintained at the summit, ministerial, and deputy levels. For example, Prime Minister Macmillan visited General de Gaulle on two occasions and Mr. Heath repeatedly traveled to the capitals of the Six to promote Britain's position and views.

The Commission, acting for the Community, participated in the negotiations. During the period from November 1961 to May 1962, which was devoted mainly to an examination of the specific problems that had to be solved before agreement on Britain's admission to the Common Market could be reached, the role played by the Commission was highly significant because this group possessed the technical data and knowledge necessary to suggest possible solutions. However, after the committees of experts had submitted their reports on these problems and had presented their recommended solutions to the ministers, the process of hard bargaining began, and during this phase the Commission's importance in the negotiations receded. At that stage, as Uwe Kitzinger observes:

> . . . the negotiations in fact came to be conducted in two dimensions: between Britain and the Six, then among the Six themselves, and then again between the Six and Britain. No small part of the time involved, and no small part of the frictions that have arisen, were due to disagreements among the Six. Faced with British demands, they felt it vital to present a united front toward the applicant state; and it is no wonder that the negotiations did not go smoothly, since, once the Six had reached a compromise among themselves, a reopening of discussion would cause immense complications each time.[8]

Of course, although this cumbersome procedure was a definite burden for the British, we must recognize that accession of a third country was a totally new experience for the Common Market, one for which no approved doctrine existed and for which, in fact, it was quite unprepared. In other words, the trial and error method had to be employed for an undertaking that was not only technically extremely difficult, but also fraught with extensive foreign policy implications for the individual member governments.

The main substantive issues of the highly complex negotiations were agriculture, the Commonwealth, and the relations with the EFTA countries. The British were most intent on moving gradually through a longer transition period toward the Community's agricultural policy—not yet implemented at that time—in order to avoid a sudden increase in prices and an abrupt end to guaranteed prices and deficiency payments. The most difficult problem in connection with the Commonwealth was that of accommodating temperate foodstuffs from Canada, New Zealand, and Australia, since they would compete with Community production. The imports of tropical agricultural products from Commonwealth countries also gave the British reason for concern. Finally, Britain had promised her EFTA partners that

71

their interests would be protected in the negotiations and therefore she demanded assurances against trade discrimination toward them.

None of these problems was solved entirely when the negotiations were broken off. No final agreement was reached on how to fit British agriculture fully into the evolving common agricultural policy of the Community. The British negotiators gave only their assent in principle to the CET and the abolition of the Commonwealth preferential system. Although the Community consented to offering associated status not only to the bulk of British colonial possessions but also to most of the independent countries of Africa and the Caribbean; and although it was agreed that comprehensive trade agreements should be concluded between the enlarged Community and India, Pakistan, and Ceylon, a number of Commonwealth problems defied all attempts at solution. Almost none of the many complex issues arising from Britain's membership in EFTA was near settlement.

It is difficult to judge what would have been the outcome of the negotiations if they had not been broken off. In the opinion of the Commission, shared by the British, substantial progress had been made and the remaining problems would have been capable of solution. Miriam Camps appears to be less optimistic, pointing out that the outstanding issues were potentially rather more troublesome than anticipated by the British government.[9] Perhaps the reflections of the Commission on the difficulties of the negotiations expressed in its report to the European Parliament point most clearly to the crux of the matter:

The question was not only one of reconciling British systems and commitments with the letter of the Treaty of Rome: it was rather one of reconciling them with a Community in the full surge of development. The British application for membership involved an obligation to accept not only the Treaty but the substantial advances made since the Treaty was signed. It was on these advances that discussion was sometimes most difficult. But the fact that, in certain fields, the content of the Treaty was still in a preliminary stage, and that, broadly speaking, the implementation of its various aspects was in an intermediary phase, may also be considered as having made matters more difficult for the negotiators.[10]

General de Gaulle's professed reasons for vetoing British admission to the Common Market were stated in his famous news conference of January 14, 1963. The General expressed grave doubts about Britain's readiness for membership in the EC because she was an insular, maritime country with the most diverse and distant commercial ties and interests and was not prepared to fully accept Community rules and institutions, a necessary precondition for admission, according to de Gaulle. British membership would weaken the cohesion of the EEC and was likely to lead ultimately to an Atlantic Community under American direction.

Probably other considerations of a more strategic and political nature motivated de Gaulle even more strongly than his expressed position. The entry of Britain into the Common Market was likely to threaten France's leadership in the EC. Rivalry for European leadership between France and Britain certainly has been an important feature of European history for centuries. Another factor was the Nassau agreement on a NATO multilateral nuclear force with Polaris missiles, concluded between the United States and Britain in December 1962. This agreement appeared to de Gaulle to be a reassertion of the special Anglo–American relationship and likely to impair Western Europe's emergence as an independent nuclear power under French leadership.

It is somewhat ironical that the British, whose concept of a united Europe was much closer to de Gaulle's *l'Europe des patries* and the Fouchet Plan than to the federal idea held by some of the other member governments, were denied admission by the General. On the other hand, there were voices heard in all member states who shared de Gaulle's notion that Britain first had to enter the "common boat" of the EC with both legs before she should be permitted to participate in determining the course of the boat. However, officially France's partners rejected the French standpoint and sought to retaliate in various ways against the action of the French government. They held up progress on the association agreement with eighteen African states, mostly former French colonies; they refused to grant special treatment for Algeria; and they blocked any agricultural agreement that would help dispose of the French dairy surplus.

After the collapse of the British negotiations the Danish, Norwegian, and Irish requests for admission to the EC were not pursued further; and Sweden, Switzerland, and Portugal saw little chance for association for the time being. The EFTA members now hitched their hopes to the revitalization of their own trade area and to a general reduction of duties through GATT negotiations.

THE SECOND BRITISH APPLICATION
FOR MEMBERSHIP

Despite the renewed emphasis on making EFTA an economic success, in the spring of 1966 Britain was again seriously considering reactivating negotiations for accession to the Common Market. In the traditional speech from the throne, on April 21, 1966, at the opening of the new parliamentary session, in which the Labour government was to enjoy a substantial majority, the Queen declared that Great Britain was ready to enter the EC, provided that her essential interests and those of the Commonwealth were safeguarded. However, Mr. George Brown, then British Foreign Secretary and an ardent pro-European, cautioned that while the political determination to enter the EC existed now in Britain, a period of probing and preparation would be necessary in order to get to the bottom of all potential difficulties and to find solutions. The French government, although expressing pleasure about Britain's renewed interest in joining the EC, continued to insist that in order to become a full member, Britain would have to accept without reservations all rules of the Common Market, including the Community's CAP. Moreover, no accession would be possible until Britain's financial and economic difficulties had been fully remedied.

The British soundings took the form of visits by Prime Minister Harold Wilson and Foreign Secretary Brown to the capitals of all member states and to the Commission during the first three months of 1967. During this round of the capitals the British leaders explained Britain's position and sought the support of the member governments if a new application for Common Market membership were to be made. In his conversations Wilson pointed out that the pound sterling had regained its strength and that the situation of the British economy had improved. It was not a "sick man" asking to be admitted to the Community, but a sound, strong organism, currently and speedily acquiring a very high degree of efficiency. He declared that the main problem to be solved would be Britain's gradual adoption of the CAP. No claim was made for a modification of the CAP but allowance would have to be made for the new scale and different economic nature of an expanded Community.[11]

Wilson's initiatives had broad support in Britain. The powerful Confederation of British Industry favored Common Market membership as offering many advantages for British industry, although it foresaw short-term adaptation problems and the need for a transition period. The National Farmers' Union was less enthusiastic because of expected serious consequences for British farming, but did not consider the problems insurmountable. Parliament in general supported the efforts of the British government, although a substantial bloc of Labour members expressed reservations about any unconditional candidature for the Common Market, and was fearful about a consequent rise in the cost of living in Britain.[12]

The reaction of the member governments to the British probing activities ranged from noncommittal in France to enthusiastic in the Benelux countries. French Foreign Minister Couve de Murville pointed out that the discussions in Paris had been exchanges of views on a possible application of Britain to join the Common Market, but had not involved negotiations and preconditions. In a statement toward the end of February 1967 he warned, however, that "Britain's entry into the EC would inevitably change the character of the organization. The number of members of the Common Market could well be eleven, and it would then be more difficult to reach unanimous decisions. Without wanting to pronounce on the pros and cons of this new situation, it is one that should be taken into consideration by Great Britain and the Six."[13]

The Germans, although in general support of British membership in the Common Market, found grounds for hesitation in the newly budding French–German friendship. Replying to a number of questions put to him by the foreign press in January 1967, Chancellor Kiesinger said that British entry was "the most serious problem for Franco–German relations."[14] German enthusiasm for British membership was further dampened by the controversy involving German financial aid for the British Army on the Rhine or its withdrawal in the absence of sufficient aid; Britain's aggressive backing of a nuclear nonproliferation treaty, which, in German eyes, might reduce the nuclear have-not countries to permanent pawns of the countries possessing nuclear power; and the view of many Germans that Britain remained perhaps the most anti-German country in Western Europe.[15]

The Italian welcome for the British visitors exceeded all expectations, but this did not mean that they broadly accepted all British views. There were nagging doubts about whether the British were ready to accept the supranational character of the Community and there was apprehension about the wide gulf that continued to separate Community and British viewpoints, especially in the field of agriculture.

The major industrial interest groups in all member states represented by UNICE expressed support for British membership. However, the French *Patronat* declared that British entry must not bring into question the provisions of the Treaty of Rome and the implementing policies; and the Confederation of Italian Industry (*Confindustria*) warned that Britain must renounce a certain degree of freedom in the making of domestic and foreign economic policy. Agricultural groups within the Community also were not adverse to British membership provided that the implementation of the CAP would be fully safeguarded. The European Secretariat of the International Confederation of Free Trade Unions (ICFTU) stressed that the entry of Britain into the Community would constitute a vital factor for strengthening European democratic structures.[16]

Although the official attitude of the EEC Commission was clearly favorable toward British membership, the views of the Commission members and of a large part of the Community bureaucracy were mixed. Some officials openly stated that British entry, while desirable, did not come at a good time and that the Community required a period of consolidation before enlarging.[17]

Although the soundings of Prime Minister Wilson and Foreign Secretary Brown in the capitals of the Six revealed that an application for EEC membership would not have smooth sailing, the British government announced on May 3, 1967, that it would formally apply to join not only the Common Market, but also the Coal and Steel Community and Euratom. Speaking on that day to the House of Commons, Wilson declared that "the Government would be prepared to accept the Treaty of Rome, subject to the necessary adjustments consequent upon the accession of a new member and provided that we receive satisfaction on the points about which we see difficulty."[18] These points, the Prime Minister stated, included the potential effects of the CAP on the cost of living in Britain and on the structure and well-being of British agriculture, balance-of-payments questions, implications of the system of financing the CAP, and certain Commonwealth problems.

The formal letter of Prime Minister Wilson requesting accession was very brief and concise and was delivered to the president of the Council of Ministers in Brussels on May 11. On the same day, the Danish government also submitted a formal application for membership in the three Communities.

Whatever the attitudes of the EC member governments and national interest groups toward the British application, there was little doubt that the French government continued to hold the key to successful British accession. This was dramatically demonstrated by de Gaulle's news conference, held only five days after the British bid for membership was received in Brussels. De Gaulle asserted that he did not want to prejudge the new British application, but then dwelt at length on the obstacles, and concluded with a listing of alternatives. He cited as main obstacles the increase in Britain's food costs, which would be caused by her acceptance of the CAP and which in turn would result in higher salaries and higher price tags for British products; the continuing danger of renewed weakness in the British pound; and the old bogy, Britain's special ties to the United States and the Commonwealth, which could not be dissolved easily. Referring perhaps to the repeatedly expressed aversion of Prime Minister Wilson and Foreign Secretary Brown toward the idea of an independent European nuclear force, de Gaulle stressed that the Six had been pulling closer together and were seeking to discern "the purely European reasons which would justify their acting in concert." This was true, he said, "whether it concerns the security of Europe or détente, or agreement and cooperation with the Eastern countries with a view toward opening the way to a settlement of the German problem."[19]

Claiming that immediate British membership would inevitably lead to applications from other EFTA countries and thereby completely alter the present organization, which would destroy what already had been built and take away the Common Market's continental European character, de Gaulle suggested two alternatives. These were (1) to wait until the internal and external economic and political evolution toward a "European" Europe that had been started in Britain was completed, or (2) to create an association between the Common Market and EFTA. Britain, however, had already rejected associated status before the de Gaulle news conference and confirmed this rejection on subsequent occasions.

It was apparent from de Gaulle's declarations that he did not want to cast an outright veto; in fact, he denied that there had been a veto in his news conference of January 1963, when he slammed the door to British entry. Rather, he seemed to indicate that British membership was not welcome now, but may be more opportune at a later date. His objective seemed to be to wear down Britain as well as his EEC partners by frustrating delays and complicated solutions such as association between the EEC and EFTA. In this connection one must not overlook that the support expressed for British membership by some of the member governments, particularly the German, and perhaps also the Italian, was perhaps more a profession of goodwill than deep conviction.

An intimation of de Gaulle's future tactics on British accession could be gleaned as early as February 1967 from Couve de Murville's statement quoted earlier, in which he pointed out that British entry would inevitably change the character of the EEC. The French tactics were an intensive effort to convince the other member states that the Community had a real personality and future in its present shape and that these might be endangered by an early enlargement. The French argued with obvious justification that progress in the Common Market is difficult enough with six foreign ministers bargaining around the Brussels Council of Ministers table. If agreement had to be sought by seven, or, more likely, eleven ministers (anticipating membership of some of the EFTA countries) the Community might become a static organization instead of a dynamic one, and past achievements would be gradually whittled away. As a consequence, solving the problem of British entry would not only be a question of finding a way out of the pound sterling problem or negotiating an agricultural transitional period; rather, insisting on accession negotiations with the United Kingdom and her EFTA partners might in fact jeopardize the future of the Community.

It was of course ironic that de Gaulle, whose government had indulged more in the determined pursuit of its own national interests and had done more to disturb the effective functioning of the Community decision-making machinery than any other government, should suddenly make himself the champion of preserving and strengthening Community solidarity. For this reason it remained a matter of conjecture how much the General could convince his Common Market partners that he was becoming a true European. To dispel these doubts, de Gaulle made slight concessions to the concept of supranationalism, but more important were his continued efforts to demonstrate that Britain's "extra-European" position made her essentially different from the present member states and inherently disqualified her from membership in the Community. In support of this contention, France tried to present the nuclear nonproliferation treaty as an attempt by the Anglo-Saxon powers to steal a march over continental Europe in an important technological field and as a serious disturbance for the proper functioning of the Euratom Treaty.

Britain's revived interest in EC membership again spurred Ireland's, Norway's, and Denmark's interest in EC membership; it prompted the Danish government's application for accession, and induced Irish and Norwegian governments to submit

79

applications for membership in May and July 1967, respectively. Interestingly, both in neutral Sweden and Switzerland voices were heard advocating full EC membership rather than associate status because political unification as a goal of the member states seemed to have faded into the background, and in July 1967 the Swedish government officially requested "affiliation" with the Common Market.

SHIFT IN PARIS AND FINAL NEGOTIATIONS

It may well have been during the waning days of de Gaulle's presidency that a change in the French attitude toward British membership in the EC was initiated. In February 1969, the General had a long conversation with the British ambassador, Christopher Soames, in which he seemed to have suggested a closer relationship between France and Britain—perhaps within the framework of a modified and looser Common Market. It is uncertain what de Gaulle's motivations were for the statements made during that conversation. He may have sought to sabotage the Common Market as was suggested by Prime Minister Wilson, who divulged the contents of the Soames–de Gaulle talks to the German Chancellor, Mr. Kiesinger, before additional clarifications were obtained. Or apprehension of Germany's growing economic prowess may have prompted the General to sound out Britain about a revival of their traditional friendship during the last two World Wars.[20] Despite the fact that de Gaulle was extremely upset by Wilson's revelation of the conversation during his Bonn talks, the "Soames affair" did not cause lasting harm. President de Gaulle relinquished his office within three months and his successor, Georges Pompidou, later used the affair to defend British entry in the face of some Gaullist reproaches.[21] In the meantime, President Pompidou, a few weeks after his victory, committed himself to the idea of a European Summit Conference in July 1969. While the French highest priority goal for this forthcoming conference was tying up the financing of the CAP, Pompidou accepted enlargement of the Community on the precondition that the CAP issues had to be settled to France's satisfaction.

The Summit Meeting of the Heads of State and Governments was held in December 1969. During that conference France advocated that the Community move toward economic and monetary union and agreed to the initiation of enlargement negotiations with the four applicant countries.[22] At the same time, France's agricultural demands were satisfied by the issuance of appropriate financial regulations by the EC Council of Ministers.

With respect to the enlargement negotiations the first task of the Six was to evolve a common basis for these negotiations. This was difficult but did not present insurmountable problems. The main elements of the common basis were (1) the acceptance of a transition period, which was to be as short as possible; (2) the institutional changes required by the enlargement, which in principle would place Britain on the same basis as France, Germany, and Italy; and (3) the procedure for the negotiations, which were to be conducted under the chairmanship of the president of the Council. This body was to be responsible for the elaboration of the common negotiating posture on all levels but could delegate this task to the Commission with respect to existing common policies. We should note that this system was to be applicable not only to the negotiations with Britain, but also to other applicant countries such as Denmark, Norway, and Ireland. In institutional terms, these countries would not be placed on the same level as Britain, but were to have a position between the Netherlands and Belgium on one side and Luxembourg on the other.[23]

As for the substance of the negotiations, the Community Council considered it necessary to ensure adequate parallelism linking the progressive introduction of the free movement of goods between the old and new members of the Community to the achievement of the common agricultural market. The former would require a phased reciprocal reduction of the tariffs in force and the latter a gradual alignment of the farm prices prevailing in the applicant countries with those inside the EEC. Finally, the United Kingdom would have to adopt the Community rules and policies toward third countries. This meant progressive application of the common external tariff of the Community on goods imported from nonmember countries and

and the common commercial policies toward these countries evolved during the Community's transitional period (1958–69).[24] To ease the burden for the Commonwealth countries resulting from the elimination of tariff preferences on their imports to Britain, the Community took the position that Commonwealth countries in Africa and the Caribbean be given associated status with the enlarged Community, similar to that granted former French, Belgian, and Italian colonies in Africa.[25] Association would provide tariff preferences for their goods shipped to the Community; in fact, some of the Commonwealth countries— Nigeria, Kenya, Tanzania, and Uganda—had already signed association agreements with the Community prior to the time the current negotiations got underway.

Once the de Gaulle obstacle to Common Market membership was safely out of the way, Britain's chief concern became the cost of joining the Community. A White Paper issued by the British government in Feburary 1970 bluntly addressed itself to the subject: "The United Kingdom and the European Communities: An Economic Assessment." Emphasizing that the British position, including the balance of payments, was now better than in previous years, it made the following significant declaration:

> . . . [T]he economy of the United Kingdom is stronger, the Six are now unanimously in favour of our entry, and the political arguments for closer unity between Britain and the other countries of Western Europe have also become stronger. The major uncertain factor still is the balance of economic advantage, particularly in the short run.
> . . . [This] demonstrates the need for negotiations to determine the conditions on which the opportunity for entry could be seized. Failure to reach agreement in these negotiations would not necessarily condemn Britain or the European Communities to political or economic sterility. But Europe would have lost another historic opportunity to develop its full economic potentialities in the interests of the welfare and security of its citizens.[26]

Stressing the difficulty of translating into quantitative terms the beneficial effects of joining the Community, the White Paper nevertheless pointed out that the increases in food costs necessitated by the high fixed market prices of the CAP could well result in a rise of between 4 and 5 percent in the cost of living in Britain. Moreover, since the currency exchange controls applied by Britain to safeguard her balance of payments would have to be ended when entering the Community, whose rules generally prohibit such restrictions, the British economy might suffer additional damage. On the other hand, the White Paper expressed the hope that by joining the EC the United Kingdom could achieve a much higher growth rate for its GNP since its industry could benefit from a market of nearly 300 million inhabitants, and therefore the gamble could clearly pay off in the long run.

Whatever its positive aspects may have been, the White Paper provided excellent arguments for those opposing British entry into the Community. This group had been growing since the time in 1966 when the Common Market again became a lively issue in British politics. At that time, public opinion expressed a slight preference for membership, but in October 1969, an opinion survey in Britain showed that only 22 percent of the respondents were in favor of entry, while 54 percent said "no," and 24 percent were undecided. Broken down by party, 58 percent of Conservative supporters, 53 percent of Liberal supporters, and 51 percent of Labour supporters believed that it would be against Britain's best interest to become a member of the Community.[27] This trend was confirmed by a public opinion survey conducted in March 1970 in the six member states and Britain. Sixty-three percent of the British respondents were opposed to membership, with only 19 percent in favor, and 18 percent undecided. On the other hand, in the six member states, 64 percent of the respondents favored British membership, 8 percent were opposed, and 28 percent were undecided.[28]

The findings of the public opinion polls correspond to the mood prevailing at the annual conferences of the three major political parties in the fall of 1969. Nevertheless, the leadership of all three parties predicted that public support for the European policy would revive once the negotiations were firmly under way. Many party leaders were convinced that the prevailing public opinion reflected the frustration of nine years of waiting and humiliation, a genuine fear of price increases, and a renewed national pride due to the obvious improvement in Britain's economic situation.[29]

At the Labour Party conference significant clues were given regarding the future negotiating strategy of the Wilson government. With the balance of payments at long last moving toward a substantial surplus, Prime Minister Wilson began to assert himself by making it clear that under these changed economic circumstances Britain intended to bargain with the Community from a position of relative strength. He pointed out that "unlike the situation in 1961, we no longer face the challenge of Europe cap in hand. Europe needs us just as much, and many would say more, than we need Europe."[30]

At the Conservative Party conference the opponents to British membership in the Community forced a vote, which they lost after the Conservative hierarchy expressed its stern disapproval of any change in the official party line of support for entry. Mr. Enoch Powell did not participate in the European debate in spite of his well-known opposition to Britain in Europe, but there was little doubt that he would remain an important factor in the development of Conservative opinion on the European question. In any case, the anti-Europeans had their say, and the arguments from the floor, similar to those at conferences of the Labour and Liberal Parties, centered chiefly on the effect of the CAP on the British cost of living and the balance of payments. In addition, Conservative spokesmen hinted that a deal with France that would bring about an Anglo–French understanding on defense problems, including the use of nuclear weapons in their respective arsenals, would have to be involved in the accession process.

It is interesting to note that Britain's apprehension about the effects of the CAP was shared by the Community Commission, which was anxious to modify the CAP's price structure and subsidy system in such a manner as to prevent the continued formation of burdensome farm surpluses. If that were achieved, the cost to the British economy from joining the EEC would be reduced and the dynamic favorable impact on the economies of old and new members expected from the enlargement would be safeguarded. At the same time, Britain's adaptation to the Community rules and procedures would be facilitated and the length of the transitional period, a very controversial subject, could be cut down. Without doubt, even though the publication of the White Paper caused considerable consternation in the EC member countries, it also spurred their governments to more rapid action in preparing the initiation of the negotiations. There was full realization that the issuance of the White Paper was a shrewd move on the part of the Wilson government—it enhanced the British bargaining position and, in view of the upcoming parliamentary elections, assured Wilson of an "emergency exit."

While some of the major obstacles to reaching agreement on Britain's accession were the same as those of the 1961–62 negotiations, several problems seemed to defy solution. The most serious obstacles were the size of the financial contribution Great Britain was to make to running the Community institutions and activities and her ability to pay it; the phasing in of the CAP preferences into the British agricultural market; the future position of the British pound sterling, up to then one of the world's reserve currencies; and the special consideration for New Zealand's dairy products and Commonwealth cane sugar producers insisted upon by Britain.

The multilevel complex negotiating procedures discussed earlier[31] may have been partly responsible for the difficulty of solving these problems. Uwe Kitzinger describes these procedures in the following passages:

> . . . the President of the Council could read to the candidates a carefully drafted compromise formula evolved between the Six, but he could hardly ever respond spontaneously to any declaration made by the candidates that did not accept the Community's terms: he had to adjourn the proceedings so that the Six could agree on a new formula in every new situation. The candidate delegations—each national delegation in turn, never the four together—would sit at the bottom of the long table, perhaps listen to a series of declarations from the President of the Council (which bored the other five to tears since they, after perhaps hours of haggling over the wording, knew it only too well) and then either "take note" or "accept" the declaration. . . . They would read their own statements and, unless they had already managed to obtain prior approval informally, would then withdraw to play bridge or poker on the floor below while the meeting transformed itself

upstairs into the Council of Ministers, until the Conference was reconvened by their being asked upstairs to listen to the new agreed position of the Six. The bulk of the formal negotiation was thus in a sense carried on not so much between each candidate and the six member states, but amongst the Six themselves on how (and how far) to meet the differing requirements of the four applicants. Certainly the Six spent far more of the formal sessions talking to each other than talking to the applicant states.

Of course not all problems were treated at the ministerial level. There were only thirteen ministerial meetings of the Conference throughout the negotiations. At the outset they sometimes lasted a bare ten minutes; at "the crunch," they could go on intermittently for several days. Far more frequent were the meetings at the level of the Ministers' Deputies—the Permanent Representatives of the Six in Brussels.[32]

In January 1971 a Committee of Deputies of the Permanent Representatives was set up. This constituted a lower-level, new forum for the deliberations and decisions on more technical, but not always politically innocuous problems. Thus a three-tier system was created, the lower tiers preparing the meeting for the upper level; and the lowest, the Committee of Deputies, being fed by reports from expert groups studying specific problems and by the proposals of the Commission. Below this whole mechanism was the whole network of the private, informal contacts between members of different national delegations and the Commission's special negotiating task force. In fact, it was in the unofficial off-the-record conversations that the ground for the solution of many problems was prepared and some of the solutions bargained out. It was the setting where differences were pared down and formulae tried out. It contrasted "to the political tactics, the sullen deadlocks and the sudden visible breakthrough on the ministerial level at the other end of the scale."[33] But certain very delicate issues such as the future of the pound sterling could not be handled in this setting and required bilateral negotiations by the chief actors in the process of enlargement, President Pompidou and Prime Minister Heath.

It was the summit meeting of Pompidou and Heath in Paris on May 19 and 20, 1971, which reached the necessary agreements to move ahead with the finalization of Britain's accession to the Community. Carefully prepared bilateral secret talks were initiated in early 1971 by Ambassador Soames and Michel Jobert, then Secretary-General of the Elysée, the headquarters of France's presidents. Supported by small, yet superb teams of British and French foreign service officials, the two men prepared the talks on the gut issues of British membership. Two days before the summit, the French president gave a talk on BBC television while the British Prime Minister appeared on French television, a ploy that Kitzinger termed "a curious little diplomatic and public relations technique of talking across each other's shoulder to each other's electorates."[34] The summit itself ended in a news conference, long handshakes, obvious cordiality, and Pompidou's confident statement concerning the Community's enlargement: "it would be unreasonable now to believe that an agreement is not possible"[35] in Brussels.

THE ACCESSION TREATY

The Paris summit resolved the log jam produced by the crucial issues separating Great Britain and the Six, and a month later, in June 1971, the negotiations on the accession of Britain and the other applicant countries concluded successfully. Ultimately, Norway did not ratify its accession treaty because in a referendum held in the fall of 1972 a majority of Norwegians (53 percent) declared themselves against EC membership.[36] The major points of the three remaining accession treaties were the following:

1. Customs duties between the new member states and the Community are being scaled down to nil by five successive steps of 20 percent each, the first scheduled for April 1, 1973 and the last for July 1, 1977. The new members' tariffs *vis-à-vis* third countries are to be approximated to the common external tariff of the Community by four steps, 40 percent on January 1, 1974 and 20 percent on January 1, 1975, January 1, 1976 and July 1, 1977.[37]

87

2. The new members accept the CAP and agree to align their food prices with those of the Six in six steps over the five-year transitional period ending December 31, 1977. Exceptions of not more than 10 percent on either side of the price adjustment for any one marketing year may be allowed. Special arrangements were made for fisheries, hill-farming, and horticulture.

3. The financial contributions to the Community budget were fixed at 19.3 percent for Great Britain; 2.46 percent for Denmark; and 0.61 percent for Ireland. However, the full contributions are becoming effective only gradually over the five-year transition period, and Great Britain was given an additional two years before it will have to pay its full share in order to avoid any financial upsets in the United Kingdom.[38]

4. The institutional changes necessitated by the enlargement resulted in an increase of Commission members to 13 from 9, with two Commissioners each from Britain, France, Germany, and Italy, and one each from the remaining countries; an increase of the Court of Justice to nine judges and three advocates general; and a European Parliament membership raised to 198 with 36 members each from the four larger countries, 14 each from Belgium and the Netherlands, ten each from Denmark and Ireland, and six from Luxembourg. Voting rights in the now nine-member Council of Ministers are: Britain, France, Germany, and Italy, 10 each; Belgium and the Netherlands, 5 each; Denmark and Ireland, 3 each; and Luxembourg, 2.

5. The enlarged Community offered the independent developing Commonwealth countries situated in Africa,[39] the Indian Ocean,[40] the Pacific Ocean,[41] and the Caribbean[42] the possibility of ordering their relations with it according to one of the following formulae of their choice:

(a) participation in the Convention of Association of Yaoundé affiliating presently eighteen African countries, Madagascar and Mauritius with the Community when the convention was to be renewed in 1974

(b) the conclusion of one or more special associations based on article 238 of the EEC Treaty and exemplified by the Arusha Convention with Kenya, Uganda, and Tanzania[43]

(c) the conclusion of trade agreements with a view to facilitating and developing trade between the Community and those countries

With respect to India, Pakistan, Ceylon, Singapore, and Malaysia the Community will be disposed to consider any trade problems that might arise in those countries and in the countries situated in the same region, with a view to finding appropriate solutions.

The territories dependent on the United Kingdom[44] will be associated with the enlarged Community, in accordance with the provisions of Part Four of the EEC Treaty.

6. With respect to the special problem of Britain, a compromise formula was found for New Zealand's traditionally large exports of dairy products to the United Kingdom under which safeguard guarantees were given for butter until 1975 and for cheese until 1977. An accord safeguarding sugar imports from certain Commonwealth countries was also reached.[45]

7. In order to underline its "Europeanness" the British government assured the Six that the pound sterling would be gradually phased out as a reserve currency and progressively align the external characteristics of sterling with those of other Community currencies.[46]

RATIFICATION OF THE
ENLARGEMENT TREATIES

Following the end of the negotiations the British government issued a White Paper in which it sought to justify the results achieved. It stated that:

89

As this White Paper shows, Her Majesty's Government are convinced that our country will be more secure, our ability to maintain peace and promote development in the world greater, our economy stronger, and our industries and people more prosperous, if we join the European Communities than if we remain outside them. The Government are also convinced—and this conviction is shared by the Governments of the present six members of the Communities—that British membership of the Communities will enhance the security and prosperity of Western Europe. The Government are satisfied that the arrangements for our entry agreed in the negotiations will enable us to adjust satisfactorily to our new position as members of the Communities, and thus to reap the full benefits of membership.

The Government will therefore seek the approval of Parliament in the autumn for a decision of principle to take up full membership of the Communities on the basis of the arrangements which have been negotiated with them.[47]

The House of Commons approved the government's decision to join the Community by a vote of 356 ayes to 244 noes on October 28, 1971. The vote for accession was considerably higher than expected, but this was not all that was needed for full legal membership. What was still required was the passage of the European Communities Bill, which would signify fully acceptance of the three Community Treaties with their considerable number of self-executing clauses and the large number of subsequent ordinances directly binding on private persons and corporations in Britain.

When, after many arduous and sometimes acrimonious deliberations, the House of Commons gave its assent to the European Communities Bill on July 13, 1972 (by a small majority of 17), a milestone was reached in British constitutional history. The Community law and legislation with its direct applicability for the people of Britain was accepted, and the path was opened for the direct introduction of Community rules and regulations into the British legal system.

Although the opposition to British entry into the EC in the House of Commons unsuccessfully attempted to make a last stand by moving for the adoption of a clause reaffirming the ultimate sovereignty of Parliament with respect to the Community Treaties, the Solicitor General maintained that passage of the European Communities Bill was, in itself, an exercise of Parliamentary sovereignty.[48] While the opposition's efforts were motivated, at least in part, by the hope of creating a basis for British withdrawal from the EC at a later date, the question of such exercise of Parliamentary supremacy is likely to be moot since the increasingly close economic and political links forged between the United Kingdom and her Community partners would make the cost of withdrawing excessively high.

Although public opinion usually plays a minor role in decisions on international policy, it is interesting to see that following the issuance of the White Paper in 1971 a slight majority of those favoring British membership in the EC became visible and that this small majority generally maintained itself during 1972 and early 1973.[49] However, toward the end of 1973, the opponents to British membership regained the upper hand.[50] To gauge the importance of this issue for the British public it is interesting to note that even during the crucial period of negotiations and ratification of the accession treaty the Common Market was regarded as a minor problem facing Britain and that "unemployment, cost of living, Ireland, and labor relations were viewed generally as more urgent."[51]

During 1972 Denmark and Ireland also ratified the accession treaties. Prior to ratification in Denmark a referendum was held, in which 63.5 percent of the voters expressed themselves in favor of Danish EC membership. By the end of 1972 the Six had also ratified the treaties and the enlarged Community became a reality on January 1, 1973.

British membership in the EC received a serious jolt when in February 1974 the Heath government was ousted and replaced by a Labour government headed by Harold Wilson, although the Labour Party was not able to gain a clear majority.[52] Prime Minister Wilson promised that if he were elected there would be a renegotiation of Britain's accession to the Community and a referendum by the people whether to accept or reject the changed relationship as a basis for continued EC membership.[53]

In June 1974 James Callaghan, the Foreign Secretary, provided details about the British position on renegotiating

91

the accession treaty and certain Community policies.

1. The British contribution to the Community budget is to be reduced to reflect the lower GNP compared to that of France and Germany. As originally negotiated, the British contribution would be eventually substantially more than Britain's fair share of the Community's operating costs. In 1980 the British GNP share would be 14 percent of overall EC GNP whereas the British contribution to expenditures would be 24 percent.[54]

2. In the agricultural field, the British government insisted on a reduction of the cost of the CAP, improvements in marketing regimes, and a reexamination of EC relations with the rest of the world, specifically a liberal import policy for foodstuffs not produced in Europe.

3. In relation with the Third World, Britain would like to see trade and cooperation arrangements worked out without regard to reciprocity and improve the system of "generalized preferences."

4. Regional aid policy must take into account the most needy areas in the Community without attempting to give each member state something in return for financial contributions to the Regional Fund, as was advocated especially by the French government.[55]

Follwing the October 1974 elections in Great Britain, which gave the Wilson government a small absolute majority,[56] Prime Minister Wilson confirmed his intention to renegotiate the accession treaty and work for a change of various EC policies. In a speech to the House of Commons, Foreign Secretary Callaghan stated that some progress had been made in these efforts. He declared:

I do not delude myself either on the subject of the budget or of the CAP. I do not believe that the walls of Jericho are likely to fall down at the first blast of the trumpet . . . but maybe we shall succeed. Progress has certainly been made on giving the Community's policy towards developing countries a more global approach. *But I am less happy about the state of affairs in the matter of regional policy. . . .* Even here, however, it seems to me that the blind acceptance of the doctrines of the market economy which has disfigured the Community in recent years is showing signs of giving way to the needs and realities of a sovereign parliament.[57]

The demands of the British government with regard to regional aid policy were met to a large degree when the Conference of Heads of Government held in Paris December 9 and 10, 1974, decided to establish a European Regional Development Fund, whose distribution was to be based generally on "need" rather than "just return" for contributions made by member states. Of the resources of the Fund, totaling in excess of $1.5 billion over a period of three years, the share for the United Kingdom was to be 28 percent.[58]

Some of the other demands made by the Wilson government for the renegotiation of the accession treaty were dealt with at the Heads of Government meeting in Dublin on March 10 and 11, 1975 (the first such meeting to be called the "European Council"). With respect to the British budget contribution, considered too high as originally stipulated in the accession agreement, a complicated correcting mechanism was adopted that takes into account the relative stance of a member country in the Community GNP.[59] This mechanism was regarded by the British as an acceptable concession by the other Community countries as was another concession made by the Conference, which made it easier for New Zealand to sell its dairy products to the Community.

With the British demand for improved Community relations with the Third World already having received sympathetic treatment prior to the Dublin meeting, the way was now open for Prime Minister Wilson to make a full statement on behalf of his government on the result of the renegotiations. Speaking to the House of Commons on March 18, 1975, after a long review of the British objectives of these renegotiations, the Prime Minister concluded:

Some [of these objectives] we have achieved in full; on others we have made considerable progress, though in the time

93

available to us it has not been possible to carry them to the point where we can argue that our aims have been completely realized.

It is thus for the judgment now of the Government, shortly of Parliament, and in due course of the British people, whether we should stay in the European Community on the basis of the terms as they have now been renegotiated.[60]

On March 28 Wilson delivered to the Parliament his government's White Paper recommending continued membership in the Community. It was approved by the House of Commons on April 9 by a vote of 396 to 180. The date for the referendum of the British people was set for June 5.

The campaign preceding the referendum was waged with great vigor by both the pros and antis. It focused more on "bread and butter" issues than on high-sounding phrases dealing with solidarity, unity, and destiny.

On food, the pros said prices had risen because of the sharp price increases on the world markets; the antis claimed that, outside Europe, Britain would be able to buy food in the cheaper markets. On jobs, the pros said the loss of access to Europe would mean higher unemployment; the antis pointed to the low jobless rate in Norway, which had voted against EC membership. On social welfare, the pros said that other partners were paying more in benefits, and membership would provide the incentive to catch up; the antis countered by saying that once Britain stopped pouring money into Europe she would have more for her own people. On defense, the pros stressed that a strong Community contributed to a strong defense; the antis, that the defense of Britain did not depend on the European Community, but on NATO, and the United States would not allow Britain to go under.

The polls suggested an overwhelming lead for the pro-Community forces, despite the opposition by half the Labour Party in the House of Commons, seven of the twenty-three ministers in the cabinet, most of the trade unions, and some vocal Conservatives such as Enoch Powell. With the leaders of the three major parties all urging a "yes" vote, the antis clearly had an uphill struggle despite the absence of real emotion within Britain for the Community.

The Commonwealth countries, the traditional trading partners of Britain, also joined the chorus. At their conference in Jamaica earlier in 1975 they made it clear that they had completed their adjustments to Britain's membership in the Community and stressed that it was now in their interest to try to broaden their access to the Community, with its 250 million people. The Commonwealth producers argued that they would stand to gain more from expanding trade with the Community than returning to the old patterns of trade with London.

From Germany, too, came an intervention in the heated debate raging in Britain. The West German defense minister, George Leber, noted that American support for Europe hinged on whether the allies showed themselves to be true alliance partners. In his view, Britain's vote would have a decisive influence on the weight of that European partnership.[61]

The outcome of the referendum was a resounding success for those who wanted continued membership in the Community. More than 67 percent voted in favor and only 32.8 percent opposed. Voter turnout was 66 percent—26 million of Britain's 40 million registered voters. All U.K. regions except two (sparsely populated Shetland and the Western Isles) showed majorities, reaching to nearly 75 percent in some cases.[62]

SOME IMPLICATIONS OF THE ENLARGEMENT

The British government's decision to seek membership in the European Community marked a significant turning point in traditional policy. Formerly having a nostalgic commitment to national independence and to its special relationships to the Commonwealth and the United States, Britain would now turn to the pragmatic policy of pooling resources and governmental powers with other European nations. To quote the late Dean Acheson, Britain had "lost an empire and not found a new role"[63] and therefore membership in the Community was the only realistic option for ensuring British economic welfare.

For Harold Wilson the strategy of renegotiating the terms of EC membership was conceived not only as an endeavor to ease the burden of accession, but as an effort to keep his Labour Party together. The national referendum was a new device in British constitutional history, one once opposed by Wilson.

The renegotiations came against the background of severe economic crisis with all indices showing that the British were falling behind their partners in economic well-being. The pound dropped on the world money market; inflation in Britain continued at a furious rate of 25 percent a year, the worst of any OECD country; businesses went into bankruptcy; and unemployment rose. The proud statements of Mr. Wilson in 1967 that Britain was not a "sick man" asking for admittance to the Community, but a "sound, strong organism" had turned out to be completely untrue by 1975.

For a year prior to the referendum much of the work of the Community had bogged down while the British government had pursued its renegotiation demands. With the surprisingly favorable response given by the British electorate to continued EC membership, the Commission embarked immediately on a program of revitalizing the affairs of the Community through concrete new initiatives that would strengthen the EC institutions and achieve greater solidarity among the member states.[64]

A major task also faces the governments of the EC member states which, despite Britain's many ailments, were anxious to ensure her continued membership. With the outcome of the referendum, Britain's problems have once and for all become European problems that require urgent solution. As a consequence, the member governments might be induced to give the EC and integration new impetus and thus work hand in hand with the Commission. But as we have seen, during the last decade, to forego national prerogatives has been a difficult undertaking for all member governments and much may depend on the conclusion Prime Minister Wilson draws from his referendum victory. As a German newspaper analyzed the situation aptly:

Should Mr. Wilson consider the poll to represent a mandate to extend the Community Britain could prove a prime mover within the Common Market.

If, on the other hand, the Labour leader concentrates on healing the wounds self-inflicted by his party, Britain may well act as a brake on further European integration.[65]

Mr. Wilson's own inclination most probably will be not to follow either alternative, but adopt a noncommittal, middle-of-the-road course, which would not actively assist in the Community's integrative progress.

The international implications flowing from British membership include the influence on future EC policies, because Britain is generally regarded as "outward looking" in its stance on foreign trade and thereby is likely to reinforce Germany's similar outlook. As a consequence, both countries can be expected to push for greater trade liberalization between the Community and third countries; and the CAP may be modified along lines that would benefit agricultural experts from temperate zone countries such as the United States, Canada, and Australia. It may well be symptomatic that the agreement on farm price increases in September 1974 was initially rejected by the German government. While a solution was evidently found on the farm price compromise reached in Brussels, the German government is just as much interested in modifying the CAP as Britain is. Moreover, British expertise in monetary affairs may be useful in finding agreement on currency relationships acceptable to both sides of the Atlantic and Japan. On the other hand, the enlargement of the Community with its accompanying increase in economic power will cause problems for the outsiders, which will create tension in the economic and political interactions among developed and developing countries. J. Robert Schaetzel, former U.S. ambassador to the Communities, put the likely implications of the enlargement in perspective when he declared:

An enlarged Community, including Great Britain, will bring new problems—but also new opportunities. I see no reason why we should not do at least as well with an enlarged Community as we have with the present Community. Fundamentally, such a large and prosperous area with fairly open economic policies should benefit American trade and investment substantially. The enlarged Community should also be

97

in an even better position to contribute to the problem of the underdeveloped world. In saying this, I am naturally assuming that both the Europeans and we will continue to follow sensible and constructive policies on international economic issues. I do not want to gloss over the problem areas. Agriculture will remain particularly difficult for some time to come, and enlargement is not likely to make things any easier in the short run. My hope is twofold: First, that we and the Europeans can settle certain pressing specific issues now and, secondly, that over a longer period of time we can come to grips jointly with the underlying problems on both sides of the Atlantic.

Beyond this it seems to me a matter of fundamental self-interest that the Community and the United States accept one another, more or less as we are. We must approach one another with a degree of maturity. This implies a recognition that any such large, democratic and evolving societies as the Community and the United States are bound to generate problems and that our relations will be marked by imperfections. Reasonable men should not lose their sense of proportion that these day-to-day problems obscure completely the broad political and economic benefits both sides of the Atlantic derive from this relationship.[66]

One of the first acts of international policy following the signing of the accession treaties have been successful negotiations for free trade agreements in the industrial field with some of the EFTA countries that for various reasons did not want to become full EC members. These countries were: Austria, Finland, Iceland, Portugal, Sweden, and Switzerland. These agreements covered not only the areas for which the EEC Treaty is competent, but included topics contained in the ECSC and Euratom Treaties. After Norway had rejected full membership in the EC, negotiations on a similar free trade agreement also led to the successful conclusion of an accord. The contents of these agreements will be discussed in the next chapter, the main topic of which is the association policy of the Community.

NOTES

1. For details of this association see Werner Feld, "The Association Agreements of the European Communities," *International Organization* 19, no. 2 (Spring 1965): 223-249.

2. For more details see Miriam Camps, *Britain and the European Community 1955-1963* (Princeton, N.J.: Princeton University Press, 1964).

3. The OEEC member states were all European countries west of the Iron Curtain. In December 1960 this organization was changed into the Organization for Economic Cooperation and Development (OECD) and the United States, Canada, and eventually Japan became members.

4. Heinrich Siegler, *Dokumentation der Europaischen Integration* (Bonn: Siegler, 1961), p. 383.

5. EEC Commission, *Fifth General Report*, sec. 184. This communication was dated August 9, 1961.

6. Cf. Randall Hinshaw, *The European Community and American Trade* (New York: Praeger, 1964), pp. 51, 52, 102-105.

7. See for example EEC Commission, *Report to the European Parliament on the State of the Negotiations with the United Kingdom* (Brussels, March 1963); and Camps, op. cit.

8. U.W. Kitzinger, *The Politics and Economics of European Integration* (New York and London: Praeger, 1963), p. 204.

9. Camps, op. cit., p. 493.

10. EEC Commission Spokesman, *Press Summary of the Commission's Report to the European Parliament on the State of the Negotiations with the United Kingdom,* March 4, 1963.

11. *Agence Europe Bulletin,* January 24, 1967, p. 2.

12. Cf. ibid., December 3, 1966, p. 4; January 9, 1967, p. 2; January 28, 1967, p. 6; February 22, 1967, p. 2.

13. Ibid., February 24, 1967, p. 3.

14. Ibid., February 24, 1967, p. 3.

15. Ibid., January 20, 1967, p. 3.

16. Cf. ibid., November 22, 1966, p. 7; January 19, 1967, p. 2; February 8, 1967, p. 7; February 14, 1967, p. 7.

17. Ibid., February 1, 1967, p. 1.

18. Ibid., May 3, 1967, p. 1.

19. *Times-Picayune* (New Orleans, La.), May 17, 1967, p. 1.

20. For details see *Le Monde,* February 21, March 11, 1969, as well as the excellent and complete account by Uwe Kitzinger in *Diplomacy and Persuasion* (London: Thames and Hudson, 1973), pp. 45-58.

21. Kitzinger, *Diplomacy and Persuasion*, p. 57.

22. Other commitments made were the provision for the Community to have its own financial resources from certain customs and tax receipts and slightly increased powers of the European Parliament over the Community budget. For details see the Communiqué in the Commisions *Third General Report* on the Activities of the Communities, 1969.

23. *Agence Europe Bulletin,* March 6, May 12, 1970.

24. Ibid., April 6, 1970.

25. *Journal of Commerce,* April 3, 1970.

26. *The Times* (London), February 11, 1970.

27. Ibid., October 24, 1969.

28. *Agence Europe Bulletin,* March 17, 1970.

29. Cf. Peter Jenkins, "Britain's Attitude to the Common Market: A Lively Issue at the Party Conferences," *Common Market* 9, no. 12 (December 1969): 262-265; and *Agence Europe Bulletin,* March 24, 1970, for the evolution of the British economy during the 1969-70 period.

30. Cited by Jenkins, op. cit., p. 263.

31. See p. 71.

32. U. W. Kitzinger, *Diplomacy and Persuasion* (London: Thames and Hudson, 1973), pp. 79, 81.

33. Ibid., p. 84.

34. Ibid., p. 119.

35. Quoted by Kitzinger, ibid., p. 121.

36. For the reasons of Norway's turndown see Frederik Bolin, "Why Norway Bolted," *European Community* (December 1972): 13.

37. *Fifth General Report,* 1971, p. 23.

38. The Commission's *Fifth* and *Sixth General Report,* 1971 and 1972, pp. 30 and 21, respectively.

39. Botswana, Gambia, Ghana, Kenya, Lesotho, Malawi, Nigeria, Sierra Leone, Swaziland, Tanzania, Uganda, Zambia.

40. Mauritius, which has already asked to participate in the Yaoundé Convention, became a member on July 29, 1969.

41. Fiji, Tonga, Western Samoa.

42. Barbados, Guyana, Jamaica, Trinidad and Tobago.

43. For details of these associations see chapter 4.

44. The Bahamas, Bermuda, British Honduras, British Indian Ocean Territory, British Solomon Islands, British Virgin Islands, Brunei, Cayman Islands, Falkland Islands and Dependencies, Gibraltar, Gilbert and Ellis

Islands, Hong Kong, Montserrat, the New Hebrides, Pitcairn, St. Helena and Dependencies, the Seychelles, Turks and Caicos Islands, Associated States in the Caribbean (Antigua, Dominica, Grenada, St. Lucia, St. Vincent, St. Kitts-Nevis-Anguilla).

45. For details see the Commission's *Fifth General Report,* 1971, pp. 43-46.

46. For details see Kitzinger, *Diplomacy and Persuasion,* pp. 138-140.

47. *The United Kingdom and the European Communities,* presented to Parliament by the Prime Minister by Command of Her Majesty July 1971 (London: Her Majesty's Stationery Office), p. 2.

48. *The Times* (London), July 14, 1972.

49. For a full analysis of public opinion trends see Kitzinger, *Diplomacy and Persuasion,* pp. 352-370.

50. *Agence Europe Bulletin,* October 10, 1973 (editorial).

51. Kitzinger, *Diplomacy and Persuasion,* provides detailed figures for this.

52. *New York Times,* March 2, 1974.

53. Interestingly, the Common Market issue ranked very low among the concerns of British voters. A poll taken early in February 1974 indicated that cost of living problems and rising food prices were the most crucial issues preoccupying the respondents (55 and 31 percent, respectively) while only 6 percent were concerned about the Common Market membership [*The Times,* (London), February 14, 1974]. Of course, rising food prices were related indirectly to the CAP's tendency of raising target prices every year.

54. *Agence Europe Bulletin,* June 4-5, 1974.

55. For details see ibid. The French method has been called the "watering can" method.

56. *New York Times,* October 12, 1974.

57. *Agence Europe Bulletin,* November 1, 1974.

58. *Bulletin of the European Communities Commission,* no. 12 (1974): 10. For background on this subject see Werner J. Feld, "Subnational Regionalism in the European Community," *Orbis* 18, no. 4 (Winter 1975): 1176-1192.

59. For details see *Bulletin of the European Communities Commission,* no. 3 (1975): 6. The formula for this mechanism was worked out exclusively by the Commission, which thereby made an important contribution to saving the Community of Nine and gained prestige from this "show of expertise."

60. Ibid., 7.

61. For additional details of the campaign see Alvin Shuster, "Britain Says 'Yes'," *European Community* (June 1975): 3-7.

62. *The Times* (London), June 7, 1975.

63. Quoted in Gerhard Mally, *The European Community in Perspective: The New Europe, the United States and the World* (Lexington, Mass.: Heath, 1973), p. 175.

64. Cf. *Agence Europe Bulletin,* June 12, 13, 1975.

65. *Hannoversche Allgemeine,* June 7, 1975.

66. Quoted in *Agence Europe Document* no. 638, July 30, 1971.

4

The
Association
Policy:
*Economic Assistance or
Extension of Political
Influence?*

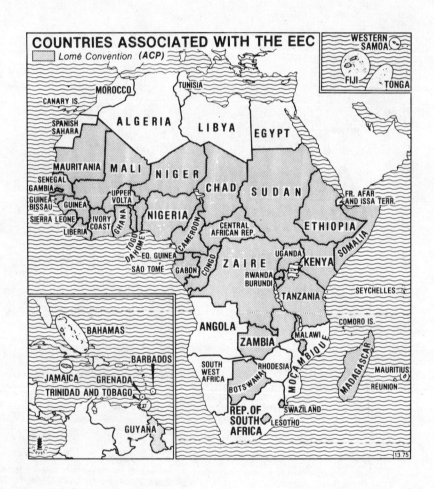

COUNTRIES ASSOCIATED WITH THE EEC

Lomé Convention (ACP)

WESTERN SAMOA

FIJI   TONGA

MOROCCO

CANARY IS.

TUNISIA

SPANISH SAHARA

ALGERIA   LIBYA   EGYPT

MAURITANIA   MALI   NIGER

SENEGAL
GAMBIA
GUINEA-BISSAU   GUINEA
SIERRA LEONE
LIBERIA

UPPER VOLTA

IVORY COAST   GHANA   NIGERIA   CAMEROON

CHAD   SUDAN

FR. AFAR AND ISSA TERR.

TOGO   DAHOMEY

CENTRAL AFRICAN REP.   ETHIOPIA

EQ. GUINEA
SÃO TOMÉ   GABON   CONGO   ZAIRE   UGANDA   KENYA   SOMALIA

RWANDA
BURUNDI

TANZANIA   SEYCHELLES

BAHAMAS

BARBADOS

JAMAICA   GRENADA
TRINIDAD AND TOBAGO

GUYANA

ANGOLA   ZAMBIA   MALAWI

COMORO IS.

MOÇAMBIQUE   MADAGASCAR   MAURITIUS

SOUTH WEST AFRICA   RHODESIA   RÉUNION

BOTSWANA

SWAZILAND

REP. OF SOUTH AFRICA   LESOTHO

13 75

The core of the Community's association policy is preferential treatment for the associate country through the reduction or elimination of tariffs for goods shipped from the associate to the Community and in many cases also by the grant of financial aid. In return, the associate countries offer certain tariff preferences, called "reverse preferences," for the import of Community products.

The first association was established with the colonial possessions of the Six by the EEC Treaty itself.[1] In 1957 France still possessed a considerable colonial empire in Africa and had special relations with Tunisia and Morocco. Algeria, in fact, was part of metropolitan France. Belgium was installed in the Congo and Ruanda–Urundi. Although Italy had lost its colonial possessions as the result of her defeat in World War II, she was authorized to administer her former possession of Somaliland as a trust territory for the United Nations. In addition, she had special relations with Libya. The Netherlands had no colonial territories in Africa, but had possessions in Southeast Asia (Dutch New Guinea) and in the New World (Surinam and Curaçao). France also had a few overseas territories outside Africa, some of them in the Caribbean and others in the Southwest Pacific. Only Luxembourg and Germany did not have any overseas possessions; Germany was deprived of her colonies after World War I.

In view of the traditionally close economic and cultural relationship between France and her dependencies, the French government threatened to abandon the EEC Treaty negotiations at a rather late stage unless the question of the overseas possessions of the member states was included on the negotiating agenda. France wanted either to extend the Common Market to the overseas territories or accord them some sort of preferential treatment. Having guaranteed its possessions a market for tropical commodities at prices often above the world level,

France felt that she could not join the EEC if it meant that the African dependencies were to be completely separated from France in the economic sphere. Moreover, the French had a tremendous investment in the overseas territories, especially in Africa, which totaled nearly $1 billion, and which would have been placed in extreme jeopardy if the colonies had to go it alone after 1958.[2]

Reluctantly, France's partners, too far committed and too eager to get started with the common venture to risk a breakdown of the whole Common Market project, agreed to an accommodation of the French demand. Germany in particular, but also the others, opposed the automatic extension of the EEC Treaty to the overseas possessions, which, in fact, would have been disastrous for the economies of the areas involved. The solution found was the establishment of an association with most of the overseas territories, especially those located in Africa. The first period of the association was to run for five years; after that the association could be renewed or revised taking into account the changed circumstances. In addition, a "Declaration of Intention" opened the way for future negotiations on association agreements with areas that had not been included in the original association. These included the autonomous parts of the Netherlands (Surinam and the Antilles) as well as the independent countries of Morocco, Tunisia, and Libya.

In general, the EEC Treaty regulations establishing the association extended most of the trade advantages of the Common Market to the overseas territories and provided for public investment capital to promote development. At the same time, they granted protection to the infant industries of these territories against the full brunt of Europen competition by permitting the retention of certain trade barriers.

The technical vehicle for the concessions granted to the associated countries was the creation of free trade areas, which opened up the whole Community—and in particular the German market—to exports of tropical products and other commodities from these countries and gave them a marked preference over similar exports from other countries. The creation of this preferential system evoked loud protests in GATT from Latin American and excluded African countries such as Ghana, who claimed that this preference would seriously harm their exports to the member states. The main counterargument of the Community was that because of the expected growth of demand in the increasingly prosperous member states the exports of third countries might well rise. As it turned out, some of the exports of tropical goods originating from nonassociated states actually increased, whereas exports from the associated countries up to 1962 rose only minimally. But the discrimination against nonassociated states has also had its effects inasmuch as long-term contracts and supply agreements covering the delivery of certain tropical agricultural products and raw materials were allocated with an eye toward the export trade of the associated countries.

Equally as important as the tariff and trade concessions were the financial aid arrangements made by the association provisions. In order to finance economic and social projects including the building of roads, ports, schools, hospitals, and the prevention of soil erosion, the member states committed themselves to paying $581 million into a European Development Fund. The two largest contributors to this Fund were France and Germany, each making available $200 million. The Fund was established in response to French claims that she could not extend trade concessions to her European partners in the EEC Treaty without receiving their assistance in financing economic development in her overseas territories; and it was France who was the major beneficiary of the Fund, receiving more than $511 million for this purpose. Germany agreed to pay her share of $200 million mainly because she anticipated large economic gains from the Common Market—in a sense it was a prepayment to France for expected benefits—but the German government also hoped, of course, that easier access to the African markets would increase her exports in these areas. Increased exports to the formerly French-controlled markets in Africa were also important motivations for the other partners of France to shoulder the financial burden involved in the association. A secondary consideration for all member states may have been the hope that during the approaching period of decolonization the associates' anticipation of increased trade with Europe and the expected financial aid from the Community would restrain these areas, especially those in Africa, from orienting themselves

107

toward the Communist bloc, and would induce them to maintain friendly political relations with the Community and the West.

THE CONVENTION OF YAOUNDÉ

With the beginning of 1960, the "Year of African Independence," most of the associated countries in Africa obtained independence, and it became clear that, after the expiration of the first five years, the continuation of the associational relationship with these countries could not be carried out by a unilateral decision of the Council of Ministers, as was stipulated by the EEC Treaty. Rather, the associational arrangement had to be based on an international law treaty with full equality accorded to the African states and Madagascar in their negotiations and relations with the Community and the member states. The EEC Commission presented pertinent proposals for such a treaty in the summer of 1961, but the discussions among the Six on these proposals immediately revealed major differences of opinion. The Germans argued that the preferences accorded to the associated states should be reduced and replaced by commodity stabilization schemes. France, on the other hand, insisted on retaining the preferences, which were especially important to her economy since the fourteen former French colonies had agreed to remain in the *Communaute Financière Africaine,* which was based on the French franc. The prospect of the British entry into the Common Market complicated the issue because the United Kingdom wanted to procure a tie with the EEC for the African Commonwealth countries, possibly by association. The Dutch felt, therefore, that the new association with the now independent former colonies of France, Belgium, and Italy could not be finalized until a decision was made about the link of the Commonwealth countries. However, the old associates did not want to wait for this decision. Backed by the French, they were anxious to shape the new associational arrangement as quickly as possible and to ensure the maintenance of their preferences. Finally, in May 1962 a ministerial meeting between the Six and the African countries succeeded in reaching a large measure of agreement on the trade and aid features for a new association, which permitted the drafting and initialing of an agreement by December 20, 1962. In January 1963, when the first British negotiations collapsed, there were general rumors that France's partners would retaliate by refusing to sign the association agreement. However, while a delay in signing did, in fact, occur that may have confirmed this rumor, the agreement was finally signed on July 20 in Yaoundé, Cameroons, and was called the Convention of Yaoundé.[3]

The broad aims of this Convention, concluded for a period of five years, were to expand trade between the associated African states and the EEC members, strengthen the economic independence of the African associates, and contribute thereby to the development of international trade. To accomplish these goals the Convention basically continued the free trade area system between the Community and the associated states established in 1958 by the EEC Treaty.

However, the Convention also made a number of important modifications. First, whereas the EEC Treaty provided for a progressive abolition of customs duties not only for trade between the member states and the associated countries but also between the associated countries themselves, the Convention did not contain such a provision. Consequently, the associated states could organize their trade relations between themselves and with third countries as they saw fit. In fact, these arrangements could even take the form of additional customs unions or free trade areas provided that such units were not incompatible with the principles and provisions of the Convention.

Second, customs duties for a number of the most important tropical products originating from the associated countries were abolished by the EEC member states as soon as the Convention entered into force, thus affording an immediate benefit to the associated countries. At the same time, the customs duties for these products were reduced for imports from third countries in order to make the new association more palatable to these countries. The reduction of customs duties by the associated countries was also speeded up, unless development needs or industrialization requirements of the associated countries made necessary the retention of existing customs duties or the introduction of new ones.

Third, when formulating its common agricultural policy, the Community had to take the interests of the associated countries into consideration with regard to those of their products that were similar to and competitive with European products. On matters of commercial policy the association partners were required to keep each other informed in order to implement the Convention effectively.

In order to achieve the long-range aims of the association agreement the Convention contained a number of provisions for financial aid and technical assistance for the economic and social development of the associated countries. The total amount to be contributed to the European Development Fund for this purpose was $730 million, of which $666 million was to come from the member states and $64 million from the European Investment Bank.

In assessing the reciprocity of the advantages and obligations of the association partners under the Convention of Yaoundé, the most important consideration must be that this agreement established a relationship between highly developed countries and states struggling to reach the first rungs of the economic development ladder. Although the immediate benefits that the associated countries derived from the Convention were vastly greater than those that the Community obtained, the African states and Madagascar undertook certain obligations that were expected to be of potential value to EEC member states. For example, the obligation of nondiscriminatory tariff treatment would offer certain opportunities for France's EEC partners, disappointed by the meager benefits they obtained from the 1958 association, to enlarge their export business to the former French colonies.

The most important associational institution under the Convention of Yaoundé was the Association Council, composed of the members of the EC Council of Ministers and the Commission, who represented the Community, and of one government member from each associated state. The governments of the EC member states were not represented individually. Reflecting the bilateralism of the agreement, the associated states collectively and the Community had only one vote each, which means that all decisions, recommendations, and resolutions had to be reached by unanimity. The main functions of the Association Council were consultation, deliberation, and supervision over the implementation of the Convention. Since most of the important details of the association had been regulated by the Convention itself, the Council's competence to make specific decisions for the operation of the association was not extensive. Such decisions were binding for the association members.

The Association Council was assisted by an Association Committee, which had the major task of ensuring the continuity of the association's satisfactory operation. Since the Association Council normally met only once a year, the Association Committee assumed considerable significance.

The third institution provided by the Convention of Yaoundé was the Parliamentary Conference. Consisting of an equal number of delegates from the European Parliament and from the parliaments of the associated states, its formal powers were very limited.

The final institutional feature of the Convention was a Court of Arbitration. It had jurisdiction over disputes concerning the interpretation and application of the Convention and could make binding decisions if prior amicable settlement by the Association Council had proven to be impossible.

It should be noted that the principle of parity, so important to the African quest for identity and self-respect, was applied strictly to the structure and procedures of all institutions of the Convention. The principle of the autonomy of the Community organs was also fully maintained by the Convention: None of the institutions created for the association of the EEC with the African states and Madagascar permitted the associated states any formal participation in the internal decision-making process of the organs of the Community. Of course, in view of the many opportunities for contact, some measure of informal participation could not be prevented at times.

111

THE EFFECTS OF THE CONVENTION

The Convention of Yaoundé became operative on June 1, 1964. Transitional provisions annexed to the Convention had extended the regulations governing the original association from January 1, 1963, until the date that the new arrangement would go into effect. How successful had the continuing association between the Community and the eighteen African states been, and how successful was the new arrangement in remedying the flaws and deficiencies of the original association?

Examining the trade figures between the association partners as shown in Table 4.1, we find that exports from the associates to the Common Market rose approximately 87.5 percent from 1958 to 1972. The big jump between 1963 and 1969 was

Table 4.1
EEC Trade with Yaoundé Associates
(millions of U.S. dollars)

	1958	1960	1963	1969	1970	1972	(Percent) Increase	1973[a]
Imports from Yaoundé associates	914	952	989	1718	1863	1714	87.5	2376
Exports to Yaoundé associates	712	603	726	1117	1265	1459	104.9	1754

[a] 1973 figures include for the first time data for all nine member states.

Source: Statistisches Amt der Europaischen Gemeinschaften, Foreign Trade, no. 2 (1973): 12, 14; and no. 5 (1975): 4.

caused primarily by shipments of bulk goods such as ores and petroleum to the EEC beginning in 1965.[4] However, the exports from the member states to the associated countries increased even more during that period, the percentage of increase being 104.9. For information purposes, we have also listed the figures of 1973, which show substantial increases over 1972. However, it must be noted that the 1973 figures are not comparable to the data of previous years, because as the result of the Community's enlargement, they contain imports and exports for the nine member states rather than the old six.

In view of the fears expressed by Latin American and non-associated countries in GATT that the association with the African states would have a harmful effect on their exports to the Community, it is interesting to take a look at the pertinent trade figures (Table 4.2). Exports to the Common Market from South and Central American countries during the period from 1958 to 1972 rose about 125 percent. During the same period, sales from the nonassociated African states (excluding the countries bordering on the Mediterranean) to the Community expanded over 500 percent, much of which has been in petroleum and minerals. Clearly, it is difficult to see that the association harmed the exports to the Common Market by those countries that compete with the African associates in many products and commodities.

Table 4.2
EEC Trade with Latin America and Nonassociated Countries in Africa Excluding Mediterranean Countries (millions of U.S. dollars)

	1958	1960	1963	1969	1970	1972	(Percent) Increase	1973[a]
Imports from								
Central and South America	1647	1870	2268	3168	3592	3608	125.13	5723
African nonassociated countries and Nigeria	524	664	802	1300	3512	3274	524.8	6353
Exports to								
Central and South America	1604	1693	1567	2578	2946	3652	127.7	4842
African nonassociated countries	364	527	596	810	1597	2007	451.3	4931

[a] 1973 figures include for the first time data for all nine member states.

Source: Statistisches Amt der Europaischen Gemeinschaften, *Foreign Trade,* no. 2 (1973): 12, 14; and no. 3–5 (1975): 4.

Under these circumstances, it is not surprising that the African associates have not been satisfied with their sales to the Community. One major bone of contention has been the large-

113

scale German importation of bananas from Latin America, especially Ecuador, Columbia, Guatemala, and Honduras, for which Germany had been granted considerable duty-free quotas during most of the EEC transitional period. Of course, the small shipments of bananas to Germany were not alone responsible for the disappointing export figures. Even where the products of the associated countries had a clear tariff preference better prices and quality, or greater regularity of deliveries by non-associated competitors diminished or at times eliminated the value of tariff preference. To remedy existing deficiencies, a working party of Community and African experts was established in the summer of 1966 to examine and make recommendations on improved production and marketing methods. It was felt that with improved quality and diversification of production and with better packaging, consumer study, and more publicity, increased exports on the part of the African associates could be achieved.

The associated countries also complained about high internal taxes on tropical products in the member states. Supported by a number of national trade organizations within the Community, they urged the member governments to reduce their taxes in order to increase the sales of products such as coffee, cocoa, and tobacco in the Community market.

YAOUNDÉ II

When the renewal of the Convention was renegotiated in 1969 for the next five years, a number of questions were raised by the associated governments. One question pertained to the degree of preferential treatment for their exports of agricultural commodities to the Community. The UNCTAD Conference (United Nations Conference on Trade and Aid) convened in Geneva in the spring of 1964 for the purpose of finding more effective means to assist the developing countries in their economic plight. It was during this conference, attended by trade and economic development experts from both the Western countries and the Communist bloc (except China), that the

Yaoundé associates voted with other developing countries for early dismantlement of their special preferential system.[5] But they made it clear that they wanted to abandon the trade advantages they had obtained from the association only if they received compensatory benefits through the application of other international measures. Pressures had been exerted by nonassociated states to reduce or eliminate the tariff preferences for the associated states but this was not an acceptable solution for the latter. Moreover, the associated governments felt that Community agricultural commodities were too much favored in comparison with their own agricultural products and wanted to breach the protective barrier that the CAP had erected around the Community's agricultural market.

The second question was whether the associated governments should be required to grant tariff preferences for Community goods imported into their countries. This was the issue of reverse preferences, the elimination of which was advocated by the second UNCTAD Conference in New Delhi in 1968. The associated governments wanted to follow this recommendation and were strongly supported in this attempt by the German and Dutch governments, which wanted to see the "Spirit of New Delhi" pervade the new Convention.[6]

The third problem involved the operations of the European Development Fund. With the advent of the second Fund under the Convention of Yaoundé, the eighteen associates began to determine expenditures on an equal basis with the Community. However, there were also considerable amounts of money left in the first Fund, which did not begin to hit its expenditure stride until 1962, and which was not fully committed until the end of 1965. Committments of the second Fund were made faster from the beginning, but actual disbursements still lagged far behind, which was a source of apprehension for the Africans. The associated governments wanted a more expeditious operation of the next Fund and an increase in the scope of projects to be considered for financing.

Although the negotiations were not concluded prior to the expiration of the Yaoundé Convention on May 31, 1969, and transitional provisions were necessary, success was scored by the end of June of that year when the new Convention (Yaoundé II) was initiated. The new Convention was to expire on January 31, 1975.

Yaoundé II was structured on much the same lines as the preceding Convention. The concept of free trade areas between the Community and the associated states was maintained as was the principle of nondiscrimination between Community countries in their relations with the associated members. With respect to the preferential treatment of the associated countries, the tariff preferences accorded remained generally the same, but as a token of goodwill toward the nonassociated developing countries, the Community did make provision to suspend certain tariffs on a number of secondary and a few primary tropical products. In relation to those agricultural products of the associated countries that were similar to and competing with European products, the Community granted the associated states more favorable treatment than that accorded to other countries. The principle of reverse preferences was retained because it was felt that in a genuine free trade area these preferences could not be lifted.

The European Development Fund's appropriations were increased to $1 billion, of which $918 million was to go to the associated countries as opposed to $730 million under Yaoundé I. The financing techniques were improved, and the scope of projects to qualify for financial aid was enlarged.[7]

Yaoundé II was concluded despite the misgivings of some of the EC member governments, especially Germany and the Netherlands and to a lesser degree, Belgium and Italy. Although the increase of exports from the member states to the associated countries was impressive, not all the member states shared equally in this expansion. Despite the safeguards against discriminatory treatment, French firms continued to obtain the lion's share of European Development Fund projects undertaken, especially in the French-speaking associated countries. In terms of monetary value, nearly half of these projects were awarded to business enterprises in France, with only about 15 percent going to Italian firms, 4 percent to Dutch enterprises, 3 percent to German companies, and 2 percent to the Belgians. The remaining projects were carried out by local companies in the associated states, whose managers, however, for the greater part were French. (At the same time, we must remember that Germany and France each contributed 34 percent to the Development Fund, with Italy, Belgium, and Holland paying only slightly above 10 percent each.[8])

The reasons for this imbalance can easily be detected. Approximately 8000 French advisors are attached to all the African countries that were formerly French colonies, and these advisors are found not only in the general administration, but also in legal, public health, teaching, and production positions. Business and industry in these countries are controlled chiefly by locally established French firms; and if proposals for development projects are not drawn up by French experts, they are at least influenced by them, and the specifications are aimed at French suppliers. In addition, French entrepreneurs, with their long experience and knowledge of African conditions, are on the spot with the necessary materials. In sum, then, the French presence persists and is a tremendous advantage for France and French business.

This very unbalanced situation has naturally displeased the Germans, Dutch, Belgians, and to a lesser degree, the Italians. Although the Belgians have also benefited from having nearly 3000 advisors in their former colonies, and the Italians from about 150 experts in Somaliland, it is the business in the 14 former French colonies in which non-French exporters and contractors are most interested. Yet, some of the non-French businessmen have at times been excluded from these areas on the most flimsy pretexts, and only the Italians have had some measure of success in their economic penetration efforts.[9]

OTHER ASSOCIATION INITIATIVES IN SUB-SAHARAN AFRICA

When the British negotiations for accession to the EEC collapsed in January 1963, the hopes of many African Commonwealth countries to be offered associated status along the lines of the Convention of Yaoundé were dashed. The Germans and Dutch had strongly favored such a status because it would have mitigated the objection of perpetuating the division of Africa into French-speaking and English-speaking parts, a division that resulted from the frontiers drawn in Africa by the colonial powers during the last century. Prompted by the Dutch government, in April 1963 the EEC Council of Ministers issued a Declaration of Intention, in which it invited African countries with economic structure and production comparable to those of the Yaoundé associates to request negotiations with the Community regarding an eventual association, either by the Convention of Yaoundé, or by setting up a separate affiliation, or by the conclusion of a simple trade agreement.

The Case of Mauritius

Mauritius, a small, independent, developing Commonwealth country in the Indian Ocean, was the first country interested exclusively in membership in the Yaoundé Convention. In 1971 the government of Mauritius addressed a letter to the presidents of the Council of Ministers and the Commission requesting membership of Mauritius in this Convention. The application of Mauritius to the Yaoundé Convention was approved in May 1972. Through participation in the Convention, Mauritius began to enjoy financial and technical assistance on the same terms as the other associated states. At the same time, Mauritius obligated itself to eliminate progressively its custom duties and charges on imports of products coming from the Community countries.

Negotiations with Nigeria

Nigeria, whose most important single trading partner is the Community, also wanted to avail itself of the opportunity for affiliation with the EEC and requested exploratory talks, which got under way in November 1963. However, the Nigerian government did not choose accession to the Convention of Yaoundé, but asked for a separate association agreement. The main reason was that Nigeria did not intend to request financial aid and also wanted to retain its membership in the Commonwealth preferential tariff system.

The Nigerian application for association was strongly supported by the Dutch and the Germans. In April 1966 the Amsterdam Chamber of Commerce issued a statement that warned that delay in acting upon the application might strengthen the impression that the EEC was primarily interested in the French-speaking countries of Africa and had the undesirable objective of establishing a special bloc. For this reason the greatest importance should be attached to extending to other countries the opportunities for concluding agreements that would enable them to establish special relations with the Community.[10]

Official negotiations opened in July 1964. From the outset two major difficulties had to be overcome. One was the problem of "double membership" in the Commonwealth and the EEC, which was opposed by France as favoring Nigeria too much over the African countries already associated. However, the French were finally persuaded that there were certain advantages in Nigeria's double membership.

The second major obstacle was the desire of the French to grant a degree of protection to those export commodities of the Yaoundé associates that would be mainly affected by the preferential treatment accorded to similar Nigerian products. Primarily involved here were cocoa, ground-nut oil, palm oil, and plywood. Although France's partners argued that any distinction in the treatment of the Yaoundé associates and Nigeria violated the spirit of the above-mentioned Declaration of Intention and that it was not in the interest of the Community to create various categories of associates in Africa, they finally agreed to a compromise. Nigeria was offered for these four commodities the same tariff preferences on the EEC market as those granted to the other associated African countries, but they were to take the form of tariff quotas based on the average Nigerian exports to the Six during the three years preceding the association. After these quotas were filled, Nigerian exports of these four products were subject to the full CET; however, all other exports would enjoy full preferences.

The United States was very opposed to the establishment of the Nigerian association. Elaborating a basic principle of American foreign policy, Undersecretary of State George W. Ball declared in 1964 that the existence of several preferential and discriminatory regimes in Africa and other developing areas tends to result in a poor use of world resources and to limit the possibilities for effective cooperation among nations seeking an increase of overall world prosperity and world peace.[11] As a consequence, the United States and Great Britain protested to the EEC as well as to the member states against the planned association with Nigeria as an unwarranted proliferation of preferential arrangements in Africa, claiming that such proliferation was inimical to the letter and spirit of GATT and was spreading discrimination in world trade.[12] Also underlying these protests may have been apprehension that the creation of additional associations would extend the Community's economic and political influence in Africa, chiefly at the expense of the United Kingdom. Another motivation for these protests may have been the American desire to protect the European export markets of its Latin American neighbors. However, the protests were rejected and the association agreement was signed July 16, 1966, in Lagos, Nigeria, by the representatives of the Community, the member states, and the Nigerian government.[13]

The content of the association agreement was relatively simple. It established a free trade area between the Community and Nigeria, granting Nigerian goods generally unrestricted entry into the Common Market at the EC internal tariff rates. In order to maintain the principle of reciprocity, Nigeria accorded marginal tariff preferences of between 2 and 10 percent to 26 EEC products. All other products imported from the EEC, constituting a vast majority, remained subject to the full duties.

The agreement created its own Association Council and a secretariat. Composed of members of the EEC Council of Ministers and Commission and members of the government of Nigeria, the Association Council could act only by unanimity. Its decisions were binding on the signatories. The Council also had the task of settling disputes; if unable to do so, the dispute was to be referred to a three-member arbitration panel for final decision.

The agreement did not contain any financial provisions and was to expire on May 31, 1969, the same date as the expiration of the Convention of Yaoundé. The coincidence of the expiration dates was intentional. If the two associations should be renewed after June 1, 1969, a fusion of the associations would have been possible with tariff treatment of Nigeria to be equal to that of the Yaoundé associates.

The Nigerian agreement never entered into force because several of the parliaments of the Community member states refused ratification in view of the civil war that had broken out as a result of the attempted Biafra secession. Even after the Biafran problem had been settled, the Lagos Agreement was not revived. Nigeria, a member of the Commonwealth preferential tariff system, then began negotiating on a future affiliation with the European Community as the Commonwealth tariff was being phased out.

Convention of Arusha

The same Declaration of Intention of the Council of Ministers that prompted Nigeria to seek association with the Common Market in 1963 also induced three other Commonwealth countries, Kenya, Tanzania, and Uganda, to request exploratory talks with the Community. These talks took place in February 1964 and involved problems similar to those posed by the Nigerian association. During the formal negotiations (opened in March 1965) the three countries declared themselves interested in a separate association with the Community. However, none of them sought financial development aid, only preferences for their exports to the Common Market. At first they were unwilling to grant even nominal tariff concessions on some of the imports from the member states, and the Community refused to negotiate on this basis because an agreement without reciprocity would violate the sensitivities of the other African associates and would not qualify for the exemption of the GATT rules. Later, possibly influenced by the precedent-breaking agreement with Nigeria, the three countries accepted the principle of reciprocity and negotiations were resumed in the fall of 1966.

Finally an agreement was reached in Arusha in July 1968 for an association that was very similar to the one between the

121

Community and Nigeria. The Arusha Convention was also limited to 1969 in order to permit parallel negotiations when the Yaoundé Convention was to be renewed, but in fact the agreement with the East African countries did not become effective until January 1, 1971. The Arusha Convention has its own association council for the implementation of the provisions of the agreement and for supervisory purposes. A joint parliamentary committee is also set up for occasional meetings between members of the East African Parliament and the European Parliament.

WHAT KIND OF ASSOCIATIONS
FOR THE FUTURE?

When in 1973 preparations were made to renew the Conventions of Yaoundé and Arusha, the Community had to take into consideration a number of additional developing countries that were promised associable status under the Declaration of Intention of 1963[14] and the accession agreement with the United Kingdom. These countries were mainly developing Commonwealth states in Africa, the Caribbean, and the Pacific.[15]

Several options were open for the negotiations of future associations. One was to continue the Yaoundé and Arusha Associations and, depending on their particular interests, offer participation to the various eligible countries in Africa, the Caribbean and the Pacific. A second option was to extend to all eligible countries the same tariff preferences and financial benefits accorded to the Yaoundé associates and obtain in return the same degree of reciprocity of tariff concessions and other rights as granted to the Community by the Yaoundé countries. The third option would be to make the Arusha agreement the standard pattern, which would mean, however, a substantial decrease of the benefits enjoyed by the Yaoundé associates and a reduction of the rights extended by them to the Community. The fourth option would be to conclude individual association agreements with the eligible countries in accordance with their special interests and objectives. While France was anxious to assure the continuation of benefits enjoyed by the Yaoundé associates and the Community under the 1969 agreement, she was ready to accept less generous treatment in the other future agreements. However, the remaining member states felt that the most important principle for the future affiliations was non-discriminatory treatment for all associates.

During July 1973 a conference was convened in Brussels by the Community. Forty-three states were invited to prepare the forthcoming negotiations regarding the renewal of the Yaoundé and Arusha Conventions. Thirty-two African states plus Madagascar and Mauritius were represented; twenty-two of these countries were already associated. In addition, four Caribbean and three Pacific states participated in the conference, and four North African states (Algeria, Egypt, Morocco, and Tunisia) participated as observers.[16] Earlier the Commission had issued a memorandum for the renewal of the Yaoundé association, which established the following principles:

1) the continuation of the free trade regime, although the associated countries were to be free to grant the non-member countries the tariff exemptions that were accorded to the shipments of Community goods to the associated countries

2) the stabilization of export revenues for the associated countries to insure stable and adequate income from certain primary commodities

3) support for efforts to initiate and enlarge regional co-operation among associated countries

4) special treatment of the very poor associated states

5) substantial increase in financial support and budgeting of the European Development Fund by the Community's own resources

6) improvement of the institutional structures

One of the difficult problems affecting not only the present and future associations but third countries as well was the question of reciprocity—reciprocity of tariff concessions by the Community and by the associated countries. The Community's attitude was not to claim "strict reciprocity," which appeared to suggest that the Community negotiators might not insist on full reverse preferences on the part of the developing countries.[17]

As already mentioned, the United States and other non-member states considered reverse preferences by the developing countries to Community exports of manufactured goods as discriminatory against U.S. manufacturers. Although the Convention of Arusha limited reverse preferences to a relatively small number of items, they were nevertheless regarded as a violation of the GATT principle of the most-favored-nation (MFN) clause.[18] However, the problem is more complex. Article XXIV of GATT permits exceptions from this clause for trade among countries participating in customs unions and free trade areas, and participation in interim agreements aiming at a gradual elimination of internal tariffs. This seems to indicate that reverse preferences are a requirement if all parties to a free trade area or an interim agreement were to enjoy the exception under Article XXIV. And it was the intention of the Community that the principle of a free trade area with the associate countries would underlie the elaboration of one or more new association agreements. However, in the middle 1960s GATT was amended to make it possible to offer developing countries preferences for their exports without reciprocity or benefits for developed member states of GATT under the MNF principle.[19] Therefore, it is possible to argue that reverse preferences for shipments from industrially advanced to developing countries are not required for free trade areas; in fact, the latter would suffer losses of badly needed revenues.

Another sensitive point in the negotiations was the maintenance of preferential margins in favor of the associated countries. A renewed commitment on the part of the Community in this respect would mean that it would not be possible in the future to make tariff concessions to other developing countries.

Despite differences of opinion between the negotiating parties, agreement on major points of principle was reached during a conference held in Kingston, Jamaica, during July 1974, in which 44 African, Caribbean, and Pacific (ACP) countries participated. The main result of the conference was a compromise on the broad outlines of a stabilization system for ACP export earnings. The ACP countries had requested a general, automatic mechanism not only stabilizing their earnings against excessive fluctuations, but also assuring specific prices of raw materials and basic products. The Community had offered a nonautomatic system involving case-by-case decisions, carefully controlling the utilization of compensatory payments, and seeking to give these payments a repayable character. In the compromise the ACP countries recognized that their demands regarding prices would place the Community members into impossible competitive situations vis-à-vis other industrialized countries and had to be abandoned until such time as a global system of price stabilization could be worked out. The Community, on the other hand, gave up the idea of controlling the utilization of compensating payments and of the need to repay these funds, although the Commission will be informed annually about the utilization of these funds.[20]

After 18 months of negotiations, final agreement was reached on a new accord, which was signed in February 1975 at Lomé, Togo, and became known as the Lomé Convention. The new Convention, scheduled to run until March 1, 1980, linked more than 250 million Europeans to nearly 300 million people in the Third World. Forty-six ACP countries joined the Convention (including some listed by the United Nations as "poorest"), three more than those initially participating in the negotiations 18 months earlier.[21] As additional countries in the ACP area become independent (for example Mozambique and Angola), they may request accession to the Convention.

The Lomé Convention assures free access to the Community member countries for all industrial and 96 percent of the agricultural products[22] originating in the ACP states, without compelling the latter to make corresponding concessions. Thus the Convention dispenses with the need for strict reciprocity in the free trade arrangements. Some of the developing countries wanted to eliminate the concept of reciprocity, thereby siding with the viewpoint of the United States, but others wanted to maintain this principle as a symbol of their equality and independence. In the Convention the ACP countries have the option

125

to grant special trade concessions to the EC countries and, equally important, are able to make such preferences available to third countries.[23] Since these provisions deviate from Article XXIV of GATT, the European Community must obtain a waiver from that organization, a stipulation that should pose no difficulties. The provisions also mean that some of the ACP countries currently providing reverse preferences to imported Community goods may continue to follow this practice if they so desire or are persuaded by the Community to do so.

Financial aid available to the ACP in the Convention was increased more than 300 percent compared with the amount provided under Yaoundé II. However, the approximately $4 billion ultimately agreed upon fell far short of what the ACP wanted originally, which was more than twice that figure. About 11 percent of the $4 billion will be used for the establishment of an export stabilization fund to aid countries heavily dependent on the export of certain raw materials and agricultural commodities susceptible to wide price and production level fluctuations. When receipts drop by a certain percentage, countries can request compensation. The mechanism triggering the fund will operate sooner for the poorest countries, which will not have to reimburse the fund. In principle, certain ACP associate states must repay these earnings when the price rises. Products affected include: peanuts, cocoa, coffee, cotton, coconuts, palm nuts and kernels, hides and skins, timber products, bananas, tea, raw sisal, and iron ore.

Many ACP countries had felt for many years that the progress in industrialization had been disappointing and that a systematic approach had to be taken by the Community, with proper financing not only by the EDF but also by other financial institutions in the member states. To help these countries develop and diversify their industrial capacity, an Industrial Cooperation Committee and an Industrial Development Center have been set up to promote the exchange of industrial know-how.

The institutions of the Lomé Convention were given broader powers than those in the Yaoundé association and were transformed into "decision making and management institutions." The new Council can meet at the ministerial level (including on the Community side members of the Council and the Commission, and on the ACP side a minister for each country), at the ambassadorial level (to prepare the ministerial meetings and to exercise the powers delegated to this level), and in the form of ad hoc groups. The second institution is a parliamentary body similar to the parliamentary conference of the Yaoundé Convention. This group is composed on a parity basis. In addition, an arbitration procedure for settling disputes regarding the interpretation and implementation of the Convention has been set up.

Prior to the conclusion of the new association agreements Claude Cheysson, the Commission member in charge of relations with developing countries, made some interesting policy statements reflecting the changed conditions as a result of the energy crisis and the steep increase in the world prices of many raw materials exported by Third World countries:

1. The poorest countries fighting a genuine battle of survival must receive their full complement of food aid, financial aid, and technical assistance.

2. Countries that have important resources of primary commodities but need help to develop them must be given this assistance with stabilization of export earnings and the promotion and marketing of their products.

3. Countries that already have developed raw materials are to be aided by industrial cooperation and the conclusion of long-term trade contracts. These countries (an example would be Nigeria) should not make an appeal for financial assistance but only for different forms of industrial cooperation.[24]

4. Agreements with the Third World countries producing raw materials should include a clause assuring access to these resources by the Community in return for the aid given to them.

Cheysson pointed out that the Community policy toward the associated countries was characterized by great flexibility enhancing the value of development aid given by Western Europe over that of other countries and international organizations. Indeed, the principles developed for the Communities' association policy should also guide development assistance for Third World countries outside the associations. In this respect Mr. Cheysson declared that the system of generalized preferences evolved by the Community outside the framework of the associations was an important tool in assisting Third World countries and perhaps superior to the policies pursued by most of the Western world.[25]

Clearly, the Lomé Convention is a remarkable achievement for the European Community. It will have great economic and also substantial political significance for the EC member states. It has reinforced the already strong ties Western Europe has with Africa and is likely to have favorable consequences for the Community throughout the Third World. An interesting psychological factor pleasing Third World countries has been the elimination of the term "associate" in the Convention because it was felt by many ACP governments that the term implied second-class status.

The overall generous nature of the Convention as well as the provision dealing with promoting industrial cooperation and assistance in the industrialization of ACP economies under EC auspices will assure business firms in the Community states goodwill, which can be translated into higher exports to ACP countries and favorable treatment for the establishment of local subsidiaries. Of course there is some serious doubt whether industrialization is the best means for all developing countries to enhance their economic welfare or whether for some of these countries the highest priority should be placed on diversification and modernization of agriculture. But given the obsession with industrialization that most Third World governmental leaders have, the Convention provisions will prove to be very attractive.

The Lomé commodity agreements will also add to the favorable image of the Community projected by the Convention. They may well become prototypes for worldwide agreements if they achieve their stated goals. Since the Lomé Convention does not contain guarantees of delivery in periods of shortage, it does not discriminate against other countries buying on the world market the commodities covered by Lomé. Of course, some concealed favoritism toward Community countries under conditions of supply shortages cannot be ruled out; indeed it should be anticipated.

Finally, a word needs to be said about the negotiating skill of the Community, and especially the Commission under the leadership of Commissioner Claude Cheysson. Considering the

complexity of the problems and the large number of participants, the Commission negotiators showed exceptional capability
and tenacity, and as a consequence increased the prestige of
that body. The negotiating stance of the Community was coherent and the solutions proposed were free of any colonialist
heritage or any neo-colonialist inclinations. Although allegations
of neo-colonialism are likely to be voiced in various parts of the
world in the years to come, the Lomé Convention is certain to
have more benefits than drawbacks for the ACP states and
thereby will have positive effects on the relations between the
developed countries and the Third World.

It is in the long-term implications and effects that the new
agreements assume the greatest political significance for the EC
member states. The continued close relationship between the
associated states and the Community is likely to give business
firms not only in France but perhaps eventually also in the
other member states increased influence and control. As a consequence the Community business world is apt to be the main
beneficiary when the economic level of the African associates
rises as the result of the massive infusion of financial aid. The
institutionalized contacts between African and European parliamentarians and civil servants are likely to contribute substantially to this development and, in addition, will promote political
cooperation between the Lomé partners. These contacts are
purposefully expanded. An illustration is the stand taken by the
Yaoundé associates in the United Nations, where most of them
supported the Dutch position in the Netherlands–Indonesia
conflict on New Guinea in the early 1960s. Political cooperation
between the association partners may in due time lead to further
extension of European influence in large parts of Africa and
indeed in the whole Third World. For example, groups of
foreign service officials of ACP countries have been taken on
carefully prepared and conducted tours in the EC countries.
The results have been cooperation and support by ACP governments for EC members' objectives in different international
fora, and thereby a subtle shift in the distribution of world
power.

Third countries must look at the effects of these conventions also in long-range terms. Up to now, their fears of major

trade diversion do not seem to have been confirmed. We have already commented on the relatively modest overall increases of Community exports to the associated states, which were much smaller than the increase of total EEC exports.

It is important to note that the Lomé Convention does not attempt to pre-empt the field of financial and technical assistance. Rather, the Convention complements the assistance efforts of some of the member states, which have bilateral "trade and aid" programs of differing scope and emphasis. France and Great Britain have by far the most extensive network of bilateral agreements, but Germany is not too far behind, followed by the Netherlands, Belgium and Italy.[26] As can be seen from Table 4.3, from 1962 to 1972 France and Belgium were in the forefront of the disbursers of aid to the Yaoundé associates and it is not surprising that most of this aid was sent to their former colonies. Great Britain has also favored its former possessions in bilateral aid agreements. The agreements of the Six with Yaoundé associates were not coordinated and include a variety of techniques—grants, loans, technical assistance, cultural cooperation, scholarships, apprenticeships, and perhaps others—with varying stress placed on the different methods. For example, France gives its financial aid in the form of grants, whereas Germany, with the exception of technical assistance, normally accords only loans. Of course, the amounts committed and expended by the member states involved vary widely, and therefore, we can observe at least five different national policies toward the African associates in addition to the Community policy. Naturally, these national "foreign aid" policies are part of the general foreign policies of the member states and are conceived in the context of their major foreign policy goals, whether they pertain to East–West relations, strategic and defense issues, or foreign economic policy in general.

Despite the pleas of the Commission and the European Parliament for a progressive coordination of the bilateral arrangements in order to evolve a common policy toward the developing countries in Africa, little progress had been made up to 1974. During that year the EC Council adopted a number of resolutions that eventually will result in the harmonization of

Table 4.3

Origin of Aid Received by the Yaoundé Associates
(millions of U.S. dollars)

	1962	1968	1969	1970	1971	1972
1.						
Bilateral aid of which:	485.5	412.1	461.2	455.3	524.5	587.1
German Federal Republic	6.5	17.6	32.9	34.0	40.7	28.9
Belgium	53.4	60.6	65.8	72.8	81.3	102.5
France	281.1	269.0	288.8	269.7	294.6	351.8
Italy	10.8	11.0	12.6	8.6	16.8	9.6
Netherlands	– –	– –	– –	2.9	4.7	4.6
TOTAL EC	358.8	358.2	400.1	388.0	438.1	497.4
United States	94.0	43.0	44.0	37.0	48.0	39.0
2.						
Multilateral aid of which:	96.4	135.6	175.7	200.6	235.8	226.9
EC	50.7	101.3	112.5	137.1	155.7	148.0
UN	15.3	25.3	41.9	38.0	56.1	56.1
Other	30.1	9.0	21.3	25.5	24.0	18.7
3.						
Total aid (1 + 2) of which:	581.9	547.7	636.9	655.9	760.3	814.0
EC	409.5	459.5	512.6	525.1	593.8	645.4

Source: European Development Fund, in Uwe Kitzinger, *Europe's Wider Horizons* (London: Federal Trust, 1975), p. 28.

bilateral aid policies and financial support to the Third World in general.[27] The implementation of these resolutions undoubtedly will also have a beneficial effect on aid to the Lomé officials but how fast this implementation will occur will depend on how ready the member governments are to reconcile their divergent national aspirations and to coordinate their foreign policies.

POLICY TOWARD THE MEDITERRANEAN BASIN

Since the establishment of the EEC, the Community has developed an increasingly determined and consistent policy toward the countries ringing the Mediterranean. The core objective of this policy as it emerged over the years has been a web of

131

preferential agreements through which these countries were linked with the Community. Some of these agreements were genuine association agreements under article 238 of the EEC Treaty. Others shunned the "association" label but nevertheless provided preferential treatment for goods imported into the Community by the affiliated countries and for the reverse flow of some Community products. Third countries, especially the United States, protested against the discrimination that some of their own exports suffered as a result of these agreements, but these protests were heeded only in a few instances. The following pages will analyze and evaluate the EC affiliations with the Mediterranean countries and the scope and direction of the Community policy.

Greece, Turkey, and Cyprus

In the late 1950s, when the British efforts to construct a Europe-wide free trade area failed, Greece and Turkey requested association with the EEC in June and July 1959, respectively.

The negotiations for the Greek association, conducted by the Commission, were protracted over a period of nearly two years. Among the reasons for the slow progress were Italian fears that Greek agricultural commodities such as oranges and dried fruit would pose a serious threat to the sales of similar Italian products if allowed free entry into the EEC. Another reason was the tenacious attitude of the Greek negotiators, who were intent on extracting the maximum on every issue despite the fact that their basic bargaining position vis-à-vis the Community was relatively weak. Finally, this was the Community's first attempt to design an association agreement. Since the text of the Treaty contains very few specifics about the content of an association, new paths had to be charted over unknown territory. To a degree, this first association was certain to set a precedent and for this reason a great deal of caution and forethought was called for.

This is also the basic reason why the Turkish government, which applied for an association only a month later than the Greeks, had to wait until after the conclusion of the Greek assoc'ation. Under the circumstances, the Commission did not consider itself able to carry on two sets of negotiations at the same time on a problem as important as an association. Another reason for the delay was the difficult political situation in Turkey. When finally, in April 1962, full negotiations were initiated, it took only a relatively short period of time—a little over a year—to initial a draft agreement.

The over-all long-range objective of both association agreements was to strengthen the commercial and economic relations between the contracting parties, with full consideration of the need to ensure the accelerated development of the economy of Greece and Turkey, and to raise the level of employment and living standards of the Greek and Turkish people. To reach this broad goal the two association agreements seek the attainment of two important objectives: the gradual establishment of a customs union and the harmonization of the economic policies of the association partners. Another long-range objective of both agreements is the accession of Greece and Turkey to full membership in the Community.

Since levels of economic development in Greece and Turkey differ, the regulations governing the introduction of the customs union are not the same in both agreements. In the Greek agreement the principle was established that with the entry into force of the agreement, customs duties would be gradually abolished over a 12-year period.[28] However, some exceptions to this principle were permitted for a number of specific items or reasons.

Turkey's low level of economic development and her economic difficulties arising from an imbalance between growing import requirements (especially capital goods) and inadequate export earnings, did not make it feasible to immediately institute machinery for progressively establishing a customs union. Rather, a "preparatory" period was considered necessary, during which Turkey would strengthen her economic posture with the aid of the Community but without making any specific concessions to the Community in return. Following the preparatory period is the "transition" period, during which the customs union is being gradually established, and which lasts 12 years, although under certain conditions a prolongation is possible.

133

It will be followed by a "final" period, during which the customs union will be fully established and the economies of the contracting parties increasingly coordinated, including the adoption of the Community's external tariff by Turkey.

Turning now to the harmonization of policy, it is not surprising that, in view of Greece's primarily agricultural economy, the Greek association agreement heavily emphasized the area of agriculture. A consultation procedure has been established to ensure that during the formation of the Community's agricultural policy the legitimate Greek interests for such products as tobacco were taken into account.

Under the provisions of the Turkish association agreement the harmonization of economic policies did not begin until the transition state. As an overall economic policy goal, the agreement requires the association members to pursue a course that will ensure the equilibrium of their balance of payments and maintain confidence in their currency while at the same time assuring a balanced and steady expansion of the economy against a background of stable prices.

The Greek and Turkish association agreements live up to the principle of reciprocity with respect to the rights and obligations of the association partners as required by the EEC Treaty. Both Greece and Turkey fall into the category of "developing countries"; they have primarily agricultural economies and are engaged in the process of industrialization. The Community is Greece's most important supplier and market, and its trade with Turkey is an important factor in that country's economy. By giving preferential treatment to Greek and Turkish agricultural products, by providing financial and technical aid, and by granting special rights to the two countries for the protection of their economies, the association agreements set the stage for the Community to further strengthen its relationships with Greece and Turkey. At the same time, the obligations undertaken by the Community appear to be reasonably counterbalanced by the eventual advantages of greater shipments of Community goods to these countries, a greater supply of needed labor for the EEC member states, and the prospects of full integration of Greece and Turkey into the Community, with all the economic and political implications that such an integration may entail.

To operate the two associations, the Greek and Turkish agreements make provisions for a number of institutions. The central organs of both associations are the Councils of Association, which have many identical features. Reflecting the principles of bilateralism and parity, both Councils are composed on the one hand of members of the nine member governments, the Council of Ministers, and the Commission, and on the other of members of the Greek or Turkish governments. Since unanimity is required for the proceedings in the Council, the weight of the vote of the associated governments is equal to that of the Community representatives, who must therefore arrive at a consensus.[29] Both the Greek and Turkish Association Councils have set up Parliamentary Association Committees composed of equal numbers of deputies from the Greek or Turkish Parliaments as well as from the European Parliament. The tasks of these Committees are to debate certain issues and to make recommendations to the perspective Parliaments.

The Greek and Turkish Association Councils have also established Association Committees, which, among other duties, are charged with ensuring the continuity necessary for the smooth operation of the association agreements. Although the Councils meet only twice a year, the Association Committees meet much more often. Taking care of all routine matters, the Committees have become very useful cogs in the institutional machinery.

For the settlement of disputes that might arise from the application or the interpretation of the provisions of the Greek or Turkish agreements, each association partner may call on the Association Council to obtain satisfaction. The Council may either seek to settle the dispute or refer it to the Court of Justice of the European Communities or to any other existing court for settlement. If these methods of adjudication cannot resolve the dispute, the parties may finally request arbitration.

How sucessful have the two association agreements been in obtaining their objectives; and what are the prospects and implications for the future?

There can be little doubt that the results of the Greek association have so far not come up to Greek expectations; and that much disillusionment prevails in the Community. The Greek government has two major complaints: the very large continuing trade deficit in the Greek–EC trade relationship, and the problems connected with the harmonization of agricultural policies.

Although there has been a steady increase of Greek exports to the Community (amounting to about 500 percent between 1961 and 1972) and although this increase is substantially higher than that enjoyed by Greek exports on a worldwide basis, imports of EC goods into Greece have quadrupled and have started from a much higher net level ($282 million versus $92 million).[30] As a result, the trade deficit at the end of 1972 was $687 million, a figure that caused concern in the minds of the Greeks. Trade deficits have continued through 1975, and the Community has pointed out that these deficits must be viewed in the light of Greece as a developing country. Many of the goods imported into Greece were not consumer goods, but capital goods for expanded industrialization. As a result, industrial production has increased by more than 10 percent, and agricultural production by 8 percent. Continued industrialization may enable the Greek economy eventually to enlarge its exports on a worldwide basis and thereby reduce its very large trade deficit.

The second grievance of the Greeks deals with the harmonization of agricultural policies between the Common Market and Greece. In the view of the Greek government, harmonization implies equal treatment and, therefore, participation in the institutional and financial machinery of the Community's CAP. In particular, the Greeks would like to benefit from the export rebates and subsidies provided by the European Agricultural Guidance and Guarantee Fund for the farmers of the member states. Only by sharing in the benefits from this fund would it be possible, according to Greece, to align Greek prices and policies with those of the EEC as was suggested by the Community.

Friction between the EEC and Greece has also arisen from the conclusion of the association agreement with Turkey. When consulted (in accordance with the provisions of the Greek agreement), Greece did not only raise objections to the Turkish agreement as incompatible with her economic interests, but it also took a hostile attitude later in GATT when the agreement with Turkey was examined for its consistency with GATT rules.[31]

The military coup of April 21, 1967, that suspended parliamentary rule in Greece, cast a pall of uncertainty over the association. Without parliamentary institutions in Greece, the Parliamentary Association Committee could not function, a fact that aroused deep apprehension among the members of the European Parliament, and raised somber questions about the operation of the association in general and about its ultimate objective of full Greek membership. A resolution adopted unanimously by the European Parliament declared that the association agreement could be applied only "if democratic structures and political . . . liberties are established in Greece."[32] The Commission, however, was reluctant to accept this line of thinking and preferred to view the operation of the association in a more pragmatic manner, although it too wanted to see Greece return to a measure of democratic government.

Although the Parliamentary Committee's operations were suspended and the Association Council did not meet until 1970 (and from then on only on the ambassadorial level), the Association Committee continued its activities at least for routine problems. Greece continued its annual tariff reductions to gradually implement the customs union; and trade between the association partners rose each year. However, the Community funds in the amount of $125 million, which were to be provided by the European Investment Bank (EIB) over a 5-year period beginning in November 1962, were stopped after the military coup, and by that time only 17 loans totaling approximately $70 million had been granted.[33]

In the summer of 1974, when the Greek military regime resigned following the Cyprus debacle and was replaced by a democratically oriented government under the leadership of Premier Caramanis, efforts were made by the Community and the Greek government to reactivate the operations of the association. Following a solemn Community statement in favor of the new regime in Greece early in September,[34] a full-fledged meeting of the Association Council took place in November. At this meeting the association was broadened to include the three member states of the Community; and the full activities of the association were resumed.

In June 1975, to the surprise of the EC member governments,

Greece submitted an application for full membership in the Community. Of course, such a step was an ultimate objective of the association with the EEC, but under the provisions of the association agreement (article 72) an "examination" of the possibility of full membership by the association partners was to precede an actual application. Nevertheless, the Community institutions set the process for Greek accession into motion quickly, although several years were expected to pass before a final decision was reached. But there seems little doubt that eventually Greece will be the tenth member of the Community.[35]

The Greek government justified its request for accession by stating that as the result of the economic benefits of the association the annual income per capita had reached $2000, and thereby stands more or less on the same level as that of Ireland. But the deciding factors for the application were essentially political. With democracy restored, Greece shares the Community's political aims, and European union would contribute to assuring freedom, justice, and dignity for Greek citizens. Another, less obvious, political motivation may have been the tensions existing between Greece and the United States in the wake of the Turkish invasion of Cyprus. The Greek government may have wanted to counteract the effects of this situation by a closer affiliation with the Community.

How would Greece's full membership in the EC affect a later similar request by Turkey? When Athens' representative to the Community was asked this question, he answered: "If Turkey would apply for membership and if this would be accepted by the Nine, we would be happy to see our Turkish neighbors enter the community."[36] Of course, what Greece's response to this question will be several years hence will depend on many circumstances that cannot be predicted now, but a full clarification of this issue may be advisable in the forthcoming negotiations for Greek membership.

The frictions and disagreements that have beset the Greek association have been absent so far from the operations of the Turkish agreement. In fact, a communiqué issued by the Joint EEC–Turkish Parliamentary Committee after its meeting in January 1967 declared its general satisfaction with the way the association is operating and praised in particular the functioning of the institutional machinery; the adequate flow of Community loans to Turkey; and the increase of Community tariff quotas for tobacco, dried figs, raisins, and hazel nuts, export items crucial for the Turkish economy, and the only Turkish products as yet receiving preferential treatment during the preparatory stage. The financial assistance granted to Turkey by the Community ($175 million) was used up at the expiration of the preparatory period and a new financial protocol providing $195 million was signed in November 1970. In the meantime, negotiations between the Community and Turkey were concluded successfully, which made it possible for the association to enter the transitional phase on January 1, 1973. By that time Turkish exports to the Community had nearly doubled, from $183 million in 1965 to $348 million in 1972, while Community exports to Turkey tripled during this period, reaching $616 million.

Evaluating both the Greek and Turkish associations from the Community's point of view, the short-term economic gains in exchange for the far-reaching concessions made by the EEC are likely to be less important than the long-range economic and political advantages. The agreements demonstrated that the European Community is not a closed society; and the prestige of the EC and the member states has been enhanced by the extension of intra-European development aid to less developed countries along Europe's fringe areas. At the same time, the economic ties linking Greece and Turkey to the Common Market prevented these countries from slipping into EFTA and permitted the Community to subtly extend its economic and political influence. Finally, the intimate continuous contacts between high government officials of the association partners within the extensive institutional structure have opened up opportunities for closer political cooperation between the associated countries. This was demonstrated by Greece's application for full EC membership.

Since Cyprus has been a source of serious conflict between Greece and Turkey, a few comments about its relationship to the Community are appropriate here. The Cypriot government requested the opening of negotiations for association in December 1962. However, in view of its Commonwealth membership, this request was not followed up when the accession negotiations with Britain broke down in early 1963. Later the climate for talks with the Community was adversely affected by the strife between the Greek majority and Turkish minority of the Cypriot population. However, in August 1970 the Cypriot government renewed its request for association. An agreement for association, concluded in December 1972, provided for two stages—the first to be completed by June 30, 1977—during which Cyprus is to move gradually into a customs union with the Community. An Association Council is responsible for the operation and supervision of the association. The Turkish invasion of Cyprus in the summer of 1974 did not disturb the basic operations of the association; to assist in the recovery of Cyprus, the Community provided large-scale emergency food for its population.[37]

Spain and Malta

Initially, Spain remained aloof from both the Common Market and EFTA because significant Spanish exports were moving to countries of both trade blocs, especially Germany and Great Britain. However, when the initiation of the British negotiations in 1961 stimulated the interest of EFTA and other West European countries to affiliate themselves with the Common Market, Spain joined the parade and in February 1962 requested association. No action was taken on this request by the EEC Council of Ministers until two years later when the Spanish government, recalling its earlier request, proposed exploratory talks to examine what form of relationship could be established between Spain and the Community. In response to this proposal, the Council authorized the Commission to open discussions with the Spaniards. These talks resulted in the submission of a very long and detailed questionnaire to the Spanish government in February 1965 asking for economic, legal, and administrative information to enable the EEC authorities to form a judgment about the economic situation in Spain.

Two major reasons accounted for the EEC Council's delayed action on the Spanish request for association in 1962. One reason was the preoccupation of the Commission and Council with the British negotiations and the subsequent disillusionment after de Gaulle had vetoed Britain's entry into the Common Market. Another reason was the sharp criticism of a Spanish association, voiced especially in Belgium, the Netherlands, and Italy. This criticism was motivated by both political and economic considerations. The socialist parties and labor unions, particularly in these countries but also elsewhere in the Community, objected to an association with a country ruled by an authoritarian government, and opposed the supply of financial and other aid to the regime of General Franco. The Italians were also concerned that preferential tariff arrangements for the import of Spanish agricultural commodities, in many respects similar to those of Italy, would unfavorably affect the sales of their own farm products in the Community.

France indicated early in 1964 that she was prepared to support Spain's request for association, and later the West German government also expressed its support for the Spanish initiatives. However, although the Spanish government had furnished the replies requested in the Commission questionnaire by August 1965, the EEC Commission did not issue a report on its findings to the Council until October 1966, the delay having been caused perhaps by opposition to Spain's affiliation that existed within the Commission and its staff.[38] In the meantime, the Spanish embarked on an intense lobbying campaign to promote their case through contacts with the Permanent Representatives of the Six in Brussels, talks with some of the member governments, and visits to influential Commission staff members. As a result, the West German government raised the issue in a Council meeting in June 1966, but pending a report from the Commission on its talks and findings, Council action was postponed until July 1967, when the Commission was given a mandate for formal negotiations with Spain.

A complex set of quid pro quo deals, which included changes in the relations with Israel and the declaration of intention to begin negotiations with the United Arab Republic and Lebanon, succeeded in balancing out opposing interests regarding Spain. It made it possible to conclude an agreement with the Spanish government in 1970 to enter into force in

October of that year, although the final result was not a true association as delineated in chapter 2. Aiming at the eventual creation of a free trade zone, the agreement seeks the gradual (in two stages) elimination of tariffs and other obstacles to trade. The first stage was to last 6 years and stipulates on the Community side gradual tariff reduction of 60 percent for most industrial products and lesser reductions for citrus fruits, olive oil, vegetables and certain wines. Spain has granted to the Community gradual reduction up to 95 percent for the bulk of industrial goods and some liberalization for agricultural products. The details of the second stage will be negotiated at a later date. A Joint EC–Spain Committee administers the agreement, which eventually may be transformed into a full-fledged association. It is too early to judge the performance of the agreement. In view of the Community's enlargement, certain changes have become necessary in the agreement. We will return to these later.

Malta petitioned the Community in 1967 to initiate negotiations for the most suitable form and best modalities for mutual relations. When Britain's entry was assured, the negotiations with Malta, a Commonwealth member state, were started and swiftly led to an association agreement in 1970, which entered into force in April 1971. A customs union is being established in two phases of 5 years each; during the first stage the Community will reduce its tariffs for industrial goods by 70 percent, while Malta will reduce the rates gradually by 35 percent or the most-favored-nation level. The details of the second stage will be negotiated later. An Association Council operates and supervises the relationship between the EC and Malta. Full EC membership is an ultimate aspiration of the Maltese.[39]

The Maghreb

In 1963 Tunisia and Morocco responded to the Declaration of Intention appended to the EEC Treaty, which invited African states with special relations to member states to request negotiations for association. Algeria, to which the EEC Treaty had extended the Common Market trade advantages and some of the other Community rules until her independence in 1962, followed suit; and during 1964 exploratory talks were held between the Commission and the three Maghreb countries. During these talks the requests submitted by the three countries were broadly similar, all aiming at the creation of a free trade area with the EEC. However, in view of the wide differences in the economic development of the prospective signatories of such an arrangement—the term "association" was disliked because of its political connotations—the Maghreb countries proposed that they reduce customs duties and quotas at a much slower pace than the member states, which, for their part, were expected to apply the tariff and quota reduction system in force between themselves. Furthermore, provisions were requested for safeguard clauses if balance of payments difficulties made it necessary to protect infant industries or if customs duties had to be reintroduced as a source of revenue.

Naturally enough, it was for farm products (their chief exports), especially fruit, vegetables, and wine, that the Maghreb countries wanted to derive substantial advantages from the association and protect themselves from adverse effects of the CAP. In addition, they asked for various types of financial and technical assistance. Finally, they were anxious to obtain the best possible conditions for those of their nationals who were employed in the member states and to arrange for vocational training courses both in North Africa and in Europe.

The importance of the EC market for the Maghreb countries is high-lighted by the fact that Algeria ships about 85 percent of its exports to the Common Market, Tunisia 60 percent, and Morocco 58 percent. Only Tunisian exports had been subject to the full third country duties of the Community. Exports from Morocco and Algeria to France were either not subject to duties or were free from quantitative restrictions. Algerian exports to other member states received until the end of 1965 the same tariff treatment that the member states accorded each other. However, only France and Germany extended the intra-Community 10 percent customs reduction that became effective January 1, 1966 to Algeria. The other member states did not grant this additional reduction to Algerian imports and expressed perplexity and reservations about the German decision, particularly as the Federal government had no diplomatic relations with Algeria.

The major economic problem that had to be overcome before an arrangement with the Maghreb countries could be concluded stemmed from the competitive positions of many of their exports with products grown in Italy and perhaps Greece. The Italian government was greatly alarmed about imports of large quantities of Algerian wine into Germany in 1966. The Italians claimed that the prices for this wine reflected disregard of any economic cost basis and that as a consequence Algerian wine was making serious inroads on the market for Italian wine. In its Memorandum of 1964 on Community association policy the Italian government had sought to establish the principle that a member state whose interests were apt to suffer from competition by a newly associated country should be entitled to compensation from other member states not affected by this competition. Although the other member states have refused to accept this principle, Italy was successful in 1966 in persuading her EEC partners to make available from the European Agricultural Fund $45 million specifically for the improvement of Italian production of olives, olive oil, fruit, and vegetables, all commodities that might suffer from preferential arrangements made with Mediterranean countries.

Additional difficulties arose from the exports of Maghreb oranges. The EEC trade agreements with Israel and Lebanon (to be discussed later) provided that if subsequent trade agreements of the EEC engendered substantial changes in the orange market of the member states, the problem would have to be examined by a mixed EEC–Israel and EEC–Lebanon Commission.

Finally, the "special relationship" between France and Algeria caused problems for the conclusion of an agreement with the Maghreb countries. In the summer of 1965 the Franco–Algerian Oil Agreement had been concluded. This pact defined the details of the cooperation between the two countries in the exploration of Sahara oil and fixing the financial and technical aid France was to grant Algeria over a 15-year period. Some voices complained that France had been acting against the spirit of the Community by seeking to strengthen her already privileged position in Algeria. Others feared that the agreement might make it much more difficult to evolve a common Community energy policy. However, nobody should have been really surprised after the experience of the previous few years that France would primarily pursue a policy to promote her own national interests.

Faced with these and other problems, the Six have found it troublesome to reach a consensus on a comprehensive negotiating mandate for the Commission, and consequently the progress of the talks with the Maghreb countries was very slow. Meanwhile, the Tunisian and Moroccan governments, more adversely affected by the existing situation than Algeria, urged the EEC authorities and member governments to speed up the negotiations. The Community responded affirmatively and agreements establishing associations with both countries were signed in March 1969.

These agreements, which came into force on September 1, 1969 and were to expire in August 1974, accorded preferential treatment to most Tunisian and Moroccan exports to the Community. Virtually all industrial products from Tunisia and Morocco can now enter the Community duty-free, which should constitute a powerful incentive to industrial development in the two countries. Substantial preferences, including outright exemption from customs duties, have been arranged for 55 percent of Community imports of agricultural products from both Tunisia and Morocco. Special import arrangements have been made for certain sensitive products such as citrus fruits and olive oil, the object of which is to step up the export revenue of the two associated countries as far as possible without upsetting the balance of the markets in these products.

For products that do not yet benefit from preferential Community treatment it was arranged that exports by Tunisia and Morocco may continue to enjoy the advantages that France used to grant to them autonomously before the agreements came into force. Association Councils have been established for the application and correct implementation of the agreements.

The negotiations with Algeria dragged on well beyond the conclusion of the associations with Tunisia and Morocco. However, when the agreements with the latter had to be reviewed in the light of the Community's enlargement and their 1974 expiration date, a comprehensive approach to all three Maghreb countries was taken, which will be examined below in connection with our overall evaluation of the Community's Mediterranean policy.

The Rim Countries of the Eastern Mediterranean

From the very beginning of the Common Market, Israel was interested in some sort of arrangement with the EEC in order to safeguard the existing and future markets for her products in the member states. The importance of these markets stems from the fact that more than 40 percent of all of Israel's exports were shipped to the EC, in particular Germany, the Benelux countries, and the EC associates, Greece and Turkey.

The talks between the EEC and Israel progressed very slowly. One reason was that a very substantial share of Israeli exports are citrus fruits, highly competitive, as we have seen, with similar Italian and Greek commodities. Manufactured goods, especially clothing and chemical products, represent another significant share, and here again pressures by competing producers in the EEC militated against granting tariff preferences to the Israelis. Finally, most member states were fearful that a comprehensive preferential arrangement with Israel might create a precedent that other states in Asia or Latin America would want to follow.

Although the Israeli government clearly preferred an arrangement in the form of an association, the EEC Council of Ministers authorized the Commission to negotiate only a trade agreement, for which formal negotiations were opened in November 1962. Large numbers of proposals by the Israeli government to improve its bargaining position led to protracted and detailed discussions between Israeli experts, relevant government departments in the member states, and Commission officials. As a consequence, the negotiations dragged on until the summer of 1964, when a trade agreement was finally signed by the EEC and Israel. It went into effect on July 1, 1964.

The agreement fell short of satisfying the aspirations of the Israelis. It gave them no exclusive preferential advantages and no protection against possible ill effects of the Community's CAP, although it did provide tariff cuts on the average of 40 percent for grapefruit; 33 percent for avocado pears; and 20 percent for a variety of chemical, aluminum, and textile products. In addition, French and Italian quotas were eased on citrus juices and bromides respectively.

Although Israeli exports to the Common Market rose slightly in 1965 and although this trend continued in 1966, the Israeli Minister of Finance declared in February 1966 that the economic relations with the Common Market had unfortunately not fulfilled Israeli expectations and that a comprehensive agreement, possibly an association, was needed to obtain satisfactory results for trade between the two parties. As a consequence, Israel filed a formal application for association on October 4, 1966. In the aftermath of the Seven-Day War, French consent to enter into negotiations with Israel was a long time in coming. It was not until October 1969 that the Council of Ministers issued to the Commission a mandate to conduct negotiations for a preferential trade agreement, but not for full association. Such an agreement was signed in June 1970 and came into force in October of that year, the same time as the Spanish agreement.

The agreement with Israel ensures a preferential system for a considerable proportion of Israel's exports to the Community. A final 50 percent reduction in customs duties is planned for industrial goods excluding a certain number of sensitive products representing about 10 percent of Israel's industrial exports. Bearing in mind the commercial, technical, and technological capacities of Israel, this system, which is accompanied by the liberalization of imports, should stimulate investments and further the country's industrial development.

Preferences ranging from 30 percent to 40 percent are provided for about 80 percent of the Community's imports of agricultural products from Israel and cover the most important products, such as oranges and grapefruit. For citrus fruit the preferential system is conditional upon the observance of price discipline in the framework of a similar system applying to all the Mediterraenean countries that are large producers of citrus fruit, and aimed at drawing maximum value from exports without compromising the balance of the markets. For its part, Israel grants tariff concessions ranging from 10 percent to 30 percent for approximately 60 percent of the Community's exports, both industrial and agricultural.

A joint committee watches over the proper execution of the agreement. It should be noted that the agreement constitutes only a first stage on the road toward closer cooperation in a context of "balanced relations" with the countries of the Near East. It is being renegotiated to take into account the enlargement of the Community and the newly defined Mediterranean policy of the EC.

Lebanon, which signed a nonpreferential trade and technical assistance agreement with the Community in 1965, petitioned in October 1969 for negotiations regarding an expanded preferential arrangement.

The United Arab Republic indicated in 1966 that she was also interested in trade talks with the Common Market. The Arab League had recommended that other Arab countries follow the example of the U.A.R. and request the negotiation of trade agreements with the EEC or perhaps a collective association. At the same time, it urged them to bring their influence to bear on the EC countries to prevent an Israeli association.[40]

During the consultations of the member states regarding a preferential agreement with Israel in 1969 France demanded that the conclusion of an agreement with Israel be linked to opening the door for Arab nations in order to assure a balance in the Community's relations with the countries of the Near East.[41] In view of this, the U.A.R. applied for a preferential agreement and negotiations were started in September 1970.

In December 1972 preferential trade agreements were signed with Lebanon and the Arab Republic of Egypt.[42] Both agreements are designed to promote increased trade between the parties and to help the general expansion of international trade. They are to run for five years, with the option of negotiating a new and broader-based agreement eighteen months before the expiration date, under which efforts to dispose of major obstacles to trade transactions could be continued. They represent only first steps toward closer cooperation between Lebanon and the Arab Republic of Egypt on one side and the Community on the other, although the agreements already accord preferential treatment to a sizeable portion of Lebanon's and Egypt's exports. Joint committees to administer the associations are institutional features of both agreements.

The agreements, coupled with an additional protocol signed in December 1972, which effect the necessary adjustment to the position resulting from the Community's enlargement, bring Lebanon and Egypt within the purview of the Community's new Mediterranean policy.[43]

THE RATIONALE OF THE COMMUNITY'S MEDITERRANEAN POLICY

The Community efforts during the last few years to create a network of preferential agreements or associations covering the states rimming the Mediterranean has been largely successful. Only a few gaps remain. Libya has not availed herself of the opportunities contained in the Declaration of Intention of 1963 and her objectives and aspirations are veiled in secrecy. Albania has also been indifferent to the Community up to now. Yugoslavia does have a trade agreement with the Community, but it is nonpreferential and we will examine it in the chapter on relations with the Communist "state-trading" countries.

The professed rationale and objectives of the Mediterranean policy have been stated succinctly by Ralph Dahrendorf, a former member of the EC Commission, in the name of this body:

(i) The quest, in relations with the Mediterranean, of a harmonious relationship between reciprocal interdependence on the one hand and the respect of mutual independence on the other;

(ii) The working-out of a joint plan for the relations of the Community with the Mediterranean countries taking into account the characteristics of each of these;

(iii) The prime necessity of going beyond the purely commercial aspect of the question and of contributing to the economic development of the region.[44]

149

A resolution adopted by the European Parliament under-lined the responsibilities and particular obligations that give the Community its economic importance in the Mediterranean basin, its situation in relation to this region, and the need to develop a spirit of true solidarity. The resolution stresses the necessity for the Community to adopt a policy of development by more appropriate means than commercial measures alone.

An examination of statistics on trade relations shows the important position that the Mediterranean countries have as-sumed in trade with the Community. Trade almost tripled between 1960 and 1970. In 1970 Community exports to the Mediterranean countries[45] reached a figure of $7 billion, as opposed to $6 billion for exports to the United States. Imports, petroleum included, from these same partners were worth $6 billion and $9 billion, respectively.[46] The economic importance of the Community–Mediterranean relationship is also illustrated by the fact that apart from Libyan oil deliveries, 36.5 percent of the exports of all of the Mediterranean countries go to the EC while 37.6 percent of their total imports come from the Community. In turn, of total Community exports to third countries 14.5 percent, a hefty share, go to these Mediterranean countries, while the share of total imports from the area, again omitting Libyan oil, is only 9 percent.[47]

The Community policy toward the Mediterranean has found broad support by the elites and public opinion in the member states. Elite surveys conducted by this author in 1965 and 1970 made one thing clear: The overwhelming majority of the re-spondents (nearly 97 percent) perceived the association agree-ments as useful instruments of policy; and there was almost unanimity that a preferential agreement policy in the Mediter-ranean was fully justified in view of the historical ties of these countries to Europe.[48] What we can see, then, is a change of role in the Mediterranean basin. While historically the Mediter-ranean was considered by the Italians as *mare nostrum*, it is now the Community as a whole that is accepting this position.[49]

The United States has strongly opposed the Community's efforts to create a sphere of influence in the Mediterranean. As pointed out earlier, U.S. policy has been basically against any kind of preferential treatment by the EC outside Europe proper.

During the last few years the U.S. government has made energetic attempts to stop the expansion of the Community's economic and political influence in the Mediterranean. In very practical terms, it was concerned about the economic effects on American exports of citrus fruits and other goods to the area, but perhaps more than that, it was the increasing worldwide influence of the Community that gave rise to serious apprehension. The United States has proclaimed again and again that the preferential agreements are violations of GATT, which only permits full-fledged customs unions and free trade areas to be exempted from the most-favored-nation clause. The Community has admitted a possible violation but continues to claim its special responsibility for the countries of the area. A good deal of the disenchantment among the American people with the Common Market, and many of the frictions that have been generated between the United States and the Common Market during the last two or three years can be attributed to the latter's Mediterranean policy.

In the summer of 1973 the EC Council of Ministers began defining a comprehensive, generally applicable concept for all associations and other preferential agreements in the Mediterranean basin. The concept was to be applied immediately to the associations with Tunisia and Morocco, which had to be renegotiated by 1975, and the new affiliation of Algeria. It was also to be applied in the renegotiations of the Israeli and Spanish agreements and changes in the Malta association.

The basic Community goal is the maximum elimination of trade barriers. In pursuit of this goal the Community proposed to remove tariff and quota barriers on imports of all industrial products either immediately, in the case of the Maghreb, or over a four and a half year schedule, in the case of Spain and Israel. It also offered tariff concessions covering a major part of its agricultural imports from each of the countries concerned, while still protecting the smooth operation of the CAP.[50]

For their part, Spain and Israel were asked to remove, according to the same four and a half year schedule, restrictions on imports of many industrial products from the Community, and to agree on concessions in favor of the Community agricultural exports. How much reciprocity was to be demanded from the Maghreb countries required further consultation.

151

The new agreements would also include a "cooperation folio," tailored to the country concerned. With regard to the Maghreb countries the Community intends economic, technical, and financial cooperation as well as certain measures for the benefit of migrant workers from these countries now in the Community. Malta will be able to benefit from the same kind of economic, financial, and technical cooperation.

As for Spain and Israel, the Community is contemplating an economic cooperation scheme insofar as it can promote the development of commercial trade. The Community has also agreed to discuss the situation of Spanish labor now engaged in the EC.

The problem of reciprocity was raised again in connection with the agreements with the Maghreb countries. Several of the governments of the member states opposed reciprocity and the creation of a full free trade zone, which by definition would involve the free circulation of goods in both directions. Others, especially France, wanted to remain faithful to the principle of the free trade area concept but would accept certain delays in its full implementation. The formulation adopted by the Council finally was the maintenance of the principle of reciprocity (which already had been specified in the Tunisian and Moroccan agreements) but to approach detailed provisions of the application of this principle with an open mind and with full consideration of any solution being compatible with the GATT rules.[51]

Another very difficult problem was the injection of the petroleum dimension. In view of the fact that Algeria and Tunisia are substantial exporters of crude and refined oil products, the delivery of oil played a major role in the deliberations of the Community. Obviously it was important to insure the stability of hydrocarbon supplies. But at the same time, could the Community authorities undertake association negotiations with Algeria, which had imposed an embargo on oil exports to one of the member states, the Netherlands? Simultaneously some Arab countries were said to have exerted pressure on the Community to give up its close links with Israel. However, the Community refused to give up its freedom of action in this respect, although the parallelism in the negotiations with the Arab countries on the one hand and Israel on the other had always been a constant source for concern for the Community authorities.[52]

In the final definition of its Mediterranean policy, the Council liberalized tariff rates for such important agricultural products from the Mediterranean countries as fruit juices and wine, although they were competing with Community-grown products and affected CAP benefits. The amount of financial assistance to Morocco, Tunisia, Algeria, and Malta was set at about $400 million over a 5-year period. Other provisions dealt with the regimes of North African labor in the Community countries.[53] Although these features were received with varying degrees of disappointment, especially by Malta and Spain, and although Israel now requested financial cooperation,[54] acceptable changes in the affiliation agreements were eventually bargained out. The first agreement concluded under the principles of the Mediterranean policy was the one with Israel, which entered into force in its entirety during the second half of 1975.

For four other countries—Egypt, Lebanon, Jordan, and Syria—negotiations for an agreement in conformance with the EC Mediterranean policy were initiated in 1975. They will modify the accords of the first three countries already in force with the Community and result in closer trade relations and economic cooperation among the parties involved.

ARRANGEMENTS WITH RESIDUAL EFTA COUNTRIES

When the Community was enlarged by the accessions of Great Britain, Denmark, and Ireland, some of the remaining EFTA countries would have also liked to have joined the EC if it had not been for certain constraints on their neutrality. The countries in question were Sweden, Switzerland, and Austria, which for various reasons have had a tradition of neutrality, and were apprehensive that membership in the Community would constitute an encroachment on their freedom of action incompatible to the principle of neutrality. However, these three countries as well as all other EFTA full and associated members entered into negotiations with the Community for free trade agreements in the industrial field. Norway, in fact,

153

had applied for full membership, and a treaty of accession had been signed by the Community and that country. But when in a referendum held on September 25, 1972, regarding entry into the Community, 53.5 percent of the Norwegian people voted against this step, the accession agreement was not ratified by the Norwegian Parliament.[55] As a consequence, Norway also negotiated a free trade agreement with the Community, which was signed in May 1973.

As of January 1, 1974, the following EFTA countries became affiliated with the Community: Austria, Portugal, Sweden, Switzerland, Norway, Iceland, and Finland. All of these agreements have one feature in common, namely free trade in industrial products. However, as far as the details of these strictly bilateral agreements are concerned, they seek to take into consideration the special trade problems of the different countries and to meet their particular economic needs. Moreover, all agreements, with the exception of Finland's, state in their preambles that the contracting parties are prepared to go beyond the scope of the present agreements if necessary to develop and expand their bilateral relations.

In view of the bilateralism of the free trade agreements, a joint committee was set up for the supervision of the proper functioning of each agreement. These joint committees in turn have formed technical committees, which are concerned primarily with the customs matters connected with the application and administration of the agreements. The work of the customs committee has been coordinated and therefore some of the rules developed by them were adopted by the Community and all the EFTA countries.[56]

The operation of the Community's preferential agreement with Portugal was influenced by that nation's political changes in 1974 that resulted in the overthrow of the Salazar regime, then its replacement by a fledgling democracy, and then the usurpation of political power by an extreme left-wing group of officers collaborating closely with the Portuguese Communist Party. During the democratic interlude, the Community responded favorably in several joint committee meetings to the requests for economic, financial, and technical support for Portugal to help the full restoration of democracy and effect an economic recovery.[57] Commission Vice President Christopher Soames and later EC Council President Fitzgerald visited Lisbon to discuss the possibility of new relations with Portugal and examine the terms of financial assistance.[58] While the presence of left-wing forces in the Portuguese government was not by itself seen as an entirely negative element, the EC Council of Ministers in its June and July meetings felt that the need to guarantee a democratic development would be implicit in any economic support action. Such action, as recommended by the Commission, could involve credits up to $400 million,[59] which could be "frozen" if the military regime were to completely prohibit all activities of political parties oriented toward a democratic political system and establish a totalitarian pro-Communist regime. Without question, the Community found itself in an unenviable dilemma: How could it avoid disappointing those segments of the Portuguese people who were anxious to make democracy a success without becoming a dupe for the military regime?

SUMMARY OBSERVATIONS

The final result of the many association and other affiliation agreements signed by the Community is a tremendous trade bloc covering all of Western Europe, the Mediterranean, most of Africa with much of the Caribbean and part of the Pacific. In view of the free trade areas that already had been created by EFTA, a combination of a customs union and free trade area quite comprehensive in nature has emerged. While the objective of the Community's bilateral agreements with the EFTA countries meets the provisions of GATT for the creation of a free trade area, the association and affiliation agreements in the Mediterranean are much more doubtful in this respect. The whole development calls into question the continuation of the GATT principles as governing rules for world trade. After all, Article XXIV of the GATT authorizing the creation of free trade areas and customs unions was considered to be an *exception* to the principles of nondiscrimination in trade. However, with such a tremendous area seeking to qualify for the exception from the basic GATT rules, we may well be witnessing the emergence of a new system for international trade. We will return to this point in our concluding comments in the last chapter.

NOTES

1. EEC Treaty arts. 131-136. Annex IV of the Treaty lists the overseas dependencies included in the association. An implementing Convention and a number of special protocols annexed to the EEC Treaty provide the details of the association.

2. For the guaranty of higher prices, the so-called *surprix*-system, the French required the African countries concerned to buy their capital and consumer goods from France.

3. The African states involved in this association are Burundi, the Federal Republic of Cameroon, the Central African Republic, the Republic of Chad, the Republic of the Congo (Brazzaville), the Congolese Republic (Leopoldville), the Republic of Dahomey, the Gabon Republic, the Republic of the Ivory Coast, Madagascar, the Republic of Mali, the Islamic Republic of Mauritania, and the Republics of Niger, Rwanda, Senegal, Somalia, Togo, and the Upper Volta.

4. *Agence Europe Bulletin,* August 23, 1966, p. 6.

5. The various UNCTAD Conferences will be discussed in greater detail in chapter 7.

6. Cf. *Le Monde,* March 26, 1969.

7. For details see *Third General Report,* 1969, pp. 350-355.

8. *European Community,* no. 94 (July 1966): 11.

9. Cf. EP, *Sitzungsdokumente* 1964-65, Document 77, November 9, 1964, Reporter: Van der Goes van Naters, pp. 43-46. The figure for the Belgian advisors is for the year 1963, but presumably it has not changed materially.

10. EP, *Monthly Bulletin of European Documentation* 6, no. 5 (May 1964): 25.

11. Department of State, *Bulletin* 50, no. 1295 (April 27, 1964): 657-662.

12. *Frankfurter Allgemeine Zeitung,* July 28, 1965.

13. For the alleviation of German fears that the Nigerian agreement might lead to a violation of the Hallstein doctrine, see p. 157.

14. See pp. 118–121.

15. For the names of these countries see footnotes 38, 40, 41, and 42, in chapter 3.

16. *Bulletin of the European Communities Commission,* no. 4 (1973). When the conference actually opened, Ethiopia, Liberia, Sudan, and Guinea were also represented.

17. *Agence Europe Bulletin,* October 18, 1973; and *Bulletin of the European Communities,* "Renewal and Enlargement of the Association with the AASM and Certain Commonwealth Developing Countries," Supplement 1/73, p. 16.

18. U.S. Senate Committee on Finance, *A Strategy for International Trade Negotiations by Senator Abraham Ribicoff,* February 9, 1973, p. 8.

19. T.I.A.S. Vol. 17, part 2, 1966, pp. 1977–1987 (6139).

20. For details see *Agence Europe Bulletin,* August 1, 1974.

21. The following is a list of the 46 independent countries in Africa, the Caribbean and the Pacific, which have entered into the new agreement with the European Community: Nineteen states hitherto associated with the Common Market until January 31, 1975 by the Yaoundé Convention: Burundi, Cameroon, Central African Republic, Chad, Congo, Dahomey, Gabon, Ivory Coast, Madagascar, Mali, Mauritania, Mauritius, Niger, Rwanda, Senegal, Somalia, Togo, Upper Volta, and Zaire. Twenty-one Commonwealth states, to which the EEC had offered special agreements on Great Britain's adhesion to the Common Market: in Africa: Botswana, Gambia, Ghana, Kenya, Lesotho, Malawi, Nigeria, Sierra Leone, Swaziland, Tanzania, Uganda, Zambia; in the Caribbean: Bahamas, Barbados, Guyana, Grenada, Jamaica, Trinidad and Tobago; in the Pacific: Fiji, Western Samoa, Tonga. Six countries of Africa with no special relationship with the countries of the EEC, which had been invited to join the above-mentioned because their economies were "comparable": Ethiopia, Liberia, Sudan, Guinea, Equatorial Guinea, and Guinea-Bissau.

22. For the small percentage of remaining products the tariff barriers will be lower for ACP states than for third countries. See *European Community,* no. 184 (March 1975): 5.

23. *Lomé Convention* art. 7.

24. For details see *Agence Europe Bulletin,* October 30, 1974.

25. Ibid., November 6, 1974. For details of the generalized preference systems of different countries see chapter 7.

26. See Uwe Kitzinger, *Europe's Wider Horizons* (London: Federal Trust, 1975), pp. 5 and 6.

27. For details see *Eighth General Report,* 1974, pp. 234–237.

28. The association agreement covers all trade between Greece and the Community except coal, coke, steel, iron ore, and scrap.

29. Following the ratification of the Greek agreement, procedures for arriving at a consensus of the Community's representatives had to be determined. The basic rule agreed upon was a unanimous vote of the EEC Council of Ministers after it had heard the EEC Commission, but there are certain exceptions to this rule: Action by EEC organs may also be required with regard to decisions and recommendations of the Association Council. Since the EEC Council of Ministers is the competent organ for their implementation, a unanimous vote is required in that body after it has heard the Commission.

30. In 1972 Greek exports to the EEC were $472 million as opposed to $1159 million for imports into Greece.

31. Greece has also taken advantage of the consultation provisions to request information about Community imports from Turkey and Iran, and has asked to be consulted on the Common Market Regulations for fats, fruits, and vegetables, as well as on the association with Nigeria. (*Agence Europe Bulletin,* May 7, 1966, p. 7.)

32. Ibid., May 11, 1967, p. 9.

33. Carl A. Ehrhardt, "EEC and the Mediterranean," *Aussenpolitik* (vol. 22, 1/71): 20–30. For additional details on the operation of the Greek association see Werner Feld, *The European Common Market and the World* (Englewood Cliffs, N.J.: Prentice-Hall, 1967), pp. 59–71.

34. *Agence Europe Bulletin,* September 18, 1974. See also October 3, 1974.

35. Cf. ibid., June 12, 13, 1975.

36. Stephan Stathatos, Athens' representative at the EEC, quoted in *New York Times,* June 13, 1975, p. L3.

37. *Agence Europe Bulletin,* September 12, 1974.

38. EEC Commission Vice-President Mansholt reflected his critical attitude toward present-day Spain's affiliation with the EEC in an address to Dutch unionists in April 1966. See *Agence Europe Bulletin,* April 12, 1966, p. 3. See also *Il Globo,* May 7, 1964; *24 Ore,* May 30, 1964; and *Il Tempo,* June 10, 1964, for Italian views.

39. Cf. *Fourth* and *Fifth General Report,* 1970 and 1971.

40. *Agence Europe Bulletin,* December 13, 1966, p. 8.

41. Cf. Ehrhardt, op. cit., 30.

42. Syria had dropped out of the U.A.R.

43. Cf. *Sixth General Report,* 1972, p. 267.

44. *Fifth General Report,* 1971, p. 307.

45. In addition to the countries already cited these figures include Jordan and Libya.

46. *Fifth General Report,* 1971, p. 308.

47. Ehrhardt, op. cit., 21-22.

48. Feld, *The European Common Market and the World,* pp. 140-142; and Feld, "The National Bureaucracies of the EEC Member States and Political Integration: A Preliminary Inquiry" in Robert S. Jordan, ed., *International Administration* (New York: Oxford University Press, 1971), p. 241.

49. Mussolini also liked to speak about *mare nostrum* when referring to the Mediterranean. Of course, France is also a littoral country.

50. See *Sixth* and *Seventh General Report,* 1972 and 1973, pp. 259 and 404, respectively.

51. See *Agence Europe Bulletin,* January 9, 1974, p. 7; February 7, 1974, pp. 8, 9.

52. For further details see ibid., January 9; February 6, 7, 1974.

53. Ibid., July 24, 1974.

54. Ibid., October 7/8, 1974.

55. *Sixth General Report,* 1972, p. 17.

56. *Seventh General Report,* 1973, pp. 402-403.

57. For details see *Eighth General Report,* 1974, pp. 245-246.

58. *Agence Europe Bulletin,* March 20, June 2/3, 1975.

59. Cf. ibid., June 23/24, 25, 1975.

5

The Evolution of Community Commercial Policies:

The Non-European Developed Countries of the Free World

In the trade of the Nine as a collective unit with nonmember states the United States has been and continues to be the largest trading partner, accounting in 1973 for approximately 17 percent of EC exports and 20 percent of EC imports. (See Table 5.1.) Non-European countries, other than the U.S., play a much smaller role, with Japan accounting for about 4.2 percent of EC imports and 2.7 percent of total EC exports. The shares of Canada, Australia, and New Zealand are even smaller.[1] In view of the position of the United States as the Community's predominant trading partner it is not surprising that in the major worldwide trade negotiations under the auspices of GATT during the 1960s—the so-called Dillon and Kennedy Rounds—the American government and the Community were the major parties involved in the drawn-out bargaining to reduce tariff barriers and to overcome some of the stubborn nontariff barriers (NTBs). In these negotiations the EC Commission assumed an increasingly important role as a negotiator, a role that was given to it by the EEC Treaty as a corollary of its responsibility to evolve a common commercial policy. But in performing this responsibility the Commission was confronted with the reluctance of the member governments and national bureaucracies to yield their traditional foreign policy prerogatives. For a full understanding of the Community's policies toward nonmember countries, it is useful to review briefly the problems that the Commission had to surmount in its struggle to develop a uniform approach to the EC's external commercial relations.

THE LONG ROAD TO A COMMON COMMERCIAL POLICY

Despite the fact that the EEC Treaty explicitly assigns to the Community organs the task of evolving a common commercial policy after the end of the transitional period, progress

163

Table 5.1
Largest EC Trading Partners, 1973
Developed Countries
(in percentage of total EC Exports and Imports)

	Exports	Imports
United States	17.0	20.0
Switzerland	8.9	5.0
Sweden	6.0	6.2
Austria	4.8	2.5
Japan	4.2	2.7
Spain	4.0	2.8
USSR	2.7	2.7
Canada	2.5	3.4
Australia	1.9	1.8

Source: Statistical Office of the European Communities, Foreign Trade (No. 3-5, 1975), p. 4.

toward such a policy has been rather slow. As early as 1962 the Council of Ministers, acting on a proposal made by the Commission, announced an action program for a common commercial policy that had as its objective the gradual harmonization of the national commercial policies of the member states. No effective implementation of this program was achieved, and in 1964 the Commission again seized the initiative with a more detailed program. In this program the Commission proposed the establishment of obligatory stages for the progressive unification of commercial policy toward third countries up to the end of the transitional period, and called for the setting up of instruments and procedures for that policy when unified. In 1965 additional proposals by the Commission aimed at establishing common regulations regarding trade liberalization, quantitative restrictions, and defensive measures against dumping (the sale of imported goods at prices below those prevailing in the country of origin).

Although major economic interest groups in all Community countries expressed support for the efforts of the Commission, the member governments showed little eagerness to accept these proposals. One of the main reasons for this reluctance was their fear of being constrained by decisions that Community officials and individual experts might make in pursuit of some questionable common "European" interests. It was not until December 1968 that the Council finally adopted three basic regulations for the beginning of an autonomous commercial policy of the Community. These regulations established a common liberalization list for goods imported from nonmember countries other than so-called state-trading (Communist) countries, a Community supervision procedure for certain imports with a common administration for import quotas, and protective measures against dumping practices. These three decisions were supplemented in December 1969 by a regulation establishing an initial common system of imports from the principal state-trading countries including a very short single list of items and a regulation standardizing export arrangements. However, these regulations did no more than reiterate the products liberalized in all the member states and they recognized the continued existence of different lists for the state-trading countries.

Despite the 1968 and 1969 decisions of the Council, a common commercial policy did not come into full bloom. While the common external tariff (CET) and the establishment of the Common Agricultural Policy (CAP) imposed specific restraints on what the member governments can do in the field of economic foreign policy, many other aspects of commercial policy remain jealously guarded by the national officials of the various foreign ministries. Although coordination of national foreign policy is increasingly practiced through the Political Committee,[2] individual commercial and economic foreign policy actions by the member governments constitute valuable tools that may be used to induce third countries to accept other segments of a member country's foreign policy goals. The implementation of these goals can frequently be carried out more successfully when a wide range of instruments, including those related to foreign economic policy issues, is at the disposal of a national government.

For all these reasons, article 113, the content of which we have discussed earlier, is being interpreted restrictively. This restrictive interpretation becomes especially clear when we look at the large number of trade agreements that continue to be concluded by the Community's member states on a bilateral basis. On the other hand, the conclusion of trade and tariff agreements by the Community as an individual contracting party has been a special concern of the Commission for many years. In order to assure that the hundreds of bilateral trade agreements concluded by the six member states with third countries and in force at the time that the Community was established would not interfere with the development of a common commercial policy, the Council of Ministers rendered a decision in July 1960, according to which member states had to include the so-called Common Market clause in future bilateral commercial agreements. This clause reads as follows:

> Should those obligations under the Treaty establishing the European Economic Community which relate to the gradual establishment of a common commercial policy make this necessary, negotiations shall be opened as soon as feasible in order to amend this present agreement as appropriate.[3]

In two other decisions rendered in July 1961 the Council postulated that agreements that did not contain this clause and that could not be terminated at a year's notice were not to be concluded for longer than one year. In addition, member states were requested to submit to the Council quarterly reports of all forthcoming negotiations with third countries, and to consult the Commission in advance or to permit the presence of an observer from the Commission at the actual negotiations.

Since it was essential for the Commission to have knowledge of the contents of the existing bilateral agreements, a systematic study of these compacts was initiated as early as 1961. Approximately 800 agreements were involved, with new agreements being signed every year since the initiation of the study. While France has indulged and continues to indulge most often in the practice of bilateralism in the field of economic foreign policy, her partners have also shared in this practice in varying

166

degrees. Even today more than 100 commercial agreements that rightfully seem to fall under the competence of the Community continue to be operative between the member countries and third states, and will have to be harmonized in due time.[4]

Since the negotiation and conclusion of Community agreements require a certain amount of time, it was not planned to enter at once into negotiations with all third countries. As a consequence, in every case where the present national agreements do not hinder the evolution of the common commercial policy the extension of national agreements is possible. However, each extension requires individual authorization by the Council, based on a pertinent proposal of the Commission. Moreover, the extension must not last longer than one year unless a specific Community reserve clause is attached to the agreement.

Up to now, the Community has concluded only a relatively small number of trade agreements under its own name. The first of these was signed with Iran in 1963; and more recently, agreements were signed with India, Pakistan, Uruguay, and Mexico. Undoubtedly, the most important trade agreements negotiated by the EC have been multilateral in nature. They have been the accords terminating the Dillon and Kennedy Rounds of tariff negotiations, which need to be discussed in some detail.

THE INFLUENTIAL ROLE OF THE UNITED STATES

In the evolution of the Community's commercial relations with all advanced countries of the free world, the goals of American foreign policy in Europe played an influential role. Hence the Dillon and Kennedy Rounds were prime factors in shaping these relations.

American Foreign Policy Factor

Ever since World War II the United States has regarded a strong and free Western Europe as essential to America's strategic interests. U.S. participation in NATO, constituting a milestone

167

in the history of American foreign policy, signified to the world that the American security zone extended in a line from Norway to Turkey. The building of a unified Europe, free from the traditional rivalries, was considered a necessary concomitant to American strategic policy. In addition, it was seen as the best means to control any German aspirations for revanche or for seeking to gain a dominant political position in Europe or the world, perhaps after the fledgling democracy in Germany had given way again to some kind of authoritarian or totalitarian government.

In the field of economic foreign policy, the United States has been basically committed since 1934 to an expansion of international trade through a reciprocal trade program. This program, technically known as the Trade Agreement Act of 1934, which was renewed and modified at intervals during subsequent years, permitted the President to reduce American tariffs provided that other countries made equivalent concessions in their tariff rates on American goods.

Utilizing these policy concepts as a basis, the U.S. State Department issued a significant statement in February 1957 defining the American position toward the then pending project of creating a European Common Market and a Free Trade Area. The statement expressed support for all steps that would further the political and economic strength and the cohesion of Western Europe within an expanding Atlantic Community, and that were aimed at making progress in the direction of liberalized, nondiscriminatory, multilateral trade and greater convertibility of currencies. In addition, it emphasized the special interest of the U.S. government in American agricultural exports to Western Europe and intimated a slight concern about the possible effects of future EEC farm regulations. However, the dominant concern was achievement of political unity in Western Europe; and for the attainment of this goal, American policy makers were prepared to accept some economic disadvantages and costs, although these costs were to be minimized as much as possible.

Despite the fact that the annual foreign policy statements of the U.S. government have continued to express support for political unification (Presidents Nixon and Ford greeted every step toward that goal, including the enlargement of the Community, with declarations of satisfaction and congratulations[5]), the premises underlying these policy goals have gradually lost strength. The new strategic diplomatic and economic relationships created by the Nixon Administration with the Soviet Union and the People's Republic of China have given the United States increased foreign policy flexibility and have lessened the dependence on Western Europe as the prime anchor of American security. What we are witnessing now is the operation of two strategic triangles: the United States, Soviet Union, and China; and the United States, the European Community, and Japan. These groups influence each other and in both of them the American government can make important moves in a double-track balance-of-power game. As a consequence, the political stake in the unification of Western Europe has become less significant for the United States; and therefore the need of the American government to accept economic cost and disadvantages in economic dealings with Europe as compensation for strategic benefits has been more or less obviated. At the same time, German democracy seems to be operating with reasonable success, and few signs of a revived German supernationalism are visible. On the other hand, the economic competition for the United States emanating from the suddenly emerged economic giantism of the enlarged Community looms large in the minds of American policy makers (official and unofficial), especially since for the first time since 1893 the United States suffered a deficit in its overall trade balance in 1971 and with the Community in 1972. Under such circumstances, political unification may be seen as a hindrance rather than an advantage to American foreign policy because it may be easier to deal with the individual member states of the Community than with a politically unified Europe. This does not mean abandoning Western Europe as a strategic base, or the withdrawal of American troops; nor does it signify a reduced interest in NATO, which remains a cornerstone of American security. Indeed, American policy makers may very well continue to foster harmonious relations with the Community institutions. But a shift in emphasis in the overall security and general American foreign policy may well have taken place, and this can not help but color the assessment of such Community policies as the CAP

169

and an explosive association policy in Africa and elsewhere, which are basically considered inimical to American interests, despite drastic changes that occurred in the area of agricultural exports and prices in 1973. We will return to this subject in considerable detail later.

Although economically disappointing, the tariff agreements with the United States and other countries during the Dillon Round were politically significant because they constituted an official confirmation of the Community's CET and therefore represented an important step in the Common Market's world-wide commercial relations. Despite the fact that the EEC was not and is not a "contracting party" of GATT, the Commission assumed a leading role in the negotiations and became internationally recognized as the proper negotiator for all agreements involving the CET, that is, all future multilateral and bilateral trade and tariff agreements. Although, in addition to the Commission officials the Council was represented by an observer, the coordination of activities worked well. The national delegations caucused each morning and elaborated the texts for the statements to be made by both the Commission and Council representatives. Nevertheless, criticism was voiced in the European Parliament that the negotiating mandates of the Council of Ministers to the Commission had been too inflexible to permit successful bargaining and that therefore representatives of the member governments had to be tied into the making of the most minute decisions. An enlarged scope of the Commission's negotiating competences was advocated in order to enable it to carry out future complex negotiations.

The Kennedy Round Negotiations

Perhaps the most crucial aspect of the relationship between the Community and the United States during the 1960s was the outcome of the Kennedy Round negotiations. Reflecting the recommendation of the GATT Ministerial Meeting in 1961, these negotiations aimed at a broad, across-the-board reduction of tariffs and other kinds of restraints upon the flow of international trade. Conducted under the auspices of GATT, the countries most affected by the negotiations were the United States, Canada, Japan, and the members of the Community and EFTA; however, the primary negotiating focus was on the United States and the Common Market.

In terms of American economic and political interests, four pertinent objectives of the Trade Expansion Act can be identified: (1) expansion of American exports and imports, thereby contributing to employment and benefiting the balance of payments; (2) persuasion of the emerging Common Market to pursue liberal "outward-looking" trade policies; (3) preventive action against the feared disastrous effects of the evolving Community CAP on American farm exports to Europe; and (4) reinforcement of the Atlantic Community ties by means of increased commercial exchanges. The Dillon Round had made only a very modest contribution to the solution of the American trade and balance of payments problems. The massive economic and military aid programs and the large volume of capital exports were continuing to cause persistent deficits in the U.S. balance of payments. Although the United States enjoyed a considerable surplus in her trade balance, including her trade with Europe, a further expansion of exports was seen as being urgently needed if the outflow of funds, some of them essential to American foreign policy, were to be maintained.

The Trade Expansion Act authorized the President for a period of 5 years to reduce tariffs by as much as 50 percent of the rates existing on July 1, 1962. In tariff agreements with the Common Market, he was empowered to completely eliminate duties on products for which the United States and the EEC together account for 80 percent or more of the world market. At the time when the Act was passed, it was anticipated that negotiations for access to the Community conducted by the United Kingdom, Ireland, Denmark, and Norway would be successful and that, therefore, heavy machinery, aircraft, automobiles, and many other important products would fall under the 80 percent provision. The Act also allowed the President to eliminate all tariffs on items on which the ad valorem duty was 5 percent or less. Finally, recognizing some of the difficult problems of the developing countries, the Act provided that the President could completely eliminate duties on tropical agricultural and forestry commodities grown in these countries on the condition that they are not produced in significant volume either in the United States or the EEC member states.

The governments of most of the member states, the Commission, and the European Parliament called for a positive approach to the proposed Kennedy Round, which had the potential of developing into the most comprehensive trade

---

Table 5.2

Disparities Between the CET, U.S., and U.K. Tariffs
Percentage of Duties Prior to Kennedy Round

	Protection	
	Above 25 Percent	Above 35 Percent
United States	28.00	10.90
United Kingdom	30.75	1.80
CET	5.00	0.05

Source: EEC Official Spokesman, *Trade Negotiations and the Problem of Disparities* (Release P–6/64), p. 3.

---

negotiations in history. France, however, expressed a number of reservations, of which the most important dealt with the inclusion of agricultural policy. There was general agreement that for a linear reduction method to be successful, it was absolutely necessary that all exporting countries of any real significance participate in the negotiations. Otherwise, under the GATT most-favored-nation clause, these countries would benefit from tariff reductions made by others without paying for them, and this would seriously diminish the willingness of the EEC members and the United States to make concessions. In the ensuring negotiations, 55 countries with significant export interests participated.

During the negotiations the French voiced apprehension about the tariff disparities stemming from the fact that U.S.

tariffs included a large number of very high as well as very low duties, whereas the CET was largely concentrated in the range of 10 to 25 percent. The degree of disparity is demonstrated in Table 5.2, which compares the pre-Kennedy Round percentage of duties imposed on imported goods above 25 and 35 percent not only between the EC and the United States, but also the United Kingdom. In the event that a 50 percent reduction were

Table 5.3

Average Tariff Rates for Imports into the U.S. and EC Prior to Kennedy Round (percent)

	All imports except agricultural products		Manufactured goods only[d]	
	Unweighted average	Weighted average	Unweighted average	Weighted average
U.S.	17.8	7.8[b]	20.2	11.7
EC	11.7[a]	5.2[c]	14.3	13.0

Source: Hinshaw, The European Community and American Trade, pp. 81, 86, 88.

[a] Takes into consideration 1961 Dillon Round adjustment.

[b] Weighted by 1960 net imports.

[c] Weighted by 1959 net imports.

[d] Figures do not take into account Dillon Round adjustments, which would reduce those percentages by slightly less than one percentage point.

to be made in all three tariffs, it is obvious that the existing imbalance of the tariff structures would be aggravated, because a high proportion of the CET would be brought down to an extremely low or zero level, whereas the U.S. tariff and, to a lesser degree, the U.K. tariff would have continued to afford a much larger measure of protection. The pre-Kennedy Round disparities between the U.S. tariff and the CET can also be illustrated by striking the average of the tariff rates for imports into the EEC and the United States as shown in Table 5.3. It is interesting to note that if the individual duty rates are weighted by taking into consideration the value and volume of imports under each tariff listing, the disparities shrink. While under three of the four calculations made in Table 5.2 the U.S. average range of duty was higher than that of the CET, it was lower if only imports of manufactured goods are used for the calculation of weighted averages.[6]

The problem of tariff disparity was compounded by the growing trade deficit of the EEC toward the United States during the period from 1958 to 1964. At the end of that year the deficit stood at $2.6 billion. We should note that during that period American shipments to the EEC increased by 93 percent and EEC exports to America by 71 percent. Prominently contributing to this deficit were American agricultural exports to the Community which, in 1964, were over six times as large as EEC exports of farm commodities to the United States.

The Problem of Agriculture

The very large trade deficit of the EC in the agricultural sector was undoubtedly one of the motivations for the French government in resisting the inclusion of farm products in the Kennedy Round tariff negotiations. Yielding to French pressures, the Community representatives protested that agricultural issues should not be part of the Kennedy Round until the CAP had been completely implemented in the years to come.[7]

This view was not accepted by the United States because the Kennedy Round was precisely the means by which it hoped to prevent the damage to her farm exports that was likely to be caused by the evolving levy-oriented CAP. In 1963 the EC countries had purchased $1.25 billion in American farm products, constituting about a quarter of all U.S. agricultural exports. A decline of these shipments was regarded by the U.S. government as a very serious matter since it would aggravate an already difficult balance of payments situation. Hence, the United States strongly insisted that both industrial and agricultural items be negotiated in the Kennedy Round, culminating eventually in a single package agreement. An essential element of the American negotiating position from the start was that U.S. exports to the Community be guaranteed not only their "historic" or "fair"

share as a source of food in the member states, but also participation in the anticipated increased demand for farm products.

The State Department expended a great deal of energy on
pursuing the accomplishment of its high-priority goal, a successful package deal in implementation of the Trade Expansion Act.
Many calls on the Commission were made by members of the
U.S. Mission to the European Communities in Brussels to urge
acceptance of the American viewpoint by the Community.
Similar demarches were undertaken also in the capitals of the
six member states. In addition, informal, personal meetings and
contacts between American diplomats and Commission members and officials of the foreign ministries in the six capitals
were used to advance the U.S. position. Orville Freeman, then
Secretary of Agriculture, actively supported the efforts of the
State Department and clamored, at times rather belligerently,
for the fair share concept of access of American farm products
to the Common Market, threatening possible retaliation by the
United States unless this concept was accepted.[8]

The conflict between the American and Community views
was aggravated by what came to be known as the "poultry war"
during 1962 and 1963. A rapid rise in American poultry exports
to Germany had caused a substantial decline in the price of
chickens and other fowl despite a steady increase in demand.
To benefit from this rise in demand, farmers in the Netherlands,
Germany, and Denmark adopted American methods of poultry
raising and quickly increased their own production. This led to
increased supply and a further decline of prices, initiating a
severe struggle for the European poultry market between American producers and EEC farmers who, saddled with high food
prices, saw their profit margins dwindle away. In August 1962
the rules of the game were suddenly changed when new EC
agricultural policy regulations established a comparatively high
barrier for poultry imports from third countries that amounted
to a nearly 300 percent increase over the original tariff of 4.8
cents per pound. As a result, American poultry exports declined
drastically in 1963, and the U.S. government threatened retaliatory tariff action on a variety of products unless the Community
authorities guaranteed a reasonably competitive position for
American poultry sales in the Community countries. In search

175

of a compromise, the United States and the EC requested a GATT advisory opinion concerning the value of poultry trade lost by the CAP regulations. The advisory panel put the amount at $26 million, $20 million less than was estimated by the United States, but $10 million more than that sought by the EC. To compensate for this loss, retaliatory increases on brandy, dextrin, and potato starch were imposed by the United States in January 1964.

Whatever the specific impact the poultry war may have had on the Kennedy Round negotiations, it highlighted the difficulty of reconciling the conflicting agricultural objectives of the two main negotiating partners. The EC gave highest priority to the successful completion of the CAP, without which a full operation of the Common Market was perceived to be impossible. For the Americans, on the other hand, the continuation of high-level agricultural exports to the Community appeared to be a dire necessity, mostly for reasons of international economics, but also because of domestic politics.

Nontariff Barriers

In addition to the problems of tariff disparities and agricultural negotiating concepts, the elimination of nontariff barriers to trade was also a matter of serious concern to all parties. These barriers stem from a variety of national laws, procedures, and regulations, which tend to impair or nullify the reduction in duties for imports. They include laws giving preference to national sources of supply for official purchases (the Buy-American Act for example), labeling regulations, quantitative restrictions, licensing controls, antidumping measures, tax discrimination between domestic and foreign goods, and customs valuations not reflecting actual costs.

One of the matters of paramount concern for the EC was the so-called American Selling Price (ASP), which relates to the calculation of ad valorem duties for certain imports into the United States. American customs laws specify that certain commodities (principally coal tar products) are to be valued on the basis of their selling price in the United States rather than their value in the country of origin. Consequently, the burden of import duties is frequently more than doubled.

Another issue troubling the EC negotiators was the application of the American antidumping laws. While the basic purpose of such legislation is considered to be fully legitimate, the administrative rules for its application have given rise to repeated criticism. The main charges against the system were that investigations into possible dumping practices are initiated automatically even if a complaint is totally unsubstantiated, and that during the usually very long investigation importers and exporters do not know what duties are to be paid.

Prominent among the sources for American apprehension about nontariff barriers was the internal tax structure of some EC countries. In certain instances, additional internal taxes have been assessed specifically against imported articles. Even when taxes were nondiscriminatory in form, they were apt to impose a disproportionate burden on imports. The American automobile industry has complained about alleged inequities of various European road taxes and has charged that taxes on automobiles of greater horsepower, such as those characteristically manufactured in the United States, were disproportionately higher than the same taxes applicable to lower horsepower vehicles, which were usually domestically produced. Other American complaints were directed against special taxes on grain liquor, high gasoline taxes, restrictive quotas for coal imports, and state monopolies on certain commodities such as tobacco in France and Italy. The value-added-tax (VAT) system has also often been criticized by nonmember countries. Although the operation of this system is not prohibited by GATT it involves the imposition of the VAT tax rates on merchandise entering the Common Market and the refunding of these taxes to firms exporting goods from the Common Market. As a consequence these taxes constitute a second kind of tariff or duty on imported goods and their refund can be seen as an export subsidy for merchandise being shipped by Community firms to third countries. Of course, the levy system introduced by the Community's CAP can also be viewed as an example of a nontariff barrier since it deviates materially from the traditional duty system. However, the Americans had become convinced that it was just as well to acquiesce to the levy system since the vast majority of the population in the Community regarded the CAP and its implementation as absolutely necessary for the successful functioning of the Common Market.

The Kennedy Round talks opened officially in Geneva in May 1964, but despite a large number of bilateral talks to define the problems existing between individual countries and trade blocs such as the EC and EFTA, no hard bargaining developed until March 1967. The delay was due partly to the Common Market crisis that broke out in the summer of 1965 and lasted until January 1966,[9] and to the subsequent pre-occupation of the member states with the broad implementation of the CAP. To ensure that France, whose attitude toward the Kennedy Round was doubtful, could not completely stall or scuttle the negotiations, the German and Dutch governments, perhaps encouraged by the Americans, attached to the EC Council agreement for the financing of the CAP reservations that stipulated that the execution of the agreement was to proceed parallel with progress in the Kennedy Round. However, progress continued to be slow during the second half of 1966, and picked up only very gradually after the turn of the year. Perhaps the most important reason for the footdragging, especially on the part of the Community, was identified correctly by William Roth, the special trade representative of the United States, when he said in February 1967, "It is in the nature of a major negotiation such as this that the toughest decisions cannot be taken until the final bargaining phase begins."[10]

In order to step up the tempo of bargaining and to bring the Kennedy Round to a conclusion, the U.S. representatives insisted on setting a deadline for the negotiations. This was necessary because time had to be allowed for preparing the details of the complex agreement document, which had to be submitted to President Johnson for his signature prior to the expiration date of the Trade Expansion Act, June 30, 1967. The various March and April deadlines set by the American negotiators had to be abandoned, but toward the end of April the pace of the negotiations increased markedly and reached a crescendo at the beginning of May. A final deadline of May 14 was agreed upon, the clock stopped at midnight of that day, according to the now time-honored tradition of the EC Council of Ministers bargaining on important issues, and on May 16 final agreement on the Kennedy Round was joyfully announced. The chief negotiators for the United States and the Common Market, William Roth and Jean Rey, expressed their extreme satisfaction with the final package bargained out and stressed its tremendous importance for greater world trade.[11]

The result was a better than moderate success. Although falling short of the 50 percent overall cut sought, tariffs on 6300 items were reduced by an average of 35 percent over a period of 5 years, and 80 countries stood to benefit from these reductions as the consequence of the most-favored-nation rule. As anticipated, the bulk of the tariff cuts were made in the industrial sector, where many items including autos, machinery, and cameras benefited from a 50 percent cut, and the average reductions amounted to 35–40 percent. However, modest concessions in the CET, ranging up to 25 percent, were also made in some of the farm products not subject to the CAP levy, including tobacco, canned fruits and vegetables, fruit juices, tallow, hops, nuts, and raisins. Finally, some headway was made on nontariff barriers; in particular an antidumping code for international trade was adopted, which provides for the concrete application of the principles already incorporated in GATT.[12] Compared with the Dillon Round result of 7–8 percent in tariff reductions and agricultural commodities completely excluded, the result of the Kennedy Round proved to be a striking improvement.

In terms of average tariff structures of the main negotiating partners in the Kennedy Round, Table 5.4 shows the substantial reduction of average tariff rates, both unweighted and weighted by actual imports, in the industrial sector. The EC has now the lowest rates in both categories (6 and 3.9 percent), while Japan is highest in the unweighted categories (9.7 and 5.7 percent), and the United States in the weighted classification. If the current average tariff rates for industrial products are broken down into raw materials, semimanufactured, and manufactured goods, we find that the weighted averages for the last groups are quite similar in the EEC, United States, and the United Kingdom (between 8 and 8.4 percent), but the Japanese rate is about 50

Table 5.4

Comparison of Unweighted and Weighted Average Tariffs for Industrial Goods
(Raw Materials, Semimanufactured Goods, and Manufactured Goods)
(1964-1971 — percent)

| | 1964[a] | | 1971 | |
	Unweighted	Weighted	Unweighted	Weighted[b]
EEC	11.7[c]	5.2[d]	6.0	3.9
United States	17.8	7.8[e]	7.1	6.1
United Kingdom	18.4	n.a.	7.6	5.5
Japan	n.a.	n.a.	9.7	5.7

Breakdown of Average Tariffs for Industrial Products as of January 1, 1973

| | Raw Materials | | Semimanufactured | | Manufactured | |
	Unweighted	Weighted	Unweighted	Weighted	Unweighted	Weighted
EEC	1.6	0.3	6.7	4.7	7.8	8.0
United States	4.5	2.7	9.5	5.1	12.8	8.4
United Kingdom	3.3	0.2	8.1	6.6	11.3	8.2
Japan	2.5	3.2	9.5	6.2	11.4	12.0
Canada	3.4	0.4	7.5	9.4	10.6	6.7

[a] The figures given stem from an EEC study. We should note that the Committee for Economic Development has also prepared a study using different criteria. Under the CED study nonagricultural commodities for the EEC carry an average tariff percentage of 13.2 and for the United States 15.2.

[b] Weighted by Importations into country or region concerned.

[c] Takes into consideration 1961 Dillon Round adjustment.

[d] Weighted by 1960 net imports.

[e] Weighted by 1959 net imports.

Sources: GATT studies 1971; Hinshaw, *The European Community and American Trade*, pp. 81, 86, 88; EEC Official Spokesman, *Trade Negotiations and the Problem of Disparities*.

percent higher (12 percent). The weighted tariff rates for raw materials are considerably higher in the United States and Japan than in the EEC and the United Kingdom.

Between the United States and the EEC the product categories in the industrial sector that caused the greatest difficulties in the negotiations were chemicals, aluminum, steel, and textiles. While for the latter three categories acceptable compromises were worked out in the last few weeks prior to the final bargaining session, the problem of chemicals seemed to defy any solution and brought the Kennedy Round to the brink of failure on more than one occasion. The reason was that the Community was most anxious to eliminate the application of the ASP method of determining duties, but offered as a quid pro quo only an average cut of 24 percent. The American negotiators were willing to seek removal of the ASP system of protection, which would require congressional approval and is politically sensitive, but insisted on a larger cut of the Community duties on chemicals than proposed by the EEC. The final compromise was that Congress would be requested to abolish the ASP system and to bring all U.S. tariffs on chemicals down to a ceiling of 20 percent except for some dyes that would remain at 30 percent. In return, the CET on these items would be cut in half, but the Community was willing to put only 40 percent of this cut into effect until Congress had acted on the ASP, with the remaining 60 percent of the reduction to follow congressional action. As could be expected, the American chemical industry vigorously assailed this compromise and called it a "blatantly one-sided bargain," because the United States had not succeeded in having other countries remove nontariff barriers that hamper American export sales.[13] With strong pressure put on Congress against the elimination of the ASP, no action was taken, and the ASP provisions have remained in force, to the dismay of the Europeans. Nevertheless, imports of chemicals into the United States have increased materially, and exports of American chemical products have fallen by more than 33 percent. Regarding the improvement over the previous antidumping rules, voices were heard in Congress expressing concern that the American negotiators appeared to have usurped congressional powers over foreign trade.[14]

The final result in the agricultural bargaining represented a dramatic shift in the U.S. position. As a partial substitute for guaranteed access to the Community's grain markets, the United States sought the creation of a 5 million ton food aid program for developing countries, to which all economically advanced countries would contribute. Requesting a Community contribution of 1 million tons, the hope was that the grain siphoned away from the EEC for food aid would be replaced by American grain sold for dollars. After considerable bargaining, during which Japan was the last holdout, a program of 4.5 million tons was accepted, with no diminution of the EEC contribution. Another concession to the Americans and other wheat exporting countries was the establishment of higher minimum world reference prices for wheat. The EC proposal for setting up a system for freezing farm price supports on a worldwide basis was dropped. Although in the light of the American expectation that agriculture would benefit materially in the Kennedy Round from a package deal with industry, many quarters considered the result in the agricultural sector generally disappointing. Of course, farm interests in the EEC, especially France, also were not fully satisfied, and complained that too many concessions had been made by the EEC negotiators.

The Kennedy Round had all the trappings of a high-stake poker game and every possible tactic, including threats of complete withdrawal from the negotiations, was used to influence their outcome. On the part of the United States, in addition to efforts by the government, nongovernmental groups were used to exercise subtle influences on similar groups sharing the same interests in the member states. For example, the Crotonville Conference of nearly 100 American businessmen and government leaders, held early in 1966, recommended that the American Chambers of Commerce be asked to appeal to their European counterparts for their vigorous support of the Kennedy Round negotiations. In May of that year American and French top-level industrial leaders met in a three-day closed session in Paris to survey their common interests. At the close of these talks all participants of this meeting expressed agreement on the need for an early, successful conclusion of the Kennedy Round negotiations and declared that such an event would be the best means to eliminate misunderstandings between the two nations.[15] Private contracts were also maintained between farm groups in the United States and in the member states, and joint meetings between American and European farmers have been held on several occasions. However, the American position on agriculture gained little from these meetings, although the International Federation of Agricultural Producers, meeting in Washington D.C. in May 1964, came up with a joint but rather meaningless statement on the Kennedy Round negotiations.[16] When toward the end of 1966 it became apparent that the results in the agricultural sector of the negotiations would be very meager indeed, American farm groups, including the powerful American Farm Bureau Federation, urged U.S. withdrawal from the Kennedy Round unless Community offers were materially broadened. As late as February 27, 1967, U.S. Special Trade Representative William Roth declared that the United States was fully prepared to leave the Kennedy Round if satisfactory negotiations could not be arranged during the next several weeks.[17] He was close to making this warning come true when in the first week of May he angrily threatened to break off negotiations and return to Washington.

Some of the European negotiators suggested that the American crisis tactics were forced upon the American negotiators because the latter had to establish their position vis-à-vis domestic political and economic groups and interests. However, contributing equally to the element of crisis was the fact that Mr. Rey's instructions were usually closely circumscribed by the Council of Ministers and that he had to shuttle with increasing frequency between Geneva and Brussels to report and receive new instructions from the Council. Even when the Commission was given a relatively flexible negotiating mandate, the final decision remained in the hands of the Council. As the end of the Kennedy Round approached, the frequency of the Council sessions was also stepped up, permitting the member governments to exercise maximum control over the negotiations.

Since every Community offer made was the result of often arduous, prolonged bargaining on all levels of Community decision making, Mr. Rey's negotiating task was perhaps more

183

complex than that of Mr. Roth, as he had to take into consideration six sets of domestic political and economic groups and
interests. In the evolving of each offer the member governments
were intent on safeguarding their national interests, economic
and otherwise, and difficult compromises had to be worked out
for the best accommodation of everyone's interests and aspirations. For example, the Germans were opposed to too much
participation in the food aid program, for which they would
have to foot a large part of the bill. The Italians, in turn, were
set against too many concessions on chemicals. The clash of
basic objectives between export-oriented Germany and the
Benelux countries, and the protectionist tendencies of France
and to a lesser degree of Italy, provided many opportunities for
tenacious holdouts and stalling, sometimes supported by strong
statements of influential Community interest groups.[18] Toward
the end of the Kennedy Round the French adopted a more
positive approach, and there seemed to be a genuine give-and-
take by the various delegations. The new flexibility on the part
of the French gave the Germans a feeling that concessions on
Community farm financing that they had made earlier had in
fact paid off.[19]

It is noteworthy that Eric Wyndham White, then the direc-
tor-general of GATT, offered on several occasions compromise
solutions when the Kennedy Round seemed to be stalled during
the final few weeks. Indeed, it was his package of compromises
submitted on the last morning of the negotiations that served
as the general framework for the settlement. Thus, the GATT
Secretary-General performed a similar role in breaking the
bargaining deadlock as the Commission has done in several
instances when its compromise package saved the day for
hopelessly stalled marathon Council of Ministers sessions.

The expertise of Jean Rey, a Belgian lawyer, and then the
member of the Commission responsible for external affairs, in
dealing not only with the negotiators of third countries, but
also with the often divergent views of the Council, further
enhanced the Commission's role as the official negotiator for
the member states in trade negotiations and strengthened the
stature of the Community in general. Although his latitude for
the negotiations was relatively limited and therefore he had to

seek frequent instructions, he clearly had the respect and confidence of the Council members who apparently accepted his arguments when the chips were down. On the other hand, it was perhaps precisely the limited negotiating discretion and the two-level arrangement for the elaboration of the Community's negotiating position that gave him considerable strength in bargaining with third countries, because negotiators on the other side were fully aware that his powers were restricted and changes were difficult. Rey's excellent performance in the Kennedy Round negotiations was undoubtedly a contributing factor to his appointment as the first president of the unified Commission of the European Communities on July 1, 1967.

ANALYSIS OF U.S.-EC TRADE 1958–1973

It is difficult to judge what effects the Kennedy Round has had on U.S.-EC trade, and whether this trade would have continued to increase even without the tariff reductions agreed upon by the Kennedy Round negotiators. The figures given in Table 5.5 from 1958 to 1973 show an overall upward trend of U.S. exports to the EC and vice versa, but they also indicate marked increases for U.S. exports in 1968, 1969, and 1970, and for EC exports for all years following the conclusion of the Kennedy Round. Note that the 1973 figures are not comparable to the earlier data as they relate to the trade with the enlarged Community of Nine.

A general analysis of U.S.-EC trade from 1958 to 1972 reveals that U.S. exports during that period almost tripled, but shipments from the Community to the United States more than quintupled. Although the United States had a surplus during the years from 1958 to 1971 it suffered its first deficit in 1972. Looking over this surplus we see that it ranged from a high of $2,300,000,000 in 1963 to a low of $413,000,000 in 1968. While this continued surplus may have been a source of satisfaction to the United States, a more thorough analysis of how American exports to the Community fared compared with those of other countries presents a somewhat different picture. When

185

Table 5.5

Trade Balance Between the United States and the European Community — 1958-73
(billions of U.S. dollars)

	U.S. Exports	U.S. Imports	U.S. Surplus
1958	2.840	1.660	1.180
1959	2.830	2.380	.450
1960	3.930	2.240	1.690
1961	4.100	2.230	1.870
1962	4.530	2.450	2.130
1963	4.860	2.560	2.300
1964	5.230	2.850	2.280
1965	5.200	4.100	1.780
1966	5.460	4.100	1.360
1967	5.582	4.457	1.125
1968	5.994	5.581	.413
1969	6.875	5.800	1.075
1970	8.325	6.612	1.713
1971	8.291	7.523	.765
1972	8.691	8.980	(.289)
1973[a]	16.700	15.500	1.200

Sources: U.N. Statistical Office, *Yearbook of International Trade Statistics* (1972); and U.S. Department of Commerce, *U.S. Foreign Trade Exports,* (1971) Products by Areas.

[a] The 1973 figures relate to the enlarged Community of Nine.

we compare the share of United States exports with those of other *nonmember* countries, we find that the American portion was 17.57 percent in 1958 and fell only slightly to 16.55 percent in 1972. However, if we compare the percentage of U.S. exports with all exports including those of European Community countries to each other, the U.S. share dropped from 12.37 to 8 percent. The reason for this is the tremendous increase in intra-EC trade from 1958 to 1972—an expected result of the creation of the Common Market. During that period this trade increased more than 8 times, while exports from third countries increased only slightly more than 3 times.[20]

Since the export of agricultural commodities has been a continuing concern of the United States, it is useful to examine the export figures from July 1, 1957, to June 30, 1973. These figures can be found in Table 5.6 and show exports both to the original six members and to the enlarged Community. The table is subdivided into figures for commodities subject to the variable-levy and nonvariable-levy products. From this table it is apparent that the variable-levy commodities shipped to the Community of the Six reached a high point in the fiscal year 1965–66 and then declined. The likely explanation for this trend is the full implementation of the variable-levy system by the end of 1964. On the other hand, the exports for non-variable-levy commodities continued to remain at a relatively high level until 1969 and in fact increased beginning with the 1969–70 fiscal year. However, it is essential to keep in mind that during the period from 1958 to 1972 the level of consumption in the Community rose steeply and that American exports of agricultural commodities were not only unable to retain their proper share of supplying this rising demand but their net volume dropped between 1965 and 1970. The figures for the agricultural commodity exports to the United Kingdom, Denmark, and Ireland exerted only a minor influence on the overall picture.

A favorable change for American agricultural exports began in 1970 and the most striking development shown in Table 5.5 is the tremendous increase in the figures for the fiscal year 1972–73. Exports of variable-levy items rose 50 percent to an all-time high of $955 million; exports of nonvariable-levy

Table 5.6

U.S. Agricultural Exports to the European Community — Fiscal Years 1957-72
(millions of U.S. dollars)

	1957/58	1958/59	1959/60	1960/61	1961/62	1962/63	1963/64	1964/65	1965/66	1966/67	1967/68	1968/69	1969/70	1970/71	1971/72	1972/73
Original Six																
Variable-levy commodities	185	309	332	373	496	414	499	519	716	522	531	402	351	479	456	778
Nonvariable-levy commodities	691	482	788	728	688	656	834	852	878	988	872	898	1060	1286	1433	2103
Total EC	876	791	1121	1101	1184	1070	1333	1371	1594	1510	1403	1300	1411	1766	1889	2882
Enlarged EC																
Variable-levy commodities	350	524	574	562	714	582	704	695	923	693	661	502	483	684	634	955
Nonvariable-levy commodities	1019	731	1105	1075	1012	961	1179	1196	1216	1389	1245	1209	1407	1655	1808	2636
Total Enlarged EC	1369	1255	1678	1637	1726	1544	1883	1892	2139	2081	1906	1711	1890	2340	2442	3591

Source: Foreign Agricultural Trade of the United States, October 1973 (Economic Research Service, U.S. Department of Agriculture), pp. 30–33.

products gained 46 percent, reaching $2.64 billion. However, it needs to be pointed out that higher prices—especially for soybeans and derivative products, hides and skins, and most fruits and vegetables—accounted for a considerable amount of this gain. Exports of oil seed and derivative products rose to $1.53 billion in the 1972–73 fiscal year from slightly less than $1 billion a year earlier. The original Six took nearly 90 percent of this amount and accounted for most of the growth. Despite the increase, the U.S. share of the EC agricultural market continued to slip because of the protectionist nature of the CAP.

The importance of the European Community to American agriculture is demonstrated by the fact that it represented a market for nearly a third of the U.S. agricultural exports in fiscal year 1973 and that it is a market without problems of currency convertibility. It is therefore understandable that the United States is anxious to make every effort to maintain a high level of agricultural exports to the Community and that the expected continuous rise of living standards in Western Europe is a particularly strong incentive.

Expectations, Frictions, and Strategies

Shortly after the Kennedy Round had been concluded, voices were heard on both sides of the Atlantic urging the start of new negotiations under the auspices of GATT that would further reduce tariffs and be especially concerned with the elimination of nontariff barriers. While the Nixon Administration seemed to be basically interested in such negotiations, the Vietnam War as well as recurring monetary crises leading to the devaluation of the dollar in December 1971 and February 1973, seemed to require the attention of American policy makers much more than a future round of trade negotiations. However, the grave deficit in the American balance of trade in 1972 and the serious monetary crisis of early 1973 compelled the economically advanced countries of the world to again focus their attention on the problems of international trade.

Faced with a mounting trade deficit in 1972 ($6.8 billion compared with $2.7 billion in 1971[21] and including for the first

189

time a deficit with the EC amounting to $289 million[22]) and concerned about the newly founded economic prowess of the enlarged Community, the U.S. government began to look toward a new round of negotiations as a possible solution to its problems. For the success of these negotiations the pursuit of three main strategies was considered essential.

The first strategy was to attack the protectionism of the CAP and to urge a modification of this policy in order to increase American exports of agricultural commodities. The U.S. government argued that in view of its high efficiency, American agriculture could offer its products at considerably lower cost than could European farmers. Therefore, increased American farm exports would benefit European consumers, and it was considered arbitrary to exclude American farm products from the Community markets.

Second, the U.S. government was intent on eliminating the discrimination that it claimed to suffer from the growing net of preferential agreements negotiated by the Community with developing countries in the Mediterranean area and Africa, a network that was likely to spread to the Caribbean and perhaps elsewhere. The preferences given to shipments from the Mediterranean countries made American exports of citrus fruit to the EC countries less competitive; and the reverse preferences given by the developing countries to Community exports of manufactured goods were seen as discrimination against U.S. manufacturers and regarded as a violation of the GATT principle of the most-favored-nation (MNF) clause.[23]

The third American strategy for trade negotiations with the EC was a linkage of trade, monetary, and military problems. The argument was that American balance of payments problems could be resolved only through a combination of monetary adjustment mechanisms tied to tariff changes and to the cost of maintaining American troops in Europe. In a report to the Finance Committee of the U.S. Senate, Senator Ribicoff stated:

> Our other outstanding problems with Europe cannot be viewed in isolation from these economic questions. It is contradictory to argue, as some Europeans do, that the U.S. must maintain troops in Europe while, at the same time, insisting that Europe must pursue a trade and monetary policy harmful

to the interests of the United States. These questions are all interrelated even if specific price tags are not put on some of our policies.[24]

While the United States was seeking concessions for alleged discrimination because of the CAP and the preferential agreements, the Community and member states insisted on reciprocity in lowering tariff and nontariff barriers.[25] They favored substantial reciprocal reductions of tariffs, but not their complete elimination, as was advocated by some American exports, although it should be pointed out, this was not the position of the U.S. government. They were prepared to bargain on the discontinuance of selected nontariff barriers employed by either the United States or the Community. However, they insisted on maintaining the principles of the CAP, but within this framework they were ready to work for an expansion of world farm trade. They were silent on the reverse preferences although the Commission recommended that in future agreements they would be excluded, while in the 40 preferential accords currently in effect with Mediterranean and African countries they would be retained.[26] Moreover, all industrially advanced countries were urged to offer generalized tariff preferences to manufactured and semimanufactured goods produced in the Third World. The Community had initiated a limited scheme for such preferences in 1971, but the United States had not taken any step in this direction, although the Administration had expressed itself in favor of this approach.

Several European worries beclouded the prospects for future negotiations. Concern was expressed about the continually growing power of American multinational corporations in Europe, and it was argued that the sales of these companies in the EC should be equated with exports of American goods to the Community. This, however, is a fallacious argument because the benefits of the production of these corporations flow to European labor and to European treasuries in the form of taxes.

Another concern of the Europeans has been that the steep devaluation of the dollar may become (or already had become) an economic warfare weapon of the United States.[27] Many Europeans would like to see a return to stable rates of monetary

191

exchange on a worldwide basis. Finally, the masses of Eurodollars floating around in Europe have been a source of worry to most Europeans. They claim with justification that the large amounts of Eurodollars have contributed to the inflationary problems in Europe and would like to see them repatriated to the United States.

In the spring of 1973 pressures built up within the Community to modify the CAP because of the effects of high food prices on inflation in Europe. The British especially wanted to substitute deficiency payments to individual farmers (subsidies) for the high guaranteed prices for farm commodities, which continued to rise year after year.[28] These pressures were fueled by the emergence of enormous surpluses of some commodities, with butter as the outstanding example. When the EC Commission approved the sale to the Soviet Union of 200,000 metric tons of butter from its 400,000 ton stockpile at 20 percent of normal Community prices, and with a loss of $362 million to be borne by the EC Agricultural Guidance and Guarantee Fund (i.e., the taxpayers), a loud chorus of criticism arose.[29]

In the meantime, however, the agricultural situation changed drastically. World prices have risen enormously and many farm commodities are in short supply. Instead of promoting the export of certain farm products such as soybeans and cotton seeds, the U.S. government has sought to limit shipments to Europe, at least on a temporary basis. Not surprisingly, this aroused shock and anger in the EC after the United States had been preaching free trade for so many years.

Fortunately, the embargo was lifted quickly, yet new demands for European self-sufficiency in these products were heard, especially in France.[30] These shortages and sharp price rises far above the target price levels of the CAP initially discouraged those in the Community who were prepared to work for modification of the CAP to narrow the gap between the negotiating stances of the United States and the EC. Nevertheless, Chancellor Brandt of Germany, in a speech on October 12, 1973, insisted that the CAP must be continually reexamined as to its true benefits for producers and consumers, and room must be left for imports from other parts of the world.[31]

New U.S. Trade Legislation

In the spring of 1973, President Nixon submitted to Congress a proposal for new trade legislation. The bill's major provisions were:

1. unlimited presidential authority to raise or lower tariffs.

2. authority to negotiate the removal of nontariff barriers, but with an after-the-fact veto reserved for Congress

3. safeguards against imports that damage domestic producers

4. balance of payments authority giving the President power to impose quotas or surcharges to improve the U.S. payments position

5. temporary import-related adjustment assistance

6. retaliatory authority against countries that "illegally" or "unreasonably" discriminate against U.S. exports and against those countries whose subsidies or other inducements to producers result in the loss of markets in third countries

7. authority for a generalized system of tariff preferences on imports of manufactured, semimanufactured, and other selected products from developing countries.[32]

The introduction of this clearly "tough" legislation was designed to win American labor's support since major trade union organizations in the United States had shifted from their previously liberal world trade positions to a high level of protectionism as imports were increasingly seen as threats to American producers and jobs. It was also an effort to take the wind out of the sails of the strongly protectionist Burke–Hartke legislative proposal which, in deference to labor's wishes, contained provisions placing stringent quotas on virtually all imports, and putting severe limitations on investments, tax advantages, and other activities of U.S. multinational enterprises.[33]

When the new trade bill was proposed it drew sharp criticism as well as strong endorsement from business leaders, including those from foreign countries. For example, Chujiro Fujino, one of Japan's leading industrialists, said that most of the trade bill seemed "reasonable." Noting, however, a section of the bill that would permit the President to restrict imports from countries considered to have "unfair trade practices" he said: "Who is going to determine what is fair or unfair?"[34] George Meany, president of the AFL–CIO, said that President Nixon's trade legislation proposals "do not meet the grave problems of trade which we have detailed time and again." He said the proposals "provide no specific machinery to regulate the flood of imports" and do "virtually nothing to close lucrative tax loopholes for American-based multinational corporations."[35]

Despite these criticisms, the House of Representatives passed the bill in December 1973, and favorable Senate action followed a year later.[36] It is noteworthy that the bill would give the President authority to grant lower tariffs to imports from less developed countries over a 10-year period. This provision is significant inasmuch as it may permit U.S. negotiators in the new round of tariff cuts to reach a compromise on the specialized preferences, which the United States finds so objectionable.

The bill gives the President authority to negotiate trade agreements over a 5-year period. Thus, the negotiators may have until 1979 to come up with a pattern of trade not only between the United States and the European Community but among all free world countries.

The Outlook

It is difficult to predict what kind of new trade relationship will emerge from this new legislation. The expectations of the American government regarding increased access to the Community for agricultural products may well change, if the shortages and high prices of many commodities persist. In view of the generally higher prices for many of the primary products sold by the developing countries, it is not unreasonable to assume that the increased purchasing power of these countries will make itself felt on the prices and sales of many of the farm commodities produced in the United States. In other words, the Americans may not be as anxious as before to push the Community on the modification of the CAP, even though it may be shortsighted not to anticipate new agricultural surpluses 5 or 10 years hence due to the high efficiency of American agriculture.[37] It is, of course, very doubtful whether U.S. strategy for modification of the CAP could be fully successful since, despite its shortcomings, the CAP remains for many Europeans an essential ingredient in their integration efforts. However, the successful British efforts at renegotiating the accession treaty and their attacks on many features of the CAP (supported in part by Germany) may finally result in modification and a more favorable situation for American agricultural exports.

As far as the preferential agreements of the Community are concerned, it must be realized that they are more than merely commercial accords. As we have pointed out, these agreements allow the Community to extend not only its economic but also its political influence. It is this political aspect that may preoccupy the American government. However, if a generalized preference scheme can be elaborated by the U.S. government, and if lower tariffs for the exchange of industrialized goods among the industrially advanced countries can be negotiated, the danger from the emergence of competing trading blocs in the world could be largely avoided. A broadly liberalized world trade pattern would be an advantage in the long run to both developing and developed countries.

The linkage of trade, monetary, and military problems sought by the United States initially generated some serious frictions and disputes, leading to sharp exchanges across the Atlantic by government officials and parliamentarians of the United States and the EC countries.[38] However, when in September 1973 new trade negotiations officially opened in Tokyo, in anticipation of favorable congressional action on the administration's proposals, the Community consented to parallel efforts aimed at the liberalization of world trade and at the establishment of a monetary system "that will shelter the world economy from the shakings and imbalances that have become apparent over recent months."[39] U.S. Secretary of the Treasury

George Shultz acknowledged the links between trade and monetary negotiations, and declared that the United States would be glad to consider any serious EC proposal ameliorating the access of American agricultural commodities to the Community. Both parties stated their desire to improve and refine the GATT provisions (article XIX) that permit the application of safeguards against imports in the event of serious injury to domestic producers. This is a difficult problem for all countries and therefore domestic adjustment for injury needs to be considered in multilateral terms instead of placing the burden exclusively on the importing country by simply prohibiting injury producing goods to enter.[40] Another major issue will be the reduction, if not elimination, of nontariff barriers, an issue with which the Kennedy Round did not really deal satisfactorily. The problems are being defined in preparatory meetings in Geneva, and their solutions are likely to be crucial for the success or failure of the Tokyo Round negotiations.[41] This can be seen by minor recurring friction between the United States and the Community arising from the threatened imposition of countervailing duties in 1975 on such products as certain cheeses and canned ham exported from EEC countries to the American market. The U.S. government claimed—perhaps on the initiative of the dairy industry lobby and other interest groups—unjustifiable export restrictions on these products.[42] Although solutions were quickly found for these problems, the United States and the Community agreed that it would be vital to avoid bilateral altercation in the future through an "early warning system" consultation mechanism.[43]

While it appears, then, that the earlier, very serious recriminations between U.S. and Community leaders on the subject of future trade negotiations have given way to a high degree of harmony, the question of American troops in Europe could continue to complicate the negotiations. Many European leaders would like to exclude this problem from any kind of trade and monetary negotiations. On the other hand, the cost of the maintenance of these troops, which amounts to $8 billion annually (including their logistical support and U.S. based training expenditures), has a significant adverse effect on the American balance of payments.[44]

Although the NATO-related balance of payments deficit of $2.1 billion in 1974 was mostly offset by German purchases of U.S. securities and purchases of U.S. military equipment by Germany and other NATO allies, the so-called Jackson–Nunn amendment to the Department of Defense appropriation act of 1974 directed the President to reduce American forces in Europe if the NATO allies failed to fully offset this deficit. McGeorge Bundy's comments regarding this problem in 1972 remain cogent. He said:

> It is a fact of life for both Europe and the United States that your "resolutely amilitary" population depends for its peace of mind, at least in part, upon the fact that *our* population is prepared to pay twice as much of its national income for the common defense. I do not lament this expense. I think that in the main it is essential for our own security, and that we should save very few dollars if there were no Europe for us to help defend. Moreover I recognize that much has already been done, and that more can reasonably be predicted, in the way of burden-sharing. Nonetheless, I think it would be asking a great deal of my fellow citizens, and even more of their elected representatives, to expect them to neglect entirely, in the reconstruction of the economic and financial foundations that are indispensable to all of us, the fact that among the open societies of the North Atlantic and Pacific, there is one which does much more than the others to provide for a defense which is still common. . . . I cannot help hoping that from time to time, as some European expert finds his temper growing short over ASP (which I do not admire), or the claims of grapefruit (which I happen not to like), he will find it in his heart to remember that these same tiresome Americans, twenty-seven years after a great common victory, are still doing somewhat more than anyone else wants to do in this matter of defense. The point is one which should not be over-bargained, but history does suggest that Americans, like others, will often trade quite a lot simply in return for understanding.[45]

It is not unreasonable to assume that understanding and offers of assistance for a greater sharing of the burdens of common defense on the part of European governmental leaders and parliamentarians might make a significant difference in the kind of trade relationship that the United States and the European

Community will have in the future. Unfortunately, such understanding is often lacking, because few Europeans are well acquainted with the political dynamics of the American system and the interaction operating among the public, influential elites, Congress, and the executive. But while arguing for greater understanding on the part of the European statesmen it should be added that similar understanding for the many political problems with which the European negotiators will be faced must be shown by the U.S. government and Congress. Moreover, European defense spending has increased since 1970, rising from $25 billion (dollars at current prices and existing exchange rates) to $42 billion in 1974. However, the percentage of the GNP devoted to defense by the Europeans has declined from 5.8 percent in 1964 to 4.2 in 1970, remaining constant through 1974. But the percentage of U.S. GNP devoted to defense has also declined from 9.4 percent in 1968 to 5.9 in 1974,[46] although it remains about one third higher than that of the Europeans. Admittedly, it is almost impossible to reach a common denominator for NATO expenditures by all the allies, especially since the thrust of the European allies is nearly totally diverted toward conventional forces and that of the U.S. must combine nuclear and conventional armaments and forces. In any case, the last thing that either the United States or the European Community can afford is what J. Robert Schaetzel, former U.S. ambassador to the European Communities, called a "dialogue of the deaf" in this crucial matter of security for the future of the free world. The redefinition of the Atlantic Relationship advocated by Henry Kissinger in 1973[47] and finally embodied in the somewhat watered-down Declaration on Atlantic Relations signed in June 1974[48] was helpful by placing a positive accent on transatlantic relations and initiatives. The need to place such an accent on these relations was also emphasized earlier by Sir Christopher Soames, Vice President of the EC Commission in charge of external affairs in a speech in October 1973 when he declared:

> . . . we have come a long way from the accumulation of interminable petty grievances, from the litany of trivial mutual reproach, and from the dialogue of the deaf which has some-

times in the past obscured the real nature and confidence of our mutual dealings. It is now up to all of us on both sides of the Atlantic to give our dialogue substance. It cannot be too strongly emphasized, what Secretary Kissinger said . . . that "we are not engaged in an adversary procedure. We are engaged in a process in which a traditional friendship is intended to be given a new vitality." That vitality will not descend from the skies. It will have to be worked for by the statesmen and the peoples here and in Europe. And it will have to stand up to plenty of buffeting, for let us face it, our interests are not always identical. As recent days have shown, events will not always conspire to favour what I profoundly believe to be this new Europe's top priority in the external field, the development with the United States of a close and constructive working relationship.[49]

EC TRADE WITH JAPAN

The significance of the EC–Japanese relationship is highlighted by the remarkable expansion of reciprocal trade since 1958. EC exports to Japan increased eightfold from 1958 to 1972, while Japanese exports to the Common Market rose from $117 million to nearly $2 billion, or twice as much as the percentage rise of EC shipments to Japan.[50] In 1973, when the trade figures included the three new EC members, Japanese exports to the EC were almost twice those of EC exports to Japan; although this gap narrowed toward the end of that year.[51]

The very strong competitive position occupied by Japan in the fields of textiles, chinaware, and steel products has led the member countries to regulate their trade relations with Japan in such a way as to ensure a measure of protection for their own industries. However, these protective measures have varied from country to country, some imposing import quotas and others a system of quotas and safeguard clauses that permit protective measures against actual or impending market disturbances. In November 1962 the Council of Ministers concerned itself with the problem of the safeguard clauses and requested the member governments to work up a model clause for uniform insertion into the bilateral agreements. Although Japan acceded to the

199

inclusion of such a clause in trade agreements with France and the Benelux countries, it refused the same to Germany and Italy, indicating different priorities of economic interests on the part of both Japan and the member states.

In June 1963 the Commission submitted to the Council proposals for a common commercial policy toward Japan. They included a liberalization policy ensuring for both Japan and the EEC the same advantages as other GATT members, application of the uniform safeguard clause suggested by the Council in 1962 for the benefit of the whole Community, and the preparation of a list of certain sensitive products for which quantitative restrictions could be imposed. These proposals did not receive a favorable reception by the Council, perhaps because they went a little too far, or were not fully thought out. Whatever the reasons for the rebuff, the Commission made a new proposal in March 1964 recommending an immediate start of exploratory talks with Japan.

Again, the conflicting views and interests of the member states could not be reconciled in the Council, reflecting the usual concern of the member governments to tie in commercial policy with the pursuit of their general foreign policy, and the divergence of economic interests. The latter factor becomes quite evident when one compares the national lists of products on which import quotas are imposed. These lists are relatively limited for Germany and the Benelux countries but are quite extensive for France and Italy.[52]

During the Kennedy Round talks the Commission sought to revive its earlier proposals for a common commercial policy toward Japan. However, only Germany and the Netherlands appeared to favor the Commission's suggestions, while the other member states, especially France, remained hostile to these recommendations. We should point out that despite the tariff reductions negotiated in the Kennedy Round, trade between the EC and Japan continues to be governed by a number of quantitative and safeguard provisions, most of which are contained in national rather than Community agreements with Japan. Progress toward liberalization of this trade on the Community level remains very slow despite a basic mandate for the Commission to engage in direct negotiations with Japan.[53] In the meantime, the Japanese government pursues its policy of encouraging bilateral arrangements. For example, the Japan Electronic Industry Association has concluded agreements with the French and British electronic industries to curb the export of Japanese electronic appliances by imposing quantitative restrictions on these goods.[54]

Japan's entry into the OECD in 1963 spurred hopes for a more normal relationship between the EC and Japan, since this step appeared to imply Japanese recognition of the general principles of trade liberalization. However, negotiations for a possible commercial agreement between the Community and Japan collapsed in 1972. The major stumbling block was the inclusion of safeguard measures aimed at the improvement of the balance of trade. This was to be accomplished by curbing the excessive growth of Japanese sales of certain electronic products in the Community, and by greater penetration of the Japanese market by European goods. To aid in achieving a more equitable balance of trade, Japan introduced ceilings on exports of certain electronic equipment in 1973, but nevertheless by the end of 1975 the trade deficit of the EC vis-à-vis Japan began to rise again.[55]

In 1974 the Community and Japan agreed on the establishment of a European Commission delegation in Tokyo with full diplomatic privileges and immunities, similar to the Washington delegation. This has created a permanent liaison instrument between the EC and Japan.[56]

EC TRADE WITH CANADA, AUSTRALIA, AND NEW ZEALAND

As Table 5.7 clearly indicates, the three old Dominions of the Commonwealth, Canada, Australia, and New Zealand, constitute important trading partners for the Common Market. A large part of the goods shipped to the EC from these three countries is composed of farm commodities such as wheat, beef, and apples, while EC shipments to these countries consist primarily of industrial products. We should note that while the EC trade balance toward the three countries is unfavorable, the gap has been narrowing between 1958 and 1972 in favor of the Community; and whereas the flow of exports to Canada quadrupled, the exports to Australia tripled and to New Zealand doubled. In 1973, with Britain a member of the Community, the EC balance with Australia became positive; it was almost even with New Zealand; but it deteriorated substantially vis-à-vis Canada.[57]

Table 5.7

EC Trade with Canada, Australia, and New Zealand (millions of U.S. dollars)

	1958	1960	1962	1969	1972
Imports from					
Canada	430	450	451	823	1088
Australia	382	418	446	574	716
New Zealand	118	162	174	164	190
Exports to					
Canada	237	293	309	713	1021
Australia	171	266	246	472	520
New Zealand	45	53	53	68	92

Source: Statistisches Amt der Europaischen Gemeinschaften, *Foreign Trade,* no. 4 (1973): 18, 20.

The attitudes of the three Commonwealth countries were of crucial importance when Great Britain decided to apply for Common Market membership in 1961. Australia and Canada were highly critical and very reluctant to support the British endeavor; and New Zealand, while somewhat more agreeable, raised the question of a separate association with the Common Market. Interestingly, since the 1961–62 negotiations, there have been significant changes in the attitudes of the three countries toward British entry into the Community. Canada, which headed the opposition to British entry in 1962, now supports it; and Australia and New Zealand, both joined since 1965 in a free trade area, also appear to have had a change of heart. However, New Zealand's agricultural exports to the United Kingdom caused some difficulties in the 1971–72 negotiations for British entry into the Community, and were a major concern for Prime Minister Wilson in the renegotiations of the accession treaty. They were finally overcome by concessions on the part of the EC.[58]

One important reason for this shift in attitude is the lessened dependence of these countries on exports to the United Kingdom. New outlets for their goods have been found in other areas of the globe, especially Asia and the United States. All three countries have begun to make individual efforts to safeguard their interests in the European Community. Although in view of the CAP, continuing access for agricultural products—for instance, Canadian wheat, Australian beef, and New Zealand dairy products—is of major importance, the three Commonwealth countries are also interested in the export of other raw materials, semimanufactured goods, and manufactured goods to the Common Market. Most prominent among these products are newsprint and aluminum from Canada, products which did not fare quite as well in the Kennedy negotiations as the Canadians had hoped.

The enlargement of the Community has greatly increased the economic dependence of Australia and New Zealand on the Community. Australia, which exported 9 percent of its total exports to the Six (11 percent of its agricultural exports), saw this percentage increase to 21 percent for the enlarged EC (24 percent of agricultural exports). Conversely, Australia imports from the Six and the Nine represent 13 and 34 percent of its total imports, respectively. New Zealand's exports to the Six and the enlarged Community constitute 11 percent (12 percent of its agricultural exports) and 43 percent (48 percent of agricultural export sales); its imports from the Six represented 9 percent of its total imports but increased to 37 percent as the result of the enlargement.[59]

Australia's relations with the Community were severely tested when imports of frozen beef were halted in the fall of 1974 because of overproduction of this commodity by Community farmers and the inability to market the growing surplus of beef and veal within the EC countries. During a visit by External Affairs Commissioner Sir Christopher Soames to Australia and New Zealand in the fall of 1974, government leaders complained about these restrictive measures as the Community "exporting its own difficulties."[60] To prevent such problems in the future, the Australian and New Zealand governments suggested institutionalized regular contacts at ministerial level in Brussels and perhaps a better adaptation of their own range of export goods to the needs of the Community.[61]

Canada and the Community have also reappraised their mutual economic relations with a view to closer cooperation. This is especially important for Canada since the Community is its second largest trading partner. A simple trade agreement was not considered sufficient to achieve this purpose, and a formal "cooperation" accord including commercial, economic, and access-to-raw materials features, which clearly would be useful for both parties, was likely to raise numerous problems. Primary among these difficulties was the need to decide whether the Community institutions had the proper legal authority to conclude such an agreement. Apart from the difficulty of evolving a common position for the Nine, a Canadian–Community cooperation agreement may set a precedent for other industrialized countries that may not be regarded as desirable by either these countries or by some of the EC member states. Nevertheless, the EC Council accepted the principle of negotiating a cooperation agreement with Canada despite initial reservations by France.[62] One cause for French apprehension was that the conclusion of a cooperation agreement implied an extension of Community competences for external relations, which were limited by the EEC Treaty to trade agreements. Indeed, it was the instrument of an "economic cooperation" accord through which some of the member states had attempted to retain a maximum amount of national foreign policy prerogatives in subtle subversion of the Treaty's assignment of common commercial policy powers to the EC institutions.

During a visit to Brussels in the fall of 1974 Prime Minister Pierre Trudeau of Canada declared that the Canadian government did not seek "preferential" relations with the Community, but that Canada would be concerned if such agreements were concluded with other industrialized nations. He also said that while Canada's bilateral relations with EC members would not cease to exist, a transfer of "parcels of sovereignty to the

Community by member states would require reappraisal of these relations, especially since the answers to questions regarding tariffs and agriculture already are mainly found in Brussels." He formally stated that in view of Canada's effort to formulate new policies in the fields of energy, natural resources, and foreign investments, it may be useful for the Community to be associated with this development.[63]

When questioned on the motivation for the search for closer relations with the Community the Prime Minister made a revealing observation. He said that it was not a question of doing something against the United States, but of seeking a counterbalance to the "massive and friendly pressure of the American giant."[64] The United States was somewhat irritated by this comment.

While awaiting the evolution of new relations between Canada and the Community, numerous procedures exist to maintain close contact. Biannual meetings between the Commission and the Canadian government cover all questions of common interest. Industrial missions from the Community countries have spent several weeks in Canada. Annual meetings between delegations of the European and the Canadian Parliaments are being held; during the meeting of November 1974 the two delegations stressed the need to stimulate economic cooperation and develop trade and investment between the two parties.[65] In keeping with these objectives, a mission of the EC Commission was opened in 1975 in Ottawa.

NOTES

1. For other details see Statistical Office of the European Communities, *Foreign Trade* No. 3-5 (1975): 4.

2. See pp. 313, 323-324.

3. EEC Commission, *Fourth General Report,* 1970 sec. 192.

4. Cf. also the *Fourth* and *Seventh General Report,* 1970 and 1974, pp. 335 and 217, respectively. Some of the bilateral treaties may have become void of significant content.

5. U.S. Foreign Policy for the 1970s, "Shaping a Desirable Peace," a Report to the Congress by Richard Nixon, President of the United States, May 3, 1973; but also see George F. Kennan, "Europe's Problems, Europe's Choices," and Zbigniew Brzezinski, "The Deceptive Structure of Peace" in *Foreign Policy*, no. 14 (spring 1974):3-16 and 35-56, respectively. See also *Agence Europe Bulletin*, May 31, 1975.

6. For an excellent analysis of the EEC-U.S. trade relationship see Randall Hinshaw, *The European Community and American Trade* (New York: Praeger, 1964), pp. 75-99.

7. For the fate of the CAP in the early 1970s, see pp. 189-192.

8. In a radio interview in Cologne in July 1965, Freeman threatened "radical import restrictions of the United States" if the EEC persisted in its protectionism. See *Frankfurter Allgemeine Zeitung*, July 31, 1965.

9. See pp. 37.

10. *Journal of Commerce*, February 16, 1967, p. 1.

11. *New York Times*, May 16, 1967, p. 1.

12. Article VI, sec. 1, states that, "dumping . . . is to be condemned if it causes or threatens material injury to an established industry in the territory of a contracting party or materially retards the establishment of a domestic industry."

13. *New York Times*, May 17, 1967, p. 63.

14. *Journal of Commerce*, May 15, 1967, p. 1.

15. Ibid., May 11, 1966, p. 1.

16. *European Community*, no. 73 (July 1964): 4.

17. *Journal of Commerce*, February 28, 1967, p. 1.

18. For example, the statement of COPA in the fall of 1966 and as late as April 1967, that the Community had already made enough concessions in the Kennedy Round and that agriculture should not be included in the over-all bargaining (*Agence Europe Bulletin*, December 2, 1966, p. 7; April 14, 1967, p. 8).

19. Cf. "Last Round for the Kennedy Round," *Common Market* 7, no. 1 (January 1967): 2-5.

20. For annual increases and other data see Statistical Office of the European Community, *Foreign Trade* 2 (1973): 12, 13.

21. *Daily American* (Rome), January 23, 1973.

22. We should note that under the accounting method used by the EC the United States showed a small surplus of $188 million. While the United States uses FOB figures for both exports and imports, the EC applies CIF figures for imports, which makes exports from third countries higher than under the FOB formula.

23. U.S. Senate Committee on Finance, *A Strategy for International Trade Negotiations by Senator Abraham Ribicoff*, February 9, 1973, p. 8.

24. Ibid., p. 13.

25. *New York Times*, April 12, 1973, pp. 69, 75. We should note that GATT negotiations have been underway since early in 1973 for the compensation of injuries suffered by American export interests due to the enlargement of the Community. The Community has contested these claims on the basis that the reduction of the tariffs of the three new member states would be sufficient to compensate for disadvantages caused the United States through the application of the CAP in Great Britain, Ireland, and Denmark. Cf. *Agence Europe Bulletin*, November 1, 1973.

26. *International Herald Tribune*, April 4, 7-8, 1973. The Federal Republic of Germany, Great Britain, and the Netherlands seemed to back the recommendation of the Commission. Interestingly, the associated and "associable" states seem to oppose reverse preferences because they would like to bury the notion of reciprocity. See *Agence Europe Bulletin*, October 19, 1973. For the position of the Community see *Agence Europe Bulletin*, October 18, 1973, and July 26, 1973. France continues to insist on some kind of reciprocity in trade between the Community and the associate states.

27. *L'Independent*, July 16, 1973, p. 1.

28. *Le Figaro*, July 6, 1973.

29. *International Herald Tribune*, April 7-8, 1973, p. 1. Iran tried to follow the U.S.S.R.'s example a month later, but was refused. See also May 29, 1973, p. 4.

30. Ibid., June 29, 1973, p. 9.

31. *Relay from Bonn*, October 15, 1973.

32. Committee on Ways and Means, U.S. House of Representatives, the Administration proposal entitled "Trade Reform Act of 1973" (Washington, D.C., 1973); and *International Herald Tribune*, March 15, 1973, p. 1.

33. Cf. *Business Week*, December 16, 1972, p. 40.

34. *New York Times*, April 12, 1973, p. 75.

35. Ibid.

36. H.R. 10710, 93rd Congress, 1st session, Facts on File, 9-15 December 1973, p. 1037.

37. New Orleans *States Item*, October 29, 1973, p. 1.

38. See for example *International Herald Tribune*, March 31, April 1, June 14, July 19, 1973.

39. *Agence Europe Bulletin*, September 1973, pp. 3, 22-23; October 1973, p. 5. For preliminary actions on the trade negotiations see *Eighth General Report*, 1974, pp. 213-257.

40. Cf. Harald B. Malmgren, *International Economic Peacekeeping in Phase II* (New York: Quadrangle, published for the Atlantic Council of the United States, 1972), pp. 146-163.

41. Cf. *Agence Europe Bulletin,* July 4, 1975.

42. Cf. ibid., April 5, 25, 1975; July 10, 1975.

43. Cf. ibid., May 31, 1975.

44. Department of State Publication 8782, *Economic Interdependence and Common Defense* (October 1974), p. 9.

45. *Europe Documents,* No. 710, December 14, 1972.

46. Department of State Publication 8782, op. cit., p. 6.

47. Initially, this attempt was not received with much enthusiasm by the governments and people of some of the EC countries.

48. For the text of the Declaration see Department of State, *News Release,* June 20, 1974.

49. European Community Information Service, German Information Center, October 1973.

50. Statistical Office of the European Communities, *Foreign Trade* 2 (1973): 12-14.

51. Ibid., No. 3-5 (1975): 4.

52. Cf. EP, *Sitzungsdokumente* 1965-66, Document 3 (March 22, 1965), Reporter: Karl Hahn, pp. 12-13.

53. For details see European Parliament Working Documents, *Report on Trade Relations Between the Six and Japan* (Document no. 212, February 2, 1970).

54. *International Herald Tribune,* March 17-18, 1973, p. 9.

55. *Sixth* and *Seventh General Reports,* 1972 and 1973, pp. 302-303 and 437, respectively; and *Agence Europe Bulletin,* June 20, 1975.

56. *Agence Europe Bulletin,* March 15, 1974.

57. Statistical Office of the European Communities, *Foreign Trade,* no. 3-5 (1975), p. 4.

58. See pp. 87, 88, 89.

59. *Seventh General Report,* 1973, pp. 438-439.

60. *Agence Europe Bulletin,* October 5, 1974.

61. Ibid.

62. Ibid., June 26, 1975.

63. Ibid., October 26, 1974.

64. Ibid.

65. Ibid., November 14, 1974.

6

The Evolution
of Community
Commercial
Policies:

Relations with Communist Countries

EASTERN EUROPE

In chapter 2 we discussed in connection with the diplomatic relations of the Community the long struggle waged by the Communists in opposition to West European economic integration and perhaps political unity, while at the same time seeking to expand their trade with the EC countries.

In their trade offensive, the Soviets attempted to create discord between the member states. For example, when a French delegation arrived in Moscow to negotiate the renewal of bilateral agreements, the Soviet government demanded that they be accorded the same preferences under the most-favored-nation clause that France had granted its Common Market partners under the EEC Treaty. When the French refused—customs unions preferences are exempt from the application of this clause—the Soviet government broke off the negotiations. Another example was the attempt by Khrushchev during an Italian industrial exposition in Moscow in the fall of 1962 to use the natural eagerness of the Italian industrialists for Russian business as a tool to shift Italian market orientation from the EEC to the Soviet Union and thereby adversely affect the progress of the Common Market.[1]

Another dimension of the Soviet attitude toward the EC became visible in 1967, when Chairman of the Soviet Council of Ministers, Alexei N. Kosygin, was interviewed during a news conference in London regarding the enlargement of the Common Market. Asked whether British membership in the EC would be good or bad for European development and security, he replied: "The very name Common Market is a drawback in that it is not 'common' because not all countries are free to join. Markets of this kind should be open to cooperation of all nations of Europe on an equal footing."[2] Reiterating the same theme in 1971, Kosygin declared during the Twenty-fourth

Congress of the Soviet Communist Party: "We are opposed to closed trade amalgamations of the 'Common Market' type."[3] The reason given for this opposition was "discrimination" in trade. At the same time, Leonid Brezhnev, the First Secretary of the Soviet Communist Party, referred again to the theory of contradictions in the capitalist camp by observing, perhaps somewhat prophetically: "At the start of the 1970s, the main centers of imperialist rivalry are clearly crystallizing: they are the U.S.A., Western Europe (particularly the six countries of the Common Market), and Japan."[4]

The Soviet Union has steadfastly maintained its policy of nonrecognition of the European Community, although from time to time discreet, indirect conversations have been taking place between Soviet and Community officials. The East European people's democracies, with the exception of Yugoslavia, have followed the Soviet position despite the fact that some of these countries, especially Romania and Poland, have had since 1964 repeated conversations and consultations with Community officials regarding the exports of agricultural commodities to the EC countries. On the other hand, Yugoslavia, which had established a diplomatic mission to the European Communities in 1968,[5] concluded in 1970 a far-reaching trade agreement with the EC as a legal unit. This agreement was renewed in 1973.[6]

Comecon, The Council for Mutual Economic Aid (also known as CEMA), which is composed of the Soviet Union and other East European Communist countries,[7] also made unofficial approaches to the Community in 1973 to initiate a discussion on economic matters of mutual interest. The Community institutions were at first hesitant to respond affirmatively to these overtures because they considered Comecon essentially different from the EC, inasmuch as the former was seen primarily as an instrument of Soviet policy and dominated by the U.S.S.R. However, the EC Council of Ministers later had a change of opinion and decided in May 1974 to inform the Secretary General of Comecon through an ambassador of one of the member countries that the Commission was ready to receive any suggestions regarding Comecon–EC relations and perhaps trade negotiations in a positive manner.[8] But since Comecon cannot make a commitment in the name of its member states, the Commission insisted that negotiations and agreements be carried out among the national governments of the EC and Comecon countries. Nevertheless, the Secretary General of Comecon, Nicolai Fadeyev, extended an invitation to the President of the Commission, Francois-Xavier Ortoli, to visit Moscow. The Commission expressed itself again in favor of the principle of establishing contacts among leading officials, and in February 1975 a delegation headed by the Director General of DGI visited Moscow and met with officials of Comecon for three days. A return visit by Comecon officials to Brussels was arranged prior to a likely summit meeting between Ortoli and Fadeyev.[9]

In connection with the Soviet Union's policy of nonrecognition of the Community it is interesting to note the rather positive attitude of the People's Republic of China. As the first comment on the expansion of the EC, the Chinese Communist newspaper, *Jenmin Jin Pao,* carried in January 1973 an article headlined "Western European Countries Strengthen Their Alignment to Counterbalance the Two Superpowers." The article stopped short of giving China's blessing to the enlargement, but depicted this development as an important step toward checking the political and economic ambitions of the United States and the Soviet Union.[10] Following up this favorable view of the Community, the People's Republic established a diplomatic mission in Brussels in 1975 and opened exploratory talks with the Commission aimed at negotiating an EC–Chinese trade agreement.[11]

Another significant factor in the Soviet–EC relationship could be the attitude of the powerful Communist parties and trade unions in Italy and France. While up to 1966, in line with Soviet leadership, these parties and labor organizations virtually boycotted all Community activities (although the Italian Communist party had been clamoring for a more positive position since 1962), Italian and French Communists are now members of the European Parliament and the Communist labor unions participate in the consultation process of different Community institutions.[12] It is difficult to judge how much the activities of the Communist members of the EP, and especially the pro-integrationist expressions of the Italian Communists, are motivated by tactical considerations rather than genuine interest in

213

advancing the integration of the Community; and it is even more difficult to appraise the type of linkages existing between the Italian and French Communist parties with Moscow, linkages that could affect the Soviet attitude toward the Community.

The Pattern of Trade

Despite the lack of diplomatic relations between most East European Communist countries and the EC, and despite the existing ideological differences, trade between them more than quintupled during the period from 1958 to 1972 (Table 6.1). It continued to soar in 1973 and 1974, with a nearly 50 percent

Table 6.1
EC Trade with Communist East Europe[a]
(millions of U.S. dollars)

	1958	1960	1963	1969	1972
Imports from East Europe	678	975	1363	2451	3607
Exports to East Europe	626	992	1080	2699	4165

Source: Statistisches Amt der Europaischen Gemeinschaften, Foreign Trade, no. 2 (1973): 12, 14.

[a] Figures exclude trade with Yugoslavia. Shipments from that country to the EEC rose from $134 million in 1958 to $895 million in 1972, and the reverse flow increased from $185 million to $1159 million.

rise in 1974 over the preceding year,[13] perhaps reflecting the climate of detente and East-West economic cooperation. Although the international trade with the East European Communist countries is still only a minor part of the total external Community trade, amounting to approximately 4 percent, the percentage increases from 1958 to 1974 are significant because they show a much larger increase of the EC trade with the Communist countries in Europe than with the rest of the world. The shares of this trade among the different member states vary: For the Netherlands, trade with the East European states represents approximately 2 percent of its foreign commerce with third countries, whereas it reaches about 6 percent in Italy, which imports appreciable quantities of petroleum from East Bloc sources. In terms of net volume, West Germany is the single most important trading partner of the Eastern Bloc.[14]

On the East European side, it is not surprising that the Soviet Union has been by far the largest EC trading partner, with Poland, Romania, and Czechoslovakia next in order of importance. For the Comecon countries the importance of their trade with the EC is substantially higher than for the Community countries because it represents a much greater share of their total international trade. Table 6.2 shows that in the case of

Table 6.2

Trade of Selected Comecon Countries with EC[a]
Percentage shares of total world trade and
extra-Comecon trade (1971)

| | Imports | | Exports | |
	World	Extra-Comecon	World	Extra-Comecon
Bulgaria	10.63	41.24	8.72	35.74
Czechoslovakia	14.93	41.38	12.83	35.69
East Germany	17.90	51.58	15.37	49.86
Hungary	17.48	47.46	15.08	42.77
Poland	17.43	48.46	17.81	43.71
Romania	27.22	52.59	23.00	46.07
Soviet Union	11.95	28.58	11.06	23.27

Source: United Nations Secretariat, Statistical Office, *Yearbook of International Trade Statistics 1970-1971* (New York: United Nations, 1973), pp. 82, 167, 250, 311, 628, 646, 777.

[a] The figures cover trade with all nine member states of the Community, including trade between West Germany and East Germany.

Romania, 1971 EC exports and imports were approximately half of total extra-Comecon trade and that it constituted approximately one quarter of total Romanian world trade. For all countries, with the exception of the Soviet Union, trade with the European Community represented very significant parts of their extra-Comecon trade, mostly above 40 percent.

Communist East European trade with the industrialized countries of the West has two major objectives. First, it serves to eliminate gaps in the economic structure and temporary shortages of goods. Second, it contributes to the rapid attainment of economic development objectives. Guided by these objectives, the purchases of the East European Communist countries from the EEC concentrated on industrial goods, and only 20 percent were devoted to raw materials and farm products. On the other hand, their exports to the Common Market consisted mainly of agricultural commodities and raw materials, whereas industrial products comprised only a minor part, and they were shipped mostly by East Germany, Czechoslovakia, and the Soviet Union.

In all Communist countries foreign trade is handled by the state itself. The governmental agencies in charge of foreign trade possess a powerful monopoly that enables them to play the offers of one supplier against those of others in order to obtain optimum terms. At the same time, they can set export prices with little regard to cost and may engage in dumping if, for one reason or another, they are anxious to sell certain commodities. One of these reasons may be the need for convertible currencies, which are in short supply in most East Bloc countries. In fact, the shortage of convertible currencies is the great dilemma of the trade with the Communist countries. It limits the opportunity to expand exports to these countries to their ability to ship in return sufficient goods for payment. The currency problem also tends to favor bilateral trade arrangements between individual EC and Comecon countries because of the need for long-term credit terms, which the latter demand from their Western trading partners. This, in turn, has increased the problems of the EC authorities in evolving a common commercial policy toward the state-trading countries of the East European Communist Bloc. Finally, bilateralism has been preferred by the Communists because of the tactical advantages it offers.

As mentioned earlier, only Yugoslavia has concluded a trade agreement with the Community, but even this agreement does not replace the existing bilateral accords with the EC member states, but represents a form of "Community cover" within which the bilateral accords spell out details of importance to individual member governments and at times may go beyond the sectors for which the EC has competences. The Community agreement contains commercial provisions, especially in the field of agriculture; safeguard clauses in the event of dumping and market disturbances; regulations about industrial and scientific cooperation; and provisions about the movements of Yugoslav labor into the Community countries. Although the agreement is essentially nonpreferential in terms of tariff treatment, Yugoslavia, as a member of the "Group of 77"[15] category of developing countries under the UNCTAD rules, benefits from the EC system of generalized preferences for the import of manufactured and semimanufactured goods into the Community.[16] After its expiration on April 30, 1973, the agreement was replaced by a somewhat broader accord, under which Yugoslavia's import policies have been liberalized in the hope that more concessions could be obtained from the Community to enhance her own exports to the EC countries. Moreover, the new agreement is designed to encourage further industrial cooperation between Yugoslavia and Western European firms.[17]

Problems of a Common Community Policy

Beginning in 1973, EC member states could no longer conclude new bilateral agreements with the East European Communist countries but must leave this to the EC as a collective organization. Although the nonrecognition of the Community by most of the East European countries and the consequent absence of official diplomatic missions from these countries made this a difficult undertaking, it did not prove impossible. In fact, technical agreements relating to the observance of minimum CAP prices and other agricultural matters were concluded in 1973 between the Commission and Bulgaria, Poland, Hungary, and Romania, without raising any particular problems.[18] Over the years the Commission has labored hard to convince the Council of Ministers that it should become the sole agent for the conclusion of all trade accords with Eastern Europe as the following brief historical review demonstrates.

In October 1961 the Council of Ministers decided to make

trade negotiations between member states and East European Communist countries subject to prior consultations among the member states. However, these consultations, to be arranged by the Commission, did not bind the member states in the negotiations they were about to conduct and therefore were not a very effective means of ensuring policy coordination. Nevertheless, they enabled the member states to have a better understanding of each other's trade relations. They provided an opportunity for member states to protest if it seemed likely that the negotiations would lead to concessions that might harm the export interests of an EEC partner. In addition, the member states were to seek the inclusion of the so-called EEC Clause in all trade agreements. Since this clause, as we have seen earlier, requires future adaptation of bilateral trade agreements to emerging EC common policies, Communist countries have so far rejected such a clause as implying recognition of the Common Market as an entity. Without such a clause, bilateral agreements either were to contain a clause providing for annual termination or be valid only for one year, a requirement with which the member states generally complied.[19]

Another Community act applying to trade with the East European countries, and potentially more incisive than the consultation procedure, was EEC Regulation No. 3/63 of January 24, 1963. This Regulation stated that if imports of certain agricultural products exceeded a certain percentage, and caused or threatened to cause such a serious disturbance on the EEC market that the objectives of the CAP might be endangered, the Commission could halt these imports after consultation with a committee of experts from the member states. This system thus added quantitative restriction measures to the usual protection accorded agricultural products in the Common Market by the CAP's levies and price systems.

In 1962, in order to prepare the basis for a future common commercial policy, the Commission prepared an action program that emphasized the need for replacing the national quotas and liberalization lists with a common quota and liberalization policy. It argued that since trade with the Communist countries is usually not subject to GATT rules, quantitative restrictions played a particularly important role. Although the Council seemed to be sympathetic to the Commission's objectives, nothing was done to give them practical implementation. In March 1964 the Commission submitted a proposal for a three-phase introduction of a common commercial policy vis-à-vis the state-trading countries, a policy that would eventually lead to generally uniform long-term agreements by the Community with the East Bloc countries. After long discussion of the proposals, they were finally adopted by the Council and eventually led to the 1973 deadline referred to earlier.

Although up to 1974 the Commission had usually given its consent to the renewal of one-year bilateral commercial agreements of member states with countries of Eastern Europe, a new practice was instituted in May of that year. At that time the Commission began to insist that all negotiations for trade agreements with East European countries be conducted exclusively by the Community, even if a temporary vacuum were created in the relations between a particular member state and its East European trading partner by the nonrenewal of a bilateral agreement. This new policy was confirmed by the Council of Ministers,[20] but we need to point out that the real effect of the new policy was more cosmetic than real. The reason for this is that since the early 1970s, economic relations between EC member states and Eastern Europe have been more and more incorporated into so-called cooperation agreements. These agreements, in effect for periods of up to ten years, are designed for economic, industrial, scientific, and technical cooperation. They include the supply and construction of factories in Eastern Europe, to be paid for by the export of the goods to be produced. They also relate to exchanges of patents, licenses, other means of technological transfers, and cooperation in the marketing of exports to specific countries. Examples of these agreements are the ten-year accords between the Federal Republic of Germany and the Soviet Union (July 5, 1972); France and Poland (October 5, 1972); and the Federal Republic of Germany and Romania (June 29, 1973).

The effect of these cooperation agreements has been a preemption of the common commercial policy that was to be the exclusive competence of the Community institutions. For the European Community this has given rise to the risk that the classical instruments of trade policy, such as customs duties and quantitative restrictions, may well be subverted or weakened by these new forms of economic cooperation which, to a large extent, remain in the field of national competence and national foreign policy, and therefore escape Community jurisdiction. In fact, no Community information and consultation procedures have been developed for this category of new agreements, and although the Commission has made proposals for such procedures, no Council action has been taken.[21] What we see then is an example of sleight of hand: The Council has given something that the Commission has wanted for a long time, namely its full competence over trade agreements; but the national goverments, perhaps inspired by the quest for detente and the desire to respond to Soviet demands for closer economic cooperation, have preempted this competence.

There are other reasons why the Commission wants to have the cooperation agreements placed into a Community-wide system of coordination, namely the necessity for a uniform credit policy toward Eastern Europe and the embargo of strategic goods instituted under NATO guidelines.

The credit policy of the Community was governed until 1963 by the Berne Convention, which was not a formal treaty, but a kind of gentlemen's agreement to which all member governments and a number of third countries, including Great Britain, adhered.[22] In 1960 a five-year ceiling was instituted by the participating countries for credits granted for large capital equipment orders, but when Great Britain deviated from the five-year rule in 1963, other countries, including Italy and France, followed suit. A resolution of the EEC Council of Ministers in May 1962 requiring consultation by member states before deviating from this rule was not effective in holding the credit line; nor were discussions within NATO aiming at a five-year limitation of credits to the East Bloc countries.

Although no specific proposals on the coordination of credit have been made by the Commission, in May 1966 the Council of Ministers instructed the Committee of Permanent Representatives to make a study of current practices. The report based on the study indicated that the longest credit terms were granted by Italy, and that the Federal Republic of

Germany led the Community in terms of total amount and number of individual credit transactions. After long discussions the Council eventually agreed on a five-year credit limit for deliveries to East Germany, and urged that the consultation procedures be strengthened. But it was also argued that the question of credit duration could not be separated from other factors, such as volume and interest rates, and that an agreement in this field would be meaningful only if it included at least all OECD countries, especially Great Britain, Japan, and the United States.[23] In the meantime, by the end of 1971 the total credits exceeding 5 years granted by firms in EC member states (then the Six) had already surpassed 3 billion dollars. This occurred despite hundreds of consultation meetings attended by government experts and credit insurers.[24]

In January 1973 the Commission asked the Council of Ministers for a regulation setting forth joint proposals and a management procedure to cover the duration of export credits and governmental guarantees; but whether this will be any more effective is highly doubtful. The anxiety of national business firms and governments to be the successful bidders in the competitive export business in Eastern Europe is likely to make a shambles out of any well-meaning regulations that may be agreed upon in the Council of Ministers, if indeed agreement can be achieved.

An interesting example of the scramble for Communist business by free world firms and governments has been the race of Italian, French, German, and Japanese manufacturers for the construction of one or more automobile factories in the Soviet Union. Vittorio Valetta, the top official of Fiat in 1966, was the first to obtain a contract for the construction of an integrated plant and housing for the 20,000 workers needed for the annual production of 700,000 compact automobiles.[25] He made the deal without prior authorization by the Italian government, but later was able to persuade his government to agree to the venture and to guarantee a necessary loan of several hundred million dollars. In fact, Fiat is now not only building cars in the Soviet Union, but is also setting up a service and parts organization necessary for the expected expansion of motoring. Since then, Renault, Peugeot, and Mercedes-Benz have also received

221

contracts for the construction of factories producing trucks and tractors. Today, the Soviet-produced Fiat is sold not only domestically, but is being exported from the Soviet Union in increasing numbers. Called the "Lada," the car is cheaper than many competitive automobiles, and if Denmark is a good example, has found rising acceptance. However, some of its features, such as brakes and steering, are not completely satisfactory. Nearly 700 Ladas were sold in Denmark in 1972, twice as many as in the previous year.[26] An equally dramatic increase of Ladas has been noted in Switzerland. The export of these cars portends that other items produced in the Soviet Union under license of and with the know-how of Western enterprises may be used for Soviet export trade in the years to come.[27]

The highly competitive nature of the export business toward the largely untapped markets of Eastern Europe has also undermined the NATO guidelines for the export of strategic goods. In view of the difficulty in finding precise definitions for the variety of goods that may fall under the embargo, there is no complete uniformity in the interpretation of these guidelines. As a consequence, an item that one NATO country may exclude from shipment to a Communist state has been delivered by another NATO partner. In view of the American promises made to deliver nuclear plants and technology to Egypt and Israel for the generation of electricity, it is noteworthy that the NATO Coordinating Committee in charge of members' trade with Communist states has indicated that it would be legal to sell nuclear reactors for peaceful purposes even to these countries.[28]

In order to assure at least some kind of uniformity in the future commercial relations between the Community and the state-trading countries, the Commission drafted a model trade agreement. With the expiration of national bilateral trade agreements by the end of 1975 (in many cases replaced by cooperation agreements, however), the Community institutions wanted to show their readiness to enter into negotiations on EC agreements with Eastern Europe as well as Communist countries in Asia.

The contents of the model agreement were marked by the following features:

1. "reciprocity" with assurance of an overall balance of advantages and obligations.

2. the reciprocal granting of the most-favored-nation clause on tariffs but no claim on the part of the state-trading countries to the tariff reductions granted by the EC to free trade or other existing preferential agreements

3. liberalization of current quantitative restrictions

4. maintenance of the principles and mechanisms of the CAP

5. payments and financing provisions to be worked out on an ad hoc basis

6. the evolution of cooperation arrangements as far as possible under EC competences

7. safeguard mechanisms to take account of the differences in economic systems between the contracting parties[29]

Although the Council of Ministers was generally sympathetic to the contents of the model agreement, several of the East European countries that received a draft of this agreement reacted unfavorably; but contacts between the EC and these countries are maintained on this matter. Meanwhile the scheme of former individual bilateral agreements on quotas and tariffs continues at least for 1975, perhaps longer, but will operate under a Community label. At the same time, long-term cooperation agreements (up to five years) between EC and East European countries also continue to be concluded, strengthening the resolve of the latter countries to negotiate with the Community institutions.[30] The Council accepted the most-favored-nation treatment in the tariff field, which up to then had not been granted by the EC countries to East European countries except to those that are members of GATT. However, in practice this treatment had been really accorded to all East European countries in one form or another, although in most cases it was not reciprocated.[31]

Prospects

Before a uniform Community trade policy toward Communist countries (including Cuba) can be fully implemented on the basis of the EC model trade agreement, the member states must commit themselves to a gradual harmonization of the various national tariff and quota schemes. Moreover, some agreement must be reached on how the overall quotas are to be allocated and managed, since quantitative restrictions vary from country to country, with Ireland having no such system at all. Finally, the prospects of the future trade relations of the Community with the East European Communist countries must also be seen in the light of two new aspects: (1) the new political and economic relations between the United States and the Soviet Union, and (2) the European Conference on Security and Cooperation.

It is evident that since President Nixon's visit to Moscow in 1972 the common political and economic interests of the United States and the Soviet Union have received heavy emphasis and attention by the decision makers of both countries. Despite the continuing, very grave problems of the maintenance of nuclear and military parity and the avoidance of a further arms race (SALT I is only the very halting beginning of solving the problems), some of the economic needs of the two countries are in the process of receiving some satisfaction. As a consequence, American exports have tripled in 1972 from $134 million to over $500 million, without considering in these figures the export of wheat, which will exceed $1 billion. This expansion of trade, with the exception of wheat shipments, has been maintained through 1974 and has made the United States the fifth largest trading partner of the Soviet Union, surpassing France and Italy, although still behind Great Britain and Germany.[32] In addition, the new political climate between the United States and the Soviet Union, within which the American government has asked Congress to grant most-favored-nation treatment to Russian exports, has induced many American firms to intensify their sales efforts in Moscow. Sales and banking offices have been opened in Moscow; an East–West trade exposition was organized in Vienna in February 1973; and joint industrial cooperation ventures have been initiated, such as the

GE contract signed with the Soviet government for the production of GE goods under license and technology of the American firm. The obvious impact of these American efforts will be to raise the level of competition for the sales of West European goods to the Soviet Union, and this impact is likely to be all the more significant since the United States is interested in purchasing large amounts of Soviet natural gas. The Soviet Union repudiated the U.S.–Soviet trade agreement signed in 1972 in anticipation of receiving the benefit of the most-favored-nation clause because the application of this clause was tied by Congress to the unimpeded emigration of Russian Jews. However, trade between the two countries continues to be promoted by American firms and Soviet trade agencies and the effect of the Soviet action on the volume of future U.S. exports is not likely to be very significant.

Although the intensified pursuit of American interests in the Soviet Union may reduce the potential of further expansion of the West European–Soviet trade relationship, the successful conclusion of the European Security Conference in July 1975 is likely to have a positive effect. These negotiations were conducted under four headings: (1) questions relating to security, (2) cooperation in economic and environmental matters, (3) the development of human contacts, and (4) the implementation of the above matters with the establishment of some kind of institutional consultation mechanism. Most important for us is the economic cooperation category, which includes industrial cooperation and collaboration in the better use of raw materials and energy resources. Progress in organizing a variety of joint industrial ventures between West European firms and East European government enterprises will most likely lead to greatly increased trade for machine tools and semimanufactured products and, in addition, could also benefit export business in general. Such ventures have been in existence for some time in several of the East European countries; and their establishment has been aided in Yugoslavia and Romania by special laws authorizing the investment of Western capital in state-owned enterprises with specific protection guaranteed the investors for the repatriation of profits and withdrawal of capital, although the management of the enterprises is controlled by indigenous

225

workers' councils. However, the number of these joint ventures, called by Howard Perlmutter "transideological" enterprises,[33] has remained small so far, but official encouragement through the successful conclusion of negotiations in the European Security Conference may increase their number materially. They may include the joint development of new production processes, joint marketing, the joint utilization of mining resources of Eastern Europe in plant facilities provided by the West, the joint production of spare parts, etc. As we have seen, the Commission would like to coordinate the national cooperation agreements and establish common Community rules and principles because it can be anticipated that cooperative agreements may become more important than traditional trade agreements, particularly since tariffs are not really meaningful for trade with countries operating under a Communist system.

The benefits of more transideological enterprises for Western countries would be not only economic, but also political. These enterprises would cross not only political frontiers, but also ideological lines. They would foster a pragmatic approach on collaboration between Communists and non-Communists and the importance of ideology would gradually recede. Working together toward a shared goal, individuals of different nationalities might adopt new values; common ways of looking at problems create feelings that common interests exist. For example, even the deep-rooted psychological antipathy in Poland toward the Germans did not inhibit the Polish Communist regime from negotiating agreements with West German companies such as Krupp and Grundig.[34] Thus, the contacts established between West Europeans and East Europeans or Americans and East Europeans could really be meaningful in terms of bridging the gap between East and West. In this respect they are likely to be much more effective than contacts artificially contrived through cultural exchanges, student exchanges, or tourism.

Another salient aspect of joint ventures such as the Fiat enterprise in the Soviet Union or similar activities in Eastern Europe is the change in the people behind the Iron Curtain resulting from the use of new products (e.g., the automobile) introduced by enterprises from the free world. Such experiences may stimulate new tastes and expectations among the people of

Eastern Europe, change the perceptions of elites and governmental leaders, and generate pressures to be exerted upon these leaders to shift from producing weapons and capital goods to manufacturing more consumer goods.

It is, of course, impossible to do more than speculate on the effects described above. Up to now, the Soviet economy has used its resources of raw materials, manpower, and capital, mainly to develop basic industries such as coal, steel, and electric power. Its performance was rather disappointing in such branches that thrive on complex modern technology as electronics and computers, as well as in the production of consumer goods generally. In these industries the centralized system of economic planning has proven to be utterly deficient compared to Western standards. The results have even been worse in agriculture, which still employ nearly 40 percent of the Soviet labor force. For these reasons it is not surprising that Soviet leaders want to expand relations with the West, since they expect such benefits as the fruits of advanced Western technology, long-term credits for the purchase of certain capital goods, and urgently needed foodstuffs. As experience has shown, Soviet gold reserves are not sufficient to purchase the variety of items needed by the Soviet Union in increasing quantities. The fact that East European currencies are not convertible also places restraints on meeting the needs of the people's democracies from the West.[35]

Concurrent with the desire to improve the economic welfare of the East European satellites, Soviet leaders hope to undermine the commitment to and the effectiveness of NATO, and achieve a reduction of American forces in Europe. In more long-range terms, they may also hope to share in the economic benefits of the EC by obtaining recognition of Comecon as an equally successful experiment in economic integration, which it clearly is not. They may try to gain some influence in the decision making of the EC through the creation of an institutional consultation mechanism regarding the implementation of the agreed-upon Security Conference decisions, although the prospects for such a mechanism are very dim. Finally, they may hope to satisfy the aspirations of the people's democracies by supporting increased trade between these countries and the EC and at the same time retain effective control over the East

227

European "satellites." But if these expectations and goals should clearly become impossible, or if overriding strategic considerations (such as an increasingly powerful China or a clear defection as seemed to develop in 1968 in Czechoslovakia) should demand it, it is likely that "the window to the West" will be abandoned and Soviet leaders will return to the use of strong military control in East Europe to protect its security and political assets.

That this may indeed be in the minds of Soviet leaders is suggested by the inherently intransigent attitude of the Soviet Union regarding the mutual reduction of conventional military forces in the talks taking place in Vienna. Moreover, the Soviet Union has never declared or given the slightest hint that for the sake of detente or a more flexible policy toward the West it would be prepared to give up its essential political or ideological objectives. On the contrary, it has been stressed many times that detente requires increased ideological vigilance and confrontation.

How well Soviet objectives are recognized in Western Europe is difficult to judge. Clearly a large segment of the population would like to filter these objectives out of their thinking because they may be disturbing to many economic interests of the member states. Considering that in the European Community nearly 20 percent of the GNP is generated by exporting industries (in some countries such as Belgium this percentage goes up to nearly 50 percent), it is understandable that trade expansion to Eastern Europe is strongly supported by industry, labor, and the governmental administration since it represents a very significant factor of the Community's economic welfare.

OTHER COMMUNIST COUNTRIES

From 1958 to 1972, trade with the Asian Communist countries (i.e., the People's Republic of China, Mongolia, North Vietnam, and North Korea) shows a mixed picture. As Table 6.3 shows, exports to the EC more than tripled, whereas shipments from the member states to these countries declined from 1958 to 1962, then increased again and returned to their former level in 1969.

Trade between the Community countries and Communist China represents the bulk of EC imports and exports to and from Communist Asia, and both have shown increases of about 50 and 100 percent, respectively from 1972 to 1974.[36] France and West Germany are the main beneficiaries of the latest increases of exports to China. This rise in shipments from member states to China may be due in part to the French diplomatic recognition of the People's Republic and French opposition to the accreditation of a mission to the EC from the Republic of China (Taiwan). However, the general race to sell goods to the Communist countries all over the world has been mostly responsible for this development. A large percentage of these exports have been in the category of capital goods; the U.S. Senate's condemnation of the sale to China of a whole steel mill by West Germany points to the strategic nature of many of these business transactions.[37] The new relationship between

Table 6.3

EC Trade with Asian Communist Countries
(millions of U.S. dollars)

	1958	1960	1963	1969	1972
Imports from Communist Asia	111	151	115	282	362
Exports to Communist Asia	354	243	122	351	318

Source: Statistisches Amt der Europaischen Gemeinschaften, Foreign Trade, no. 4 (1967): 18, 20.

the United States and the People's Republic of China may well portend a rise in future exports of American and other Western goods to China in the years to come.

The difficulties besetting the development of a common policy toward the East European Communist countries are equally troublesome in the situation with the Asian Communist states. No uniform credit policy exists, nor are other effective policy guidelines available to govern the increasing volume of trade in Communist Asia (indicated by the present trends). West European trade with Communist countries continues to involve quotas by the member states, bilateral balancing of accounts, and even barter. No one has as yet found a satisfactory way of establishing a set of rules between private enterprises and state-trading countries.

Despite these difficulties, it needs to be recognized that the Community is one of China's most significant trading partners, accounting for about one-seventh of China's foreign trade. It is perhaps for this reason that the Chinese economic press now devotes a surprising and ever increasing degree of attention to Western European integration and its economic problems. To China, the Community does not constitute the kind of un-comfortable political challenge that may exist in the case of the United States, and which certainly is a major barrier for eco-nomic relations between the Soviet Union and China. This may well be the reason that China has looked with favor upon the enlargement of the European Community and appears to be interested in seeing the enlarged Common Market flourish. Indeed, the Chinese government welcomed the introduction of the model trade agreement as a useful basis for its commercial relations with the Community.[38] We should note that this positive view of the Community is of fairly recent origin. Up to the end of 1970 the government of the People's Republic of China followed the line of the Soviet Union and regarded the European Community as belonging to the circle of "imperialist" powers.[39] The leaders of China gave European unity scant prospects that integration would be successful, and Peking was of the opinion that EC policy would be determined more by a conflict situation than by a community of interests, a view which in retrospect may not have been too far from reality. Nevertheless, the strategic and economic interests of the People's Republic of China dictated a change of judgment regarding the Community. In 1971 the *Peking Review* stated:

> The Common Market is intended to promote cooperation and unity among the West European countries. In this way they want to assert their position and protect themselves against threats and interferences by the two super powers, U.S. imperialism and social-imperialism.[40]

Chinese commentators stated that the establishment of an economic and monetary union and the creation of a common

West European currency, scheduled to take place in 1980, were signs of the common struggle of these countries against the privileged position of the dollar. This new climate of opinion in China will undoubtedly favor the expansion of trade and other relations between the Community and the People's Republic of China. With a Chinese diplomatic Mission to the Community headed by an ambassador now established in Brussels we can anticipate an increasing flow of goods between Europe and China although the new ties between the United States and China are likely to create competitive pressures on Community exports.[41]

All Asian countries except Japan fall into the category of underdeveloped. Many of the Third World countries constitute special problems for the economic policy of the Community and it is to these problems that we will address ourselves in the next chapter.

NOTES

1. Karlheinz Neunreither, *Das Europa der Sechs* (Cologne: Westdeutscher Verlag, 1964), p. 106.

2. *The Times* (London), February 10, 1967, p. 11.

3. *Pravda*, April 4, 1971.

4. Ibid., April 1, 1971.

5. *Second General Report*, 1968, p. 389.

6. *Seventh General Report*, 1973, p. 411.

7. These countries are East Germany, Poland, Czechoslovakia, Hungary, Bulgaria, Romania, and Yugoslavia. We should note that Yugoslavia is only an associate member. Prompted by the success of the EEC, extensive changes in the structure of Comecon were made in 1962, but the hopes for the success of Comecon as an economic force similar to the EEC have not been realized.

8. *Agence Europe Bulletin*, May 9, 16, 1974. See also May 6/7, 1974.

9. Cf. ibid., October 16, 24, 1974. See also Gerald Segal, "The East Looks West," *European Community*, no. 170 (1973): 18-20; and *European Community*, no. 184 (1975): 19.

10. *International Herald Tribune*, January 6-7, 1973.

11. *Agence Europe Bulletin,* July 3, 1975.

12. For background see Werner J. Feld, *The European Common Market and the World* (Englewood Cliffs, N.J.: Prentice-Hall, 1967). See also Werner J. Feld, "National-International Linkage Theory: The East European Communist System and the EEC," *Journal of International Affairs* 22, no. 1 (1968): 107-120.

13. *Eighth General Report,* 1974, p. 212.

14. Cf. F. A. M. Alting von Geusau and Woiciech Morawiecki, *Subregional Organizations in Europe and the Changing European System* (Tilburg, Netherlands: John F. Kennedy Institute, 1973), p. 34.

15. The initial group of developing countries seeking, as a bloc, financial aid and trade concessions from the economically advanced countries. This group now numbers over one hundred countries, but continues to be referred to as the "Group of 77."

16. This system will be described in detail in chapter 7. Romania also benefits from these preferences since January 1, 1974.

17. *Agence Europe Bulletin,* February 9, 1973; May 3, 1974.

18. *Seventh General Report,* 1973, p. 443.

19. An Italian treaty with Albania concluded for two years (1965-67) did not contain such a clause and for this reason the Commission filed action against Italy before the Community Court.

20. *Agence Europe Bulletin,* May 18, 1974.

21. Ibid.

22. The Berne convention is technically the International Credit Insurers' Union, established in Berne in 1933. Its members are organizations from 16 countries including all EEC states except Italy and Luxembourg However, these two countries accepted the 5-year rule for credits in 1960.

23. We should note in this connection that the United States now applies the most-favored-nation clause to imports from Poland and Yugoslavia, placing these countries on the same footing as GATT countries. Application of this clause is being considered in the future also for other East Bloc countries.

24. *Agence Europe Bulletin,* January 11, 1973.

25. We must keep in mind that under terms of construction contracts the factories and housing built by the foreign firms become the property of the Communist government.

26. *States-Item* (New Orleans), December 22, 1972.

27. General Electric and the Soviet government have concluded a contract under which hundreds of millions of dollars of GE products are to be manufactured in the Soviet Union. Some of these items may be for

domestic consumption to satisfy the needs of Soviet customers, but others may be reexported since the use of low-cost Soviet labor may make them highly competitive. Cf. *New York Times,* January 18, 1973.

28. Richard F. Staar, *The Communist Regimes in Eastern Europe,* 2d rev. ed. (The Hoover Institution on War, Revolution and Peace, 1971), p. 255.

29. Cf. *Agence Europe Bulletin,* October 28/29, 1974.

30. See ibid., April 22/23, 24, 1975.

31. Ibid., November 14, 1974.

32. *International Herald Tribune,* January 18, 1973. Japan and Finland also have more trade with the Soviet Union, but the grain deal would push the United States temporarily ahead of these countries too.

33. For details see Howard V. Perlmutter, "Emerging East-West Ventures: The Transideological Enterprise," *Columbia Journal of World Business* (September–October 1969): 39-50.

34. Staar, op. cit., p. 254.

35. Recently these countries have turned to the Eurodollar market in order to find relief for their shortage of hard currencies. But this has not been an adequate remedy and long-term credits, hopefully at preferential interest rates, remain a continuing necessity.

36. OECD, *Statistics of Foreign Trade* (May 1975): 52-53.

37. *New York Times,* July 26, 1966, p. 1. The new, benevolent attitude of the People's Republic of China toward the EC, about which we have commented earlier, points to a further increase in trade with Community member states.

38. *Agence Europe Bulletin,* November 1, 1974.

39. W. B. Findorff, "China and the European Community," *Aussen Politik,* 24, no. 2, 1973, pp. 210-216.

40. Quoted in ibid., p. 213.

41. See also the perceptive editorial in *Agence Europe Bulletin,* March 26, 1975.

7

The Evolution of Commercial Policies:

Relations with the Third World

Approximately 100 countries, containing about 70 percent of the world's population, constitute what is generally known as the "Third World." Most of these countries are in Central and South America, Africa, and Asia—notable exceptions are the Union of South Africa and Japan. All of these nations have certain common characteristics. The masses in these countries have a very low per capita income; the degree of disease and illiteracy is high; their economies are mainly oriented toward a relatively primitive type of agriculture and a low level of industrialization; and the political stability of most of them is low. Of course, the level of development varies from country to country; some, especially in Africa, are extremely poor,[1] while others are economically more fortunate. It is noteworthy that despite the very high income enjoyed by some of the oil producing countries, very few members of their societies benefit from the influx of funds.

The relations of the Community with the countries of Africa, the Caribbean, and the West Pacific have already been discussed in chapter 4. The countries in these areas either have a special relationship with the Community, through association and preferential arrangements, or fall into the category of "associable" countries, which means that some kind of special arrangement may be concluded with them in the future. We also have examined previously the Community's relationship with the Communist developing countries in Asia. The characteristics of this relationship are determined more by the political system of these countries than by their underdevelopment. Nevertheless, all of these countries belong to the United Nations Conference on Trade and Development (UNCTAD), which was organized in Geneva in 1964. It is therefore useful to focus briefly on the activities and accomplishments of UNCTAD, especially because they may affect the evolution of commercial policy by the Community.

The major impetus for UNCTAD was the dissatisfaction of the developing countries of the world with the economic trends appearing in the later 1950s. Looking toward the industrially advanced and wealthy countries of the world for assistance, UNCTAD became a special forum for discussion and hopefully the solution of the awesome problems faced by the Third World countries. UNCTAD is now an organ of the United Nations General Assembly and consists of a triennial conference open to all U.N. member states; a Trade and Development Board elected by the conference and meeting twice a year; and four permanent committees dealing with the functional problems of commodities, manufacturing, financing, and shipping.

The first conference of UNCTAD took place in Geneva in 1964; a total of 120 countries, representing both developing and developed countries, participated. The major goals of the conference were to expand international trade in such a way as to benefit mainly the developing countries, to find solutions to the violent fluctuations in the prices of international commodities, to permit greater access of manufactured and semimanufactured goods produced in the developing countries to the markets of the industrially advanced states through special tariff concessions, and to find new methods of financing the international trade of the Third World.

A second conference was held in New Delhi in 1968, and a third in Santiago, Chile, in 1972. Despite the fact that each of these conferences were huge affairs attended by approximately 1500 delegates, and lasting for several weeks, the results of UNCTAD have not been spectacular. In fact, although the Geneva conference appeared to be the beginning of a very fruitful period of cooperation between developing and developed states, the New Delhi and Santiago conferences were generally disappointing. Perhaps the most important aspect of the conferences has been the establishment of a high level of solidarity among the developing countries and a means of producing common positions on many problems. However, reaching agreement on various issues required some compromises; and the acceptance of the positions of the developing countries by the industrially advanced states of the world has been very slow, despite much rhetoric to the contrary.

The Commission was represented in all three conferences; and its representatives have acted as spokesmen both for the Community as a collective unit and for the member states. At the 1964 conference the Community was represented—as an observer—by the Commission as well as by the Council. Member governments consulted each other before and during the conference. However, a unity of views could not always be reached during the conference and therefore the Commission representative had to limit himself frequently to general exhortatory declarations rather than the presentation of specific policy proposals.[2]

Similar procedures were applied during the second and third UNCTAD conferences. The representatives of the Commission met regularly with those of the member states to coordinate their viewpoints. However, these attempts to act in unity failed in most cases, although the European Parliament had urged the member states to designate the Commission as their exclusive spokesman for customs, tariffs, agricultural policy, and other matters for which the Community was competent according to the EEC Treaty.[3]

DEMANDS OF UNCTAD

One of the demands of UNCTAD during the conference of 1964 was the improvement of conditions for exports from the developing countries. This included the early dismantlement of the special preferential system that the Yaoundé association provided for its members in Africa. We have mentioned that in fact the Yaoundé associates voted with the other Third World countries for this objective although they did not want to give up their trade advantages without compensation.

During the second UNCTAD conference, in New Delhi in 1968, special demands were made for the establishment of a generalized system of preferences for the semimanufactured and manufactured goods produced in the developing countries. It was the contention of the Third World countries that such a system should be introduced without requiring reciprocity of concessions on the part of the developing countries and without discrimination against any of the approximately one hundred members of UNCTAD. A particular request in this connection was the elimination of reverse preferences which, as we have seen, was a principle underlying all of the Community associations. Another demand was the stabilization of prices for agricultural commodities and other raw materials exported from Third World countries with a price policy increasing and maintaining high revenues from these exports. Finally, the problems of financing development and aid were a major concern of the New Delhi conference.[4]

The Community responded to the request for a generalized preference system by adopting a series of regulations and measures in 1971, which went into effect July 1, 1971. The system offers preferential tariff advantages for finished and semifinished manufactured goods from developing countries as well as for processed agricultural products. However, in order to provide continuing protection for the associated countries, the Community imposed quotas on the goods that could be imported into the Community under the generalized preference system. These quotas were based on prior shipments of specific items into the Community countries and therefore were not considered a really satisfactory remedy to the problems of nonassociated Third World countries.[5] We need to point out, however, that the Community is the only entity among developed countries that has introduced a generalized preference system. The United States has talked about the introduction of such a system but up to this writing has not implemented it, despite congressional approval, given in the 1974 Trade Reform Act. Japan has made a half-hearted effort; and the remainder of the developed world has expressed sympathy with the problems of the Third World countries without doing much to help the exports of these countries.

During the third UNCTAD conference, in 1972, many complaints were heard about the insufficiency of the Community system and the continuation of the reverse preferences. In response to these complaints the Community modified its generalized preference system with a view to increasing the volume of trade from nonassociated countries. At the same time, the

Commission organized a series of seminars in Latin America to familiarize these countries with the details of the rather complicated generalized preference system.

It was obvious during the Santiago conference that the Community was unable to meet the expectations of many developing countries that were becoming impatient. They found it difficult to understand how a Community wishing to move forward on the road to economic and monetary union could not come up with a coordinated policy in the field of development cooperation. Of course, part of this inability is due to the political system of the Community, which does not give a clear-cut assignment of policy formulation and implementation to the Community institutions in external relations. As a consequence, Community institutions were not and could not be authorized to make fundamental decisions that might commit all of the member states. An additional difficulty during the Santiago conference was the prospective enlargement of the Community, which placed constraints on the definition of broad and coherent policies toward the Third World.[6]

PATTERNS OF TRADE

Table 7.1 shows the trend of trade between the European Community and the Third World. This table includes trade relations with the associated and associable countries as well as with all other developing countries. We observe that imports into the Community from 1958 to 1973 have tripled, while exports from the Community to the developing countries have increased by 250 percent. We also note that the trade balance between the European Community and the Third World has become increasingly unfavorable for the former.

When we analyze this trade in greater detail, we find that petroleum imports account for 50 percent of the total value of Community imports from developing countries. At least for the last 2 or 3 years inflation must also be taken into account when evaluating both imports and exports. The growth rates shown in Table 7.1 do not accurately portray imports of manufactured

241

Table 7.1

EEC Trade with the Developing Countries and Territories Generally In Units of Account, approximately valued at $1.24

Year	EEC Imports			EEC Exports			Net balance of trade value
	Value[a]	Index	Year-to-year growth rate (percent)	Value[b]	Index	Year-to-year growth rate (percent)	
1958	6824	100	–	6125	100	–	– 699
1959	6669	97.7	– 2.3	5926	96.8	– 3.2	– 743
1960	7485	110	12.2	6738	110	13.7	– 747
1961	7575	111	1.2	6765	110	0	– 810
1962	8168	120	7.8	6197	101	– 8.4	–1971
1963	8822	129	8.0	6355	104	2.5	–2467
1964	9843	144	11.6	6892	112	8.5	–2951
1965	10522	154	6.9	7501	122	8.8	–3021
1966	11312	166	7.5	7955	130	6.0	–3357
1967	11592	170	2.5	8299	135	4.3	–3293
1968	12506	183	7.9	9309	152	12.1	–3197
1969	14222	208	13.7	10217	167	9.7	–4005
1970	16105	236	13.2	11546	189	13.0	–4559
1971	17669	259	9.7	12895	211	11.7	–4774
1972	18903	277	7.0	13998	229	8.5	–4905
1973[c]	21164	310	12.0	15116	247	8.0	–6048

Source: Statistical Office of the European Communities, October 10, 1973.

a. At ruling rates cif.   b. At ruling rates fob.   c. Estimates based on the first three months.

goods from the developing countries, which have been 19 percent in 1970, 29 percent in 1971, and 23 percent in 1972; their total volume has increased 88 percent in 3 years.[7] Without doubt, this growth is due at least to some extent to the introduction of the Community system of generalized preferences. However, the net amount of this category of imports is relatively small and amounted in 1972 to only $1.8 billion or approximately 10 percent of total imports.

Changes in this system introduced in 1974 forecast the possibility that imports of many semimanufactured and manufactured items from the developing countries will further increase. These changes include a substantial rise in the ceiling of quotas, the elimination of quotas from a number of products, and selected tariff reductions. In addition, with the enlargement of the Community, new markets are available for the imports from developing countries to benefit from the generalized preference system.

The Community further broadened the generalized preference system in 1975. It was prodded especially by the Dutch government, which felt that the system required major improvement and that some of the benefits granted had become illusory, since inflation had made increases in quotas and ceilings meaningless. In general, the very poor countries were given greater opportunities for exports to the EC by limiting the imports from developing countries whose industries had already achieved a high level of competitiveness. In particular, in the processed food field the preferential margins for Third World countries were increased and new items added to the preferential list. In the industrial sector quotas for duty-free imports were enlarged on a number of products including certain textiles.[8] In order to circumvent inflationary erosion of quotas, some were expressed in volume (tons or cubic meters) rather than in monetary value. Of course, the expansion of the generalized preferences required consultation with the Community's association partners whose shipments to the EC countries were likely to suffer as a consequence. The associated states wanted special compensation for prospective losses and they received various types of satisfaction from the Community, either in the form of industrial cooperation and the stabilization of export earnings or indi-

243

vidual measures such as specific new duty-free quotas for a particular commodity or product.

Of course, regardless of how well the preference system may work, there are other factors that may impede the expansion of imports from developing countries. Especially disturbing in this respect is the world energy crisis, which may lead to a diversion of convertible currencies to the procurement of petroleum and thereby reduce the funds available for general imports. Moreover, the energy crisis could seriously crimp the economic expansion of the Community countries and make it more difficult to combat inflation. A declining economy within the Community could reduce the capacity of the nine member states to import goods from the developing countries by a considerable amount.[9]

For most of these countries primary commodities still constitute the main sources of export earnings. Up to 1975 it was precisely in primary commodities that progress was least satisfactory in terms of access and prices. Although increasing shortages of primary commodities are likely to ameliorate this picture, it is too early to judge whether a tighter supply situation and increasing prices will be a continuing expectation in the years to come. In the second half of 1974 the prices of many commodities, for example copper, dropped sharply but some recovery set in toward the end of 1975. Although the Community has offered to participate in a number of commodities stabilization programs, very little has been done by all advanced countries to satisfy the demands of the Third World for stabilization measures regarding export earnings. At the same time, access to raw materials is crucial for the economies of the Community countries (although the alarm sounded during the height of the petroleum crisis in 1972 and 1974 with respect to many other primary commodities may have exaggerated the situation and been caused more by political and economic manipulation than absolute resource deficiencies).

The dependence of the Community on Third World raw materials to fuel its industrial machine is illustrated in Table 7.2. While dependence on individual commodities varies greatly, the table illustrates a high degree of vulnerability of the Community, which its institutions and member states must seek to

Table 7.2
Third World Regions Supplying EC Imports of Selected Industrial Raw Materials
(imports as a percent of consumption)

	Africa	Latin America	Other
Aluminum	2	3	2
Bauxite	13	3	–
Chromium ore	17	–	21
Copper	27	17	13
Iron ore and conc	15	15	–
Lead	8	8	–
Manganese ore	31	10	1
Nickel	1	–	1
Phosphates	66	1	–
Tin	10	28	47
Tungsten ore and conc	5	31	22
Zinc	4	9	3

Source: *International Economic Report of the President,* March 1975, p. 162.

alleviate. We have noted in chapter 4 that in the Lomé Convention the Community resisted the temptation to make guaranteed access to specific raw material part of the treaty objectives. This probably pleased the Lomé affiliates as well as other industrially advanced countries such as Japan and the United States, which also are in need of these items. The cooperation provisions included in the Convention and also the concern with cooperation beginning to appear in negotiations of bilateral accords—for example with Canada and the expanded agreement with India[10]— reflect the Community's full awareness of this issue. Cooperation may take the form of joint ventures in extraction and processing of raw materials with developing country governments and could encompass increased local processing (a long-standing Third World demand) and the encouragement of Community and private stockpiles.

During the October 1972 summit conference of the Community member states one of the objectives elaborated was the formulation of a coherent Community policy toward the Third World. As always in such matters, progress is agonizingly slow and it may be years before a comprehensive Community policy can be agreed upon; although in 1974, as mentioned in chapter 4, the Council began to adopt a number of resolutions for the harmonization of aid policies. Such a coordinated policy must address itself to financial support and technical assistance toward the Third World in general, and cannot limit itself in this respect to the associate memberships and preferential agreements in existence or to be negotiated in the future. It must deal with the volume of aid related to the GNP of the member states, the financial terms of this aid, and its geographic distribution.[11] As already noted, the Convention of Lomé has not preempted national aid measures, and many bilateral trade and aid programs continue to exist. Indeed, France, Great Britain, and Germany have extensive networks of such bilateral arrangements and Italy and Belgium are also involved in bilateral foreign aid activities. Naturally, France, Britain, and Italy have favored their former colonies in these arrangements.

Although a long-term Community policy must aim its development activities at all developing countries, including those in Asia and Latin America, whether or not these countries are associated or were former colonies, its formulation does not exclude the possibility of placing a greater emphasis on one area than another. In other words, while a future development aid policy must be global in orientation, it does not mean necessarily that the countries in Africa and the Mediterranean, which have enjoyed a good and mutually fruitful relationship with the Community, may not continue to benefit more from such a policy than other Third World countries.

THE NONASSOCIABLE DEVELOPING COUNTRIES

The figures in Table 7.2 provided an overall picture of Community trade with developing countries. In Table 7.3 we offer data on trade with those countries which, under the terms of the accession agreement with Great Britain, Ireland, and Denmark, will not be offered opportunities for associated status with the Community. It is interesting to note from this table that imports and exports between 1958 and 1972 from the nonassociables (Latin America and Asia) increased in the same manner as overall trade.

It is also interesting to note that trade with the nonassociables is larger than with the associated and associable countries and that the percentage share has changed very little, and has if anything increased between 1958 and 1972. Thus, the hopes of the associated countries to gain special advantages through the particular preferences given to them have not really been fulfilled.

On the other hand, since many of the African associates fall into the category of very poor countries with very limited resources it may well be that without the special preferences granted to these countries their share in the Community trade would have dropped materially. Therefore, from the point of view of the Community as well as of the associated countries, the Yaoundé, Arusha, and other associations and preferential agreements have performed a useful function at least temporarily.

247

Table 7.3

Trade of Nonassociable Developing Countries
1958–1972

	Imports				
	1958	1960	1963	1969	1972
Central and South America	1647	1870	2268	3168	3608
Asia and others[a]	2582	2791	3042	4811	8505
Total	4229	4661	5310	7979	12113
Percent of total EC imports from the Third World	62	62	60	56	64

	Exports				
	1958	1960	1963	1969	1972
Central and South America	1604	1693	1567	2578	3652
Asia and others[a]	1700	1954	1955	3547	4601
Total	3304	3647	3522	6125	8253
Percent of total EC Exports to the Third World	54	54	55	60	59

Source: Statistical Office of the European Communities, *Eurostat:* Foreign Trade, Monthly Statistics, 2/1973, pp. 12–14.

a. Includes Caribbean countries.

Latin America

Traditionally Latin American countries have exported three categories of commodities to Western Europe: tropical foodstuffs, farm products from the temperate zones, and raw and partially processed materials. In the first category coffee, cocoa, and bananas comprise 20 percent of total exports.

When the EC embarked on its original association policy, which the EC Treaty prescribed for the former colonies of the Six, the Latin Americans feared that their exports to the member states would be harmed, because the special preferences granted to associated states were likely to result in a wide-reaching trade diversion. However, these fears were not substantiated as can be seen from Table 7.3. On the contrary, the exports of tropical foodstuffs have increased at a greater rate than those from the African associates. Yet, there were new fears when the preferential treatment accorded by the Community was extended in 1970 to other African countries, but again, up to 1974 these fears proved to be unfounded. Nevertheless, the Latin Americans have strongly demanded the abolition of the preference systems; proportional access guarantees; and the creation of market organizations on individual products, by international agreements, possibly on a worldwide basis.

The exports of temperate zone farm commodities to the Common Market also cause concern to the Latin American countries. The products chiefly affected are grain, meat, and perhaps sugar. Like the United States, Latin America is anxious to ensure increasing access to the Common Market, and objects to the effects of the CAP levy system. Beef and veal exports, very important to Uruguay and Argentina, appeared to be most threatened because of the high import levies, whereas the rules for pigmeat and poultry seem to be less worrisome. Of course, the shortage of beef in Europe and throughout the world temporarily reduced these fears, but offered little consolation in longer terms. On the other hand, the Latin American countries have been fairly well satisfied so far with their exports of vegetables and fruit, especially apples and pears, although possible new restrictions on vegetables and vegetable oils could cause a reduction of Latin American shipments.

Raw materials such as wool, cotton, copper, lead, zinc, and oil are not subject to any duties, and the problems caused by fluctuating prices are not limited to exports to Europe but are worldwide. However, partially processed materials such as copper wire and cotton yarn are subject to duties and suffer not only from competing products manufactured within the Common Market, but also, and this is more painful, by preferences accorded to the associated countries in Africa and Europe.

Members of the European Parliament and officials of the Commission felt that the Community had neglected its relations with Latin America. In 1962 the Commission advanced an action program of closer cooperation with Latin America, which, with the exception of a few secondary points, was not approved by the Council of Ministers. In 1964 a delegation from the European Parliament visited several Latin American capitals and made a number of proposals for the expansion of trade between Latin America and the EEC, technical assistance, and enlarged investments of European capital in Latin America. In support of these measures and in order to improve the image of the Common Market, a Press and Information Office was set up in September 1965 in Montevideo, Uruguay, the headquarters of the Latin American Free Trade Association.[12] As an important by-product of these measures, and as a result of aggressive sales methods and generous long-term credits, Common Market exports to Latin America have expanded substantially.

In talks between the Commission and Latin American diplomatic missions in Brussels (carried on from April 1965 to January 1966), the Latin Americans suggested the establishment of a Standing Joint Committee composed of EC representatives and the Latin American Heads of Mission to the Common Market. As envisaged by the Latin American side, this Committee was to have the power to influence Community deliberations regarding Latin American affairs. However, such power would have affected the principle of institutional autonomy of the Community and therefore was rejected. Yet in a more limited sense the Commission supported the idea of a joint committee, provided it would act mainly as an overseer of the relations between the EC and Latin American countries and would review periodically the policies pursued by all partners. Demarches by

Latin American diplomats made in the capitals of the member states in support of such a committee were favorably received by the member governments, and in November 1966 the Council gave its approval to an informally constituted liaison group, composed of members of the Commission and the chiefs of Latin American missions. Perhaps as the result of this committee, Latin American fears that, in view of its preoccupation with Africa, the Community might develop a common commercial policy *against* South and Central America have been somewhat alleviated. We should point out here that the Latin American trade balance with the Community since 1958 has been generally favorable, although in 1972 and 1974 it showed small deficits. However, much of the favorable trade balance was due to oil exports from Venezuela; while semimanufactured and manufactured goods, a special concern of all developing countries, constituted only a very small percentage of Latin American goods shipped to Europe.

In 1972 the Community concluded the first trade agreement with a South American country, Argentina. It is essentially a nonpreferential accord, and pays particular attention to the questions of beef and veal exports. To oversee the functioning of the agreement, a joint EC–Argentine committee has been established, an institutional device that the Argentine government would like to expand by the creation of permanent subcommittees for cooperation in the sectors of agriculture, industry, finance, and meat. A sensitive issue that has not been as yet fully resolved is the desire of major Latin American countries including Argentina to build up their own commercial fleets and the insistence that at least half of all shipments between Europe and Latin America be carried in Latin American ships. Otherwise, the joint committee, in its meeting early in 1973, declared itself generally satisfied with the operation of the trade agreement. Reciprocal trade was increasing, the balance of trade of Argentina with the Community was improving, and cooperation developing favorably.[13] Nevertheless, the Argentine government would like to broaden the current agreement to assure a higher level of beef exports and to set up procedures for closer cooperation in industry, technology, and finance.[14]

In 1973 Uruguay signed a trade agreement with the Community similar to that concluded with Argentina. Again, the problem of shipping seemed to be the most difficult to overcome, but an acceptable compromise was found.[15] The negotiations for a trade agreement with Brazil were more complex because some of the major export commodities of Brazil, such as coffee and cocoa butter, competed with the same products sold by associated countries of West and East Africa, and therefore these countries had to be consulted. The final result has been a nonpreferential agreement of three years' duration, with concessions on the importation of beef and veal, cooperation clauses in the agricultural sector, and some customs reductions for all suppliers of some products such as soluble coffee. Again, the maritime problems cropped up in the negotiations because for Brazil shipping in its own vessels was considered important for its balance of trade. In both the Uruguayan and Brazilian agreements provisions have been made for the establishment of joint committees to watch over the implementation and functioning of the agreements.[16]

Mexico, the only Latin American country with a continuing deficit in its trade balance with the EC, also expressed an interest in a trade agreement with the Community, but was seeking some special preferences in order to speed its economic growth and diversify its industrial activity. Some support for a preferential agreement was indicated at least obliquely by Germany.[17] An agreement between the Community and Mexico was signed in 1975 but it is nonpreferential. Rather, major emphasis was placed on cooperation between the Community and Mexico to assist in the development and diversification of industry and trade; and a joint committee set up under the agreement has been given wide powers in this respect.[18] Paraguay has also expressed a wish to hold preliminary talks with the Commission in the hope of negotiating a trade agreement.

Although the liaison group composed of Latin American ambassadors and Community officials has not met frequently (two meetings a year are now foreseen), it has served to alleviate anxieties of Latin American countries regarding present and future EC policies and, therefore, has become a safety valve for accumulated grievances. One of the major problems in the eyes of the Latin American governments continues to be the application of the principle of "Community preferences" in relations with associated developing countries and those granted preferential treatment outside formal associations (an example is Egypt). They would like to receive similar treatment specifically tailored to Latin American needs, and are dissatisfied with the operation of the Community system of generalized preferences toward the remainder of the Third World, including of course Latin America. In the absence of specific action for them, they demand that the generalized preferences be broadened to encompass all primary agricultural and industrial products. These demands are made with the hope that more and more products manufactured in the Third World and imported into the Community would become substitutes for goods produced in the advanced countries. Other demands are the expanded coverage of the European Development Bank in order to provide loans for projects in Latin America and an assurance that the EC would not adopt any new measures prejudicial to the present situation of Latin American trade or to the latter's relations with other countries of the Third World.[19]

It seems reasonable to assume that the intensification of the institutionalized contacts between the EC and Latin American governments, the growing attention paid by the Community to its relations with South and Central America, and the traditional concern about Yankee imperialism are likely to strengthen an already existing Latin American orientation toward Europe.[20] Expanding investments by European multinational corporations, and revelations of undue interference by American multinational enterprises in Latin American domestic politics (e.g., the ITT affair in Chile) may well reinforce this trend. The foreign policy program of the Peronista government illustrates this trend. Among the points stressed in this program are the "termination of political and economic dependency" and the "decisive rapprochement to the European Community."[21]

South and Southeast Asia

Although Table 7.3 shows that imports from developing countries in Asia have more than tripled from 1958 to 1972 and that by 1973 the Community had a very serious trade deficit exceeding $6 billion, this does not mean that all countries in South and Southeast Asia participated in this expansion of trade. The reason is that oil exports from the Persian Gulf, Indonesia, and other parts of Asia are included in this rising trend. Such countries as India, Pakistan, and Malaysia (including Singapore) showed only a very modest increase of their exports to the Community, with relatively unimpressive net totals. India's exports rose from $103 million in 1958 to $253 million in 1972; Pakistan's shipments during the same period expanded from $93 million to $122 million; and Malaysia's exports to the Community increased from $180 million to $345 million.[22] However, these figures rose substantially in 1973, mostly due to Britain's accession to the Community.

During the same period, exports from the Community to all of Asia nearly tripled, suggesting that despite the large Community trade deficit caused by oil, EC sales have done much better than most products shipped from Asia to the Community.

The trade problems that South and Southeast Asian countries were likely to face were recognized by the governments of these countries almost as soon as the Common Market had been established. During the 1961–62 negotiations for British access to the Community, the Asian Commonwealth countries—India, Pakistan, Ceylon, and Malaysia—were fearful that in the event of success they might not only lose their Commonwealth preferences for imports into Britain, but that they would also suffer general disadvantages from the emerging CET. To counter these fears, the British and Community negotiators decided that comprehensive trade agreements should be concluded between the enlarged EC and India, Pakistan, and Sri Lanka (Ceylon). With the failure of the British negotiations, the three Asian Commonwealth countries were on their own as far as trade concessions from the EC were concerned. In order to bring the need for Community concessions before the public eye, the Indian Minister of Trade, Mambhai Shah, toured the Common Market capitals in the spring of 1963 and discussed the problem with the appropriate authorities. In these discussions particular attention was drawn to the large deficits in the Indian balance of trade with the Community, which, if allowed to continue, would be apt to injure EC sales to India as well as Indian investment projects. In order to reverse this trend the Indians proposed suspension or large-scale reduction of duties on products for which India is the principal supplier or one of the principal suppliers. Such products include pepper, jute products, handknit carpets, and coir mattings, among others.[23]

The Commission was ready to support many of the Indian suggestions, but its proposals for negotiations in 1963 were rejected by the Council of Ministers, which considered them premature in view of the forthcoming U.N. Conference on Trade and Aid (UNCTAD) and the Kennedy Round talks. However, to show its desire to cooperate with India and other developing countries, the Council suspended or temporarily reduced the tariffs for tea, mate, cashew nuts, shellac, tropical woods, and various spices. The total amount of trade affected was $221 million, but since exports from India to the EC represent merely 7.2 percent of total exports, her trade benefited in the amount of only $20 million. In the summer of 1966 India again urged the Community authorities to find means for the improvement of Indian exports to the EC. However, no concrete steps appeared to be feasible until the nature of the future trade relationships between developing and economically advanced countries had been clarified in GATT and UNCTAD consultations. Since the UNCTAD conferences in Geneva (1964) and New Delhi (1968) did not have any major positive results, the Community concluded an initial nonpreferential trade agreement in 1968 covering silk and cotton fabrics, followed by two others in 1968 dealing with certain handicrafts and coconut products, and two in 1970 on jute products and cotton textiles.

Pakistan's problems are similar to those of India, except that she ships about 25 percent of her total exports to the EC. The Pakistanis export mainly jute and cotton and are anxious to broaden the range of their products for shipment to the Common Market. In 1969 and 1970 the Community concluded two agreements with the Pakistani government, covering handicrafts and silk and cotton goods. Afghanistan has also shown an interest in improving her commercial relations with the Common Market and talks to this effect have been held between the Commission and an Afghanistan delegation.

Ceylon (Sri Lanka) sells primarily tea and rubber. It benefited from the temporary tariff concession on tea, but the sales of this commodity to the EC have been insignificant. Malaysia's export trade with the Community is mainly in rubber and tin, which are both important for the EC. Rice, the main export of Burma and Thailand, competes with the Common Market's own production, and imports into the EC from the two countries may also suffer by future preferences to North African rice.

Britain's entry into the Community in 1973 has further complicated the problems of the Commonwealth countries. They are now faced with a complete loss of Commonwealth preferences for shipments into the United Kingdom market and are apprehensive about further trade diversion as a result of the proliferation of preferential arrangements with Mediterranean countries, and the EC affiliation of African Commonwealth countries and some of the Caribbean and Pacific states under the Convention of Lomé. Although the Community's generalized preferences offer some compensation for the loss of Commonwealth preferences, the exclusion of certain items such as textiles and shoes make the benefits doubtful. Moreover, as we have seen, the Community's scheme of generalized preferences is limited by a quota system and thereby is considerably less attractive than it may appear at first glance.

Although the Commission's Memorandum to the Council on Community policy regarding development cooperation[24] devoted only three paragraphs to Asia, the Community showed some awareness of Asian difficulties in the Joint Declaration of Intent attached to the Treaty of Accession. In this declaration it agreed to examine (with the individual Commonwealth countries in Asia) trade problems caused by the enlargement, and to seek appropriate solutions. Initial steps were taken toward attaining these objectives by the improvements made to the system of generalized tariff preferences, which included the raising of quota ceilings, transfer of products to more flexible categories, and adding new processed agricultural products to the list of items benefiting from the preferences. Some of the earlier agreements with India were renegotiated in 1973 to include the markets of the new Community member states, and to raise the annual quotas for the imports of handicrafts, silk and cotton

fabrics, and various other textiles. In addition, a trade cooperation agreement was concluded in 1974 for a period of five years.
This agreement sets up a joint committee with the task of seeking and promoting the implementation of genuine economic
and commercial cooperation between the Community and
India.[25] Its dynamic aspect is the intention of the Community
to go beyond the narrow framework of commercial relations to
provide cooperation for general economic development.

In the fall of 1974 the EC Council of Ministers decided to
instruct the Commission to open negotiations with Pakistan,
Sri Lanka, and Bangladesh for the conclusion of trade and cooperation agreements similar to those concluded with India.
Future increases in the production and shipment of textiles
were to be emphasized. The new accords will set up joint committees as permanent bodies with powers in the field of cooperation.[26] The agreement with Bangladesh is a follow-up to a trade
agreement on jute textiles signed in 1973.[27]

Other countries in Asia also signed limited trade agreements
in 1973—Thailand, the Philippines, and Indonesia—and they as
well as Malaysia and Singapore (all ASEAN members) expressed
their intentions in 1974 to negotiate broader agreements. The
accords are not likely to be as comprehensive as the Indian
model. The main instrument for economic relations with the
ASEAN states is the generalized preference system, supplemented by Community assistance in the marketing of their
products and the establishment of a regional study group to
survey cooperation possibilities and promote training in marketing and other economic activities useful for the exports of their
products. Joint committees probably will be important features
of all agreements. Closer relations with the Community also
have a political dimension: They provide a new option for the
ASEAN countries in addition to their relations with Japan and
the United States. At the same time, they may offer the Community some guarantees for access to needed raw materials.[28]

Iran had a 10-year trade agreement, which expired in 1973.
Since then it insisted on negotiating a preferential accord, but
was supported only by France and Denmark. The solution may
be an overall cooperation agreement that would include joint
ventures between local and Community firms and take into ac-

count, at least indirectly, the petroleum resources of Iran, and the need professed by Iran to have special arrangements for her manufactured goods.[29]

In the minds of many Latin American and Asian governments, the institution of associations and preferential arrangements such as those found in the Mediterranean countries has become the political dividing line in the Community treatment of all the Third World. There emerges the distinct impression, whether accurate or not, that the associated and associable countries (as well as the Mediterranean) are the preferred parts of the Third World. Most attention by the Community is focused on this part, while Asia and Latin America are dealt with with "benign neglect." The justification of the Community policy of discriminating between various developing countries has always been "special links shaped by geography and history"[30] between Community member states and certain developing countries. However, with the enlargement of the Community this justification appears to lose its force inasmuch as many Asian countries belong to the Commonwealth and therefore have as much right to preferential treatment as have the associates and the associables. As far as Latin America is concerned, there are strong cultural affinities with European countries that could be used for justifying a claim for preferential treatment.

While vested interests of some of the Community member states and the associates may call for a continuation of present policies, inasmuch as better access to the Common Market by outsiders may well damage producers in Europe and hurt the associates, the Community must find means of overcoming the present policy dilemma.[31] Several instruments are available to assist in solving the problem.

One obvious means would be the further improvement of the generalized preference scheme by raising ceilings of the quotas for many products, and perhaps eliminating both tariffs and quotas altogether on less significant items. Another means for helping the Third World as a whole would be the conclusion of commodities agreements that would help to stabilize prices and permit access for primary agricultural commodities and other raw materials to the Community. Such agreements should take into account not only the interests of the suppliers but also those of the purchasers, because increasing shortages of certain raw materials will impose responsibilities on Third World supplier countries to make their resources available on an equal basis to the advanced countries. A third tool may well be a comprehensive Community aid policy (discussed earlier) that would offer not only grants and long-term loans but also technical assistance. Since public aid may not be sufficient for this purpose, the Community may well have to come up with some kind of guarantee for private investments in the Third World similar to the Overseas Private Investment Corporations (OPIC) of the United States. How far the member governments would agree to such a policy and whether the Community would have the means to provide the necessary guarantees to private investors is difficult to predict at this stage. Previous experiences with Community attempts for the coordination of the foreign policies of the member governments do not augur well for rapid success. Finally, the recently concluded cooperation agreement with India may become the prototype of economic arrangement between the Community and Third World countries. It is interesting to note that up to now the member governments have used the instrument of cooperation agreements as a subtle means to remove the Community's competences in foreign economic policy (competences that had been assigned to the EC institutions by the EEC Treaty). The cooperation agreement with India may be a new departure that could be employed in Community relations with Third World countries as a substitute for bilateral arrangements. The cooperation agreement could also be conceived of as an intermediate step between mere trade agreements and associated status, inasmuch as they include institutional devices (such as a joint committee between the treaty partners) and aim at a close cooperative scheme approximating the association agreements under article 238 of the EEC Treaty. In fact, the institutional framework is likely to be expanded. This can be seen in the Indian agreement: the joint committee has established specialized subcommittees with responsibilities to survey the cooperation activities in various economic sectors. Links could also be created between the parliamentarians of the cooperation agreement partners in a way similar to what has been done in the association agreements.

259

Periodic conferences can be set up between select members of the European Parliament and of the legislatures of the particular states, joint study groups can be formed bringing together especially qualified parliamentarians, and guided tours to the national legislatures of the EC member countries can be organized for visiting legislators. Such links would be useful in the relationship between the partners, and at the same time would permit the Community to expand its political influence over additional segments of the Third World.

NOTES

1. They are sometimes called the "Fourth World."

2. Frans A. M. Alting von Geusau, *Beyond the European Community* (Leyden: A. W. Sijthoff, 1969), p. 82.

3. Ibid., p. 83.

4. *Second General Report*, 1968, pp. 391–394.

5. For details see the *Fourth General Report*, 1970, pp. 312–314, and *Fifth General Report*, 1971, pp. 343–347.

6. *Sixth General Report*, 1972, pp. 286–293.

7. *Seventh General Report*, 1973, pp. 383. It is noteworthy that despite these impressive growth figures the import of iron, steel, and non-ferrous metals has dropped.

8. Cf. *Agence Europe Bulletin*, November 14, 15, 1974.

9. *Seventh General Report*, 1973, p. 387.

10. Cf. pp. 204, 254, 255, 259.

11. *Eighth General Report*, 1974, pp. 234–237.

12. EP, *Sitzungsdokumente*, 1964–65, Document 98, November 24, 1964, Reporter: Eduardo Martino.

13. *Agence Europe Bulletin*, March 15, 1973.

14. Ibid., May 22, 1974.

15. Ibid., February 21, March 19/20, 1973.

16. Ibid., February 7, March 19/20, 1973.

17. *Relay from Bonn*, February 8, 1974, vol. 25.

18. *Agence Europe Bulletin,* June 11, 12, 1975.

19. For details of the meeting of July 1975 see ibid., July 2, 1975.

20. It is noteworthy that the EC has sent observers to several Latin American conferences dealing with economic integration; and has offered advice based on its own experience to LAFTA, the Andean Common Market, and the Central American Common Market. Both the OAS and the Organization of Central American States have established liaison bureaus with the EC.

21. *Frankfurter Allgemeine Zeitung,* March 31, 1973, p. 8.

22. Statistical Office of the European Communities, *Eurostat:* Foreign Trade, Monthly Statistics, 2 (1973):12.

23. EP, *Sitzbungsdokumente,* 1965–66, Document 98, November 22, 1965, Reporter: L. G. Morox. This report provides a good analysis of the Indian problems.

24. Commission of the European Communities, *Memorandum on a Community Policy on Development Cooperation,* 1972.

25. *Seventh General Report,* 1973, pp. 429–430. The Community has also agreed to supply 1,000,000 tons of wheat to India, of which 300,000 are given in the form of food aid (*Agence Europe Bulletin,* November 6, 1974).

26. Cf. *Agence Europe Bulletin,* June 8, 28: July 5, 1975.

27. Ibid., May 17, October 16, 1974.

28. Ibid., September 18, October 5, 1974; July 2, 1975.

29. Ibid., May 16, 1975. Note that preferential agreements with Iran would be a precedent outside the ACP and Mediterranean areas.

30. Memorandum on a *Community Policy on Development Cooperation,* 1972, p. 16.

31. For details see John Pinder, "The Community and the Developing Countries: Associates and Outsiders," *Journal of Common Market Studies* 12, 1 (September 1973):53–77.

8

Monetary, Energy, and Security Problems

If the member states of the European Community are really serious about wanting to "speak with one voice" in world affairs, they must attempt to formulate common external policies in the monetary, energy, and security fields. The EEC Treaty contains provisions for member governments that deal with recommended balance of payments policies and actions to be taken in the event of currency crises (articles 104–109), but does not assign to the Community institutions any particular competences regarding external monetary policies. In particular, there is no common balance of payments on the part of the Community as against the rest of the world and each member state controls its own exchange rates. The Euratom Treaty includes authority for the Community institutions to evolve external policies and to take appropriate action with respect to certain nuclear matters falling under Euratom competences (mainly articles 101 to 106, but also others), but no assignments have been made for external policies on energy problems in general. Military security matters are of course completely outside the competences of Community institutions, although some aspects of European security negotiations during 1972–75 (such as economic cooperation between Eastern and Western Europe) clearly have touched on the interests of the EC organs.

MONETARY POLICIES WITH EXTERNAL EFFECTS

During the summit conference of heads of state and chiefs of government of the EC member states held in The Hague in December 1969 it was decided that an economic and monetary union should be created among the member countries. The inclusion of this objective was motivated to a great extent by the currency disturbances in 1968 and 1969, which were to a

265

considerable degree the consequence of divergent economic trends within the European Community, and which ultimately led to the devaluation of the French franc and the revaluation of the German mark.

Recognizing that the harmonization of the disparities in economic trends was the only alternative to a constant repetition of these undesirable events, the Council of Ministers adopted on January 26, 1970, an initial program of coordinating economic and monetary policy in the European Community. This program contained not only guidelines for short-term economic development in 1970 but also plans for a common definition of medium-term indicators and specific economic guideposts for 1970–75, as well as an inventory of the main structural reforms to be accomplished at national and European Community levels.[1]

About two weeks later, the European Community's five central banks (Belgium also representing Luxembourg) activated arrangements for making available $2 billion as short-term monetary aid to member countries running into temporary balance of payments difficulties. The agent for this arrangement was the Bank for International Settlements in Basel; and drawings could be made in any currency.

The Monetary Committee

Prior to the decision to establish an Economic and Monetary Union, a Monetary Committee was set up in 1958 under article 105 of the EEC Treaty. It was to cooperate with another committee which was assigned the function of examining economic trends.

The Monetary Committee consisted of two members appointed by each member state for a term of two years; in addition, two alternates were appointed. One member and one alternate must be proposed by each member state's central bank. It has been the practice of each member state to make the appointments at the highest official level within the Finance Ministries and at the level of Deputy Governor of the central bank. The Commission has been represented on the Committee by the Director General for Economic and Financial Affairs and by the Director in charge of Monetary Policy in the Directorate-General for Economic and Financial Affairs.[2] From its inception in June 1958 to the middle of 1974, the Committee has met nearly 200 times. These meetings often extended to two-day sessions.

Among the tasks assigned to the Committee was the promotion of the coordination of monetary policies of the member states.[3] This task included attempts to coordinate the balance of payments adjustment policies of the member states, particularly external measures and financing of deficits. However, despite the legal basis for this task contained in the EEC Treaty, the member states have not always felt it necessary to consult the Monetary Committee before taking action on international credit problems or on changes in exchange rates. For example, when in March 1964 a severe speculative attack hit the Italian lira, the Bank of Italy turned to the United States and the International Monetary Fund (IMF) for massive credits rather than make use of the Community processes. On the other hand, during the crisis of the French franc in 1968, a number of consultations on French policy were undertaken, although eventually the recommended solution of an 11 percent devaluation of the French franc was not adopted by the French government. When the same problem cropped up again nine months later, the French devalued the franc without effective prior consultation.[4]

The Monetary Committee also took an early initiative to bring about a common approach by the Community countries to problems arising in the international monetary system. In particular, it was anxious to contribute to a better equilibrium in this system; and a number of studies for this purpose were conducted by experts from each central bank and a Commission representative. These studies influenced consideration of the General Arrangements to Borrow (GAB), which was concluded among the Group of Ten countries in December 1961.[5]

During 1962 the Committee examined such matters as swap credit agreements between the Federal Reserve system of the United States and certain European central banks and the selection of currencies for drawing on and repayments to the IMF.[6]

In 1966, when the Committee pursued its effort to restore the international payments equilibrium, a split developed between France and the other five EEC countries on how the Special Drawing Rights (SDRs) of the IMF should be organized. Despite considerable efforts of the Monetary Committee, the Commission, and the finance ministries and central bank governors of the member states, a common EEC position on SDRs could not be reached until 1970.[7] Nevertheless, the Six were able to establish a unified position in most international meetings regarding the activities of the IMF; and they were able to reform the procedures and practices of this body, including receiving a higher value for their votes. It is interesting to note that international monetary problems have increasingly occupied the meetings of the Monetary Committee. Indeed, by the end of 1972, international monetary problems ranked second to policy harmonization in terms of topics discussed.

The Evolution of the Economic and Monetary Union

In March 1970 the EEC Commission transmitted a communication to the Council of Ministers defining the steps that would eventually lead to economic and monetary union. Three stages were envisaged: the first to finish by the end of 1971; the second, by the end of 1975; and the third, by the end of 1978. The third stage, however, could be extended for two years. The EC Commission pointed out that balanced progress must be made between the economic union and the monetary union and that no priority should be given to one element over the other.[8]

Action by the Council of Ministers in March 1971 extended the first phase until the end of 1973, but confirmed the goal of monetary union in order to have the Community "form an individual monetary unit within the international system."[9] Fluctuations in the rates of Community currencies were to be narrowed gradually until they became fixed again, and ultimately one currency (the Europa) would emerge for all member states. Part of this scheme was the establishment of a European Monetary Cooperation Fund to help EC countries in national currency crises and balance of payments difficulties.

The French government, not always known to favor common policies, basically gave strong support to the idea of a common monetary unit. A persuasive reason was that changes and extensive fluctuations of member state currencies threatened to impair the proper functioning of the CAP inasmuch as quasi-duties had to be imposed on the flow of farm products across intra-Community frontiers to compensate for the currency changes.

The traditional reluctance of the member governments to accept limitations on their policy-making autonomy, and the floating of the German mark and Dutch guilder in response to the weaknesses of the U.S. dollar in the spring of 1971 combined to not only halt any progress toward the monetary union, but to seriously endanger the continued operation of the Common Market as a whole. This situation was further aggravated by President Nixon's imposition of the 10 percent surcharge on individual imports and the closing of the "gold window" in August 1971. Nevertheless, this action served to galvanize efforts by the Six toward defining the common interest, despite continuing internal policy differences in 1971 among the member governments and especially between Chancellor Brandt and President Pompidou as to the principles of currency relationships and permissible spread of currency fluctuations.

In the ensuing negotiations among the IMF members of the Group of Ten on the readjustment of currency relationships and the elimination of the surtax, the Six adopted a common stand and thereby emerged as perhaps the most powerful unit in world economic politics. We should stress that this stand of the Six toward the United States and the outside world did not stem directly from the proposed move toward an economic and monetary union. Rather, faced with possible harm from the international environment, the policies of the Six were consolidated, and it was hoped at that time that this external show of solidarity would have long-range beneficial effects on internal political cohesion as well. Evidence of such effects was seen in the resolution passed by the Community Council of Ministers on March 8, 1972, to initiate on July 1, 1972, the maximum fluctuation margins of 2.25 percent between EC currencies, and to defend these margins through Community short- and

269

medium-term credits to member states with insufficient reserves to maintain the margins. In addition, an arsenal of antispeculation measures was to be employed by each member state to curb speculative attacks on its currency; and the establishment of a European Monetary Cooperation Fund was to be expedited.[10]

The 2.25 percent margin restriction in the fluctuation of the Community currencies (also known as the snake arrangement), to which the original six member states had obligated themselves in 1972, was not accepted by the British and Irish governments. Both new member states allowed their currencies to float independently. However, Denmark, the third new EC member, accepted the snake. A new monetary crisis erupted in January 1973. Italy, beset by a heavy outflow of capital, decided to let the lira float.[11] In February the United States announced a 10 percent devaluation of the dollar. The disarray of the exchange markets that followed led to a revaluation of the mark by 3 percent in March, and a further revaluation of 5.5 percent in June. The guilder was also revalued by 5 percent in September. Thus by the end of 1973 a new system of exchange rates had been set up in the Community, yet at least six member states (Germany, France, Denmark, and the Benelux countries) agreed to continue the snake system under the new conditions.

In the meantime, the European Monetary Cooperation Fund was established in Luxembourg in April 1973. Its main functions are:

1. the proper functioning of the progressive narrowing of the margins of fluctuation in Community currencies against each other

2. interventions in Community currencies in the exchange markets

3. settlements between the central banks of the member states leading to a concerted policy on reserves, especially a progressive pooling of their reserves of gold, SDRs, and foreign exchange[12]

Despite the establishment of the Monetary Cooperation Fund, the snake arrangement was buffeted again in January 1974 when the French government decided to float the franc and to suspend interventions on the exchange markets for six months. As a consequence the French franc depreciated about 5 percent and thus nearly half of the Community member states had abandoned the monetary restraints of the snake arrangement. The remainder, Germany, Denmark, and the Benelux countries, vowed to continue this arrangement and expressed the hope that the others would return to Community exchange rate agreements.[13]

In 1974 the economic and monetary solidarity of Community received additional jolts as the result of balance of payments deteriorations in some of the member states, caused mainly by the steep increases in world oil prices. Denmark had to impose special tax measures on the importation of goods, and Italy introduced temporary customs duties against Community imports and a deposit requirement of 50 percent of the value of merchandise purchased from abroad. Italy faced a current payments deficit exceeding $3 billion and was forced in March 1974 to draw the entire amount agreed as short-term monetary support, nearly $2 billion. However, this large sum was not sufficient to remedy Italy's money problem and in September the West German government came to the rescue by providing a short-term $2 billion swap loan.[14] To legitimate this loan, Italy received additional Community aid in November of that year in the form of a medium-term loan amounting to about $1.5 billion with repayment stretched to 1978. All of Italy's EC partners with the exception of Britain made varying commitments to underwrite this loan.[15]

The situation improved in 1975. Italy and Denmark lifted their import curbs and Italy's balance of payments improved. At the same time, France announced its return to the snake, although some conditions were attached to this decision; and Italy's Finance Minister Emilio Colombo stated that extended return to the snake remained an important Italian goal. In the meantime, Austria, Norway, and Sweden had become associated with the snake arrangement and Switzerland hoped to follow suit.[16]

Prospects

Despite the French decision to return to the snake, the outlook for the implementation of the monetary union is bleak. One important external reason is the disarray in the international payments conditions brought about by the extraordinary rise of petroleum prices since 1972. Another reason, mostly internal, is illustrated by France's abandonment of and later return to the snake: the high degree of economic and political egoism displayed at the time of the oil crisis, when solidarity among the EC partners should have been the first order of business. But given the many examples in the Community's history that demonstrate that in an emergency national interests and national solutions are preferred by the member governments to Community interests and solutions, France's action and later change of mind are not surprising.[17] The French action was one of the major causes of the inability of the economic and monetary union to proceed to the second stage at the end of 1973, as had been planned. That phase was to see a further restriction in the disparities between currency rates to 1 percent and concerted intervention in the exchange markets by the Monetary Cooperation Fund. Clearly, the day of monetary union has not arrived, and may never arrive. This judgment is corroborated by a careful study made under the auspices of the Commission by a group of European economics professors and business experts, published in March 1975. It states:

> Europe is no nearer to [the] E.M.U. [Economic and Monetary Union] than in 1969. In fact if there has been any movement it has been backward. The Europe of the Sixties represented a relatively harmonious economic and monetary entity which was undone in the course of recent years; national economic and monetary policies have never in 25 years been more discordant, more divergent, than they are today.

> The only thing to be said is that each national policy is seeking to solve problems and to overcome difficulties which arise in each individual country, without reference to Europe as an entity. The diagnosis is at national level; efforts are

made at national level. The coordination of national policies is a pious wish which is hardly ever achieved in practice.

The result is that when one speaks of Europe one is talking basically about a geographical entity situated between the U.S.A. and the U.S.S.R., composed of States which trade intensively among themselves but which in most other respects behave in their national affairs and in world affairs according to the trends and the particular interests of each.[18]

The study suggests as first steps toward a realistic economic and monetary union the formulation of a comprehensive industrial policy that aims at developing the potential of the large-scale market of the Community, the rapid liberalization of capital movement to support and to benefit from this large market, increasing cooperation of firms at the European level, and a far-reaching uniform energy policy built around the International Energy Agency, constituted in Paris by the OECD.[19] In the meantime, some means must be found to bridge the gap between the snake and floating currencies of some of the member states if the Common Market is to continue its proper operation. The achievement of a judicious reform of the international monetary system would represent major progress in that direction.

The Reform of the International Monetary System

The increasing inconvertibility of the U.S. dollar that began in the early 1960s and was made official by President Nixon's decision in August 1971 to "close the gold window" completely, recurring monetary crises in Western Europe caused by the dollar's problem, and disparate national economic policies of the EC member states have created continuing international monetary chaos. Although the Smithsonian agreement of December 1971 (described euphorically by President Nixon as the most significant monetary agreement in the history of the world) was to produce new stability when the ten major countries of the world accepted new exchange rates vis-à-vis the dollar, this pleasant vista was short-lived. The agreed-upon

273

margin of permissible fluctuation of 4.5 percent was insufficient to cope with the growing deficits of the U.S. balance of payments for 1970 to 1972 and the transnational shifts of large masses of national currencies. As a consequence, the Smithsonian system broke down in early 1973 despite a second devaluation of the dollar, and the central rates were abandoned by all major countries that allowed their currencies to float freely on the exchange markets.[20] Since then, a number of meetings have been held by the IMF and its Committee of Twenty[21] to find a way back to monetary order, but these worldwide negotiations have not achieved any concrete results. Indeed, as Robert Triffin states, these negotiations "proceed at such a slow pace that they are inevitably by-passed by recurrent crises," while "crisis management entails at best hurried consultation among a handful of countries, or at most unilateral action by individual countries."[22] All these conditions have been further aggravated by the high price for crude oil that must be paid to the OPEC countries, a problem to which we will turn later.

The failure of the Community to create a joint float of all member state currencies vis-à-vis the dollar means that only six EC currencies are moving together now, but as mentioned earlier, the Norwegian, Swedish, and Austrian currencies are at present linked to this joint float. Yet at least in terms of international trade it is the West European monetary area that should be the center of gravity for world exchange rates since the EC trade with the world is three times as large as that of the United States, and 67.3 percent is conducted within Western Europe.[23]

During the negotiations on the reform of the international monetary system in the IMF and the Committee of Twenty[24] the EC member states sought to present a common front. Meeting in London in July 1972 the EC Ministers of Finance arrived at an agreement on the general objectives of such a reform. They include the following principles: fixed, but adjustable parities; the general convertibility of currencies; effective international regulation of the world supply of liquid resources; and a reduction in the role of national currencies as reserve instruments.[25] The Community is very much in favor of a compulsory and multilateral system of convertibility in which all national currencies have equal rights and obligations. Previous inequalities should be corrected by a system of intervention in one or several currencies. At the same time pressure should be brought to bear on countries that accumulate excessive reserves to ensure equilibrium and stability of parities.[26]

Despite the apparent reasonableness of these objectives, detailed implementation is difficult and very slow. A number of disagreements exist among the Group of Twenty countries:

1. Under what circumstances could pressures or sanctions be applied to a country that had failed to take adequate corrective measures of adjustment on surplus or deficits in its balance of payments, and what kind of pressures should be applied? Should these pressures be other than financial? With the European Community holding a powerful position on any authorized IMF body (its voting strength is almost 50 percent larger than that of the United States) would member states be reluctant to take adjustment action against any other member government and be accused of being a "protective society"?

2. In the area of convertibility, should settlement arrangements between countries that hold currencies in official reserves and the country whose currencies are so held be mandatory or optional?

3. What transactions in gold will be permissible to the monetary authorities, including the IMF, other than the normal settlement at the current official price? With the SDRs agreed to become the principal reserve asset, the role of gold and reserve currencies is being reduced, as indicated by the IMF decisions of September 1975.

It seems necessary that a fairly detailed code of international conduct must characterize the new international monetary system, which legitimizes actions of one state impinging on the sovereignty of another. Only in this manner can governmental leaders explain unpleasant monetary actions to their national constituencies and reduce adverse domestic political reactions

275

to a minimum. With every country having its particular national interests to be protected or promoted, many objective rules must be elaborated to guide national monetary action, and to ensure that the whole system will work. This applies also to the Community countries, despite their agreement on common objectives, because these objectives are in the nature of principles and require detailed regulations to make the new system palatable to individual member states. Although the snake arrangement reflects the objective of six Community countries to return to generally fixed exchange rates for the international monetary system (this also seems to be the long-term desire of the three member states outside the snake—Italy, Great Britain, and Ireland),[27] the floating rate system is likely to remain the governing principle for many years to come. The United States and Japan seem to prefer it this way and as long as they hold to their positions, it is doubtful that Great Britain and Ireland will give up the floating of their currencies. However, efforts are under way to refine the floating rate system[28] in order to prevent the type of wide fluctuation of exchange rates that could seriously harm international trade.

Within the EC one of the continuing problems is the disparity of national economic policies. For example, in July 1974, while Germany pursued a restrictive and deflationary policy, more or less in keeping with EC antiinflation guidelines and as a partial result of having accumulated a large balance of payments surplus, Great Britain embarked on an expansionist policy, although with certain safeguards. Under such circumstances Community monetary solidarity is difficult to achieve, and concrete working rules can hardly be elaborated.[29] Harmful deficits caused by the rise in petroleum prices ought to be remedied, at least in part, by specific EC solidarity measures, but remedies are applied on an ad hoc basis—witness the Italian problem discussed earlier—and few general, long-term policy devices and mechanisms for this purpose have been shaped.

One of these measures, created by the Council of Ministers in October 1974, is a Community loan mechanism.[30] We should note that this mechanism is limited to the expenditure of $3 billion, covering both borrowed capital and interest. In view of the "petroleum deficit" of the Community member states, expected to reach $20 billion in 1975, and perhaps a higher figure in later years, the loan operation will satisfy only 10 percent of the needs.

There is no conclusive evidence that the Monetary Committee has been able to increase its capacity to produce common Community positions. The Commission's role in the Monetary Committee's meetings, the meetings of the Finance Ministers of the Community, and other international meetings has tended to be that of the silent guest. Although the Commission has been represented at sessions of the Group of Ten[31] and OECD working parties since 1971, and has been invited to participate in the deliberations, the common position of the Community is not presented by a Commission member but by the Chairman of the Council of Ministers. Nevertheless, despite the weakness of the Commission's position, and the activities in the Monetary Committee (which more often than not resemble an inter-governmental rather than a Community process), some cautious attempts have been made to correct balance of payments inequalities within the Community. For example, EC countries with payment surpluses (Germany and the Benelux countries) were encouraged in 1974 to moderate internal production in order to give the deficit-ridden member states (Italy, France, and Great Britain) opportunities to expand exports to the former. Despite these efforts the problem of adjusting the economies of the member states to the outflow of enormous funds for petroleum purchases and of recycling these funds, which the Arab countries invest in various parts of the world, remains far from being solved satisfactorily. We will analyze the troublesome energy problem and its effect on the Community in the next section.

ENERGY PROBLEMS

Although many warnings were given beginning in the early 1970s that the gradual exhaustion of the world's petroleum resources would someday lead to increased prices for crude oil, it was the embargo of the Arab oil producing countries on shipments to the United States and Western Europe following the Arab–Israeli war that caused the steep rise in petroleum costs during the latter part of 1973. This embargo was coupled with a progressive reduction of crude oil production and was designed to cause a shift from generally pro-Israeli attitudes to a more friendly position toward the Arab countries. Whether this action was conceived exclusively by the foreign ministries and chancelleries of the Arab oil producing countries or whether politically sophisticated executives of the multinational oil companies participated in devising this plan is difficult to determine. Clearly, the oil companies had an interest in leveling up their revenues through higher prices and they may have seen in the Arab frustrations of the aftermath of the Yom Kippur war an opportunity to achieve this goal by careful collusion with the Arab governments. In view of the finite nature of oil resources and the need to find additional reserves and alternate sources of energy, which requires huge outlays of capital, the objective of the oil companies to increase reserves may be understandable despite the questionable methods used. However, the international and domestic consequences of this endeavor may well be long-lasting and could seriously damage the economic, political, and social fabric of most nations of the world. Several factors account for this.

1. Instead of an expected balance of payments surplus of $10 billion in 1974, the OECD countries suffered a deficit of over $30 billion in that year. Some countries found their economies hurt more than others. Italy experienced a $12 billion deficit, but West Germany managed to hang onto a balance of payments surplus.[32] For 1980 the United States anticipates a deficit of $20 billion as a result of the higher oil prices, a deficit that may reach $30 billion in 1985.

2. The huge outflows of funds to pay for oil have a damaging impact on the normal international trade pattern, inasmuch as national governments resort to protectionist measures to curb imports and at the same time use various means such as subsidies to pro-

mote exports in order to find the foreign currencies to pay for petroleum products. We have already noted that in 1974 Italy was forced to reintroduce temporary tariffs in intra-Community trade to reduce imports, and Denmark had to resort to similar measures on certain goods. These types of restrictive action to international trade may be only the beginning as governments search for national solutions to their problems, and among these solutions may be further devaluations of currencies to stimulate exports.

For developing countries without their own oil resources the rise in their bills for petroleum products is equally, if perhaps not more serious than for the economically advanced states. It is estimated that the annual cost for oil products needed by these countries will rise by $10 billion, which would almost wipe out the foreign aid they receive from the OECD member states.[33] In view of the very serious political ramifications of such cuts in foreign aid, other means must be found to provide minimum financial support to many developing countries, but Western advanced countries will be hard put to raise additional foreign aid or provide low interest loans unless such aid comes from Arab oil producers. Despite rhetoric to this effect from some Arab countries, little concrete help has been offered so far.

3. The rise in oil prices has materially contributed to worldwide inflation. As a result, disposable income has been reduced, new wage demands stimulated, giving added impetus to higher prices and thereby leading to continued upward movement in the vicious spiral of inflation. While businessmen may be able to protect themselves somewhat from the cancer of inflation, the bulk of wage earners and retirees suffer. Moreover, lowered disposable income and purposeful deflationary policies by national governments are apt to produce greater unemployment and perhaps depression. As can already be seen in many Western

279

countries, increasing inequalities of income lead to sharpened political polarization, and this in turn diminishes political stability. If national governments are unable to cope with the increasing difficulties, internal turmoil may ensue, and international conflict and chaos may not be far behind. It is thus evident that the problem of energy needs far-reaching international solutions and that only comprehensive energy policies transcending national boundaries and national egoism may prevent worldwide depression and economic and social decay.

Attempts to Develop Community Energy Policies

During the last few years efforts have been made by the EC Commission and Council of Ministers to define comprehensive energy policies covering not only petroleum, but also natural gas, coal, shale, hydropower, and nuclear fission materials. With respect to the last energy source, Euratom had been expected to play a central role when it was established in 1958. It was hoped that atomic energy was a functional area that would lend itself to rapid integration, because by giving Euratom the task of developing the peaceful uses of this new energy source it entered a field where long-existing national industries such as coal and steel and their vested interests did not exist. Hence, it seemed that a truly "European" industry could be developed without hindrance by vested national interests. But this hope was not fulfilled. In fact, despite initial efforts by the United States to deal exclusively with the Euratom institutions on matters of nuclear energy[34] in order to give them backing and legitimacy, the Euratom program never really got off the ground. The prestige factor of being a nuclear nation, which was of paramount importance to France,[35] and the desire of the other member states to develop their own nuclear electric generating facilities and research programs emasculated any real cooperation within Euratom. Its main activities today are the coordination of research and inspection services for the International Atomic Energy Agency (IAEA), but carrying out even these limited activities has been hampered by a continuing struggle to obtain sufficient budgetary support.

Euratom and the IAEA

Despite its very minor role in the generation of electricity from nuclear sources, Eruatom was given an important international responsibility in the inspection of the effectiveness of safeguards to insure that member states not possessing nuclear weapons capabilities did not divert fissionable materials for military purposes. The nuclear cooperation agreement between the United States and Euratom concluded in 1958 provided for the latter to carry out such inspections of member states' peaceful nuclear activities subject to U.S. verification. When the Nonproliferation Treaty (NPT) had been concluded in 1968 and the IAEA was given the dominant authority for the application and inspection of safeguards, the question was raised as to how this would affect the self-inspection system of Euratom. All member states except France sought to elaborate a common stand with the Commission, which would ensure continuation of the basic Euratom system. France argued that the issue was one for the member governments to work out without any involvement of Euratom institutions. In the end, however, the Community view prevailed.[36] Arguing that the NPT–IAEA provisions would violate the preceding U.S.–Euratom inspection arrangements that some nuclear facilities were controlled by Euratom and thus not fully under the authority of the member states,[37] Euratom was given a special role in acting as inspection representative of the IAEA vis-à-vis the EC member states. As Paul Szasz points out, Euratom began

> to act in part as agent of its member states, in part as an instrument of the Agency, in part as an independent actor carrying out its peculiar responsibilities, and in most respects as a buffer between the Agency and the Euratom states.[38]

281

As a consequence, Euratom continues to carry out inspections of member states' activities in the field of peaceful uses of nuclear energy; the IAEA is limited mainly to observing these inspection services. Moreover, Euratom, rather than the member states, keeps the necessary records on the receipt, use, and disposition of fissionable materials, and the reports normally made by states to IAEA are made by the member governments to Euratom.[39]

Guidelines for Comprehensive Policies

Voices were heard again and again in the Community during the 1960s that the formulation of a comprehensive energy policy was a necessity. Although no stipulation to this effect is found in the EC Treaties, such a policy is needed to ensure the continuous and effective operation of the Common Market. Moreover, it has been argued that the energy sector of any country is by nature transnational, since energy sources are unevenly distributed and that therefore energy problems cannot be solved in the national context.

In December 1968 the Commission submitted to the Council of Ministers a document entitled "First Guidelines for a Community Energy Policy." The principles underlying such a policy are competition and the interest of the consumers. Security of supply must be ensured at prices that are relatively stable and as low as possible. Recourse to governmental intervention in the energy market is to be only a last resort, but supervisory functions are necessary. Supply difficulties must be presented by regular examination of supply conditions, and all impediments to a truly common market for energy within the Community—for example discriminatory indirect taxation—have to eliminated.[40] The guidelines were approved by the Council in November 1969.

Of course, from the acceptance of general guidelines on an energy policy to a concretely formulated policy is a long and difficult path, especially when one takes into account the often demonstrated tendencies of the member states to go their own way and pursue what they perceive to be their own high-priority national interests. Between 1969 and the middle of 1973 some small steps were taken to initiate a general energy policy. For example, the maintenance of a minimum level of crude oil and petroleum products was made compulsory.[41] In 1972 the Council adopted regulations notifying the Commission of all hydrocarbon imports and of investment projects in the oil, natural gas, and electricity sectors that would be of interest to the Community.[42]

In April 1973 the Commission forwarded to the Council a memorandum in which a number of precise guidelines and actions were proposed for future relations with energy exporting and importing countries. In addition, suggestions were made for the organization of the Community oil market and for policies in the atomic energy, coal, and natural gas sectors, as well as for environmental protection. With rumblings of forthcoming oil shortages as reserves were being depleted, the Council requested the Commission on May 22, 1973, to prepare concrete and comprehensive policy proposals by the end of that year.[43] With respect to nuclear fuels the Council set up a Standing Committee on Uranium Enrichment (COPENUR), which was charged with ensuring the sufficiency of the Community's uranium supply, most of which had been coming from the United States.[44]

The use of the oil weapon by the Arab petroleum producing countries in the aftermath of the Israeli–Arab conflict, whereby oil production was progressively reduced and embargoes imposed on selected consuming nations considered "too friendly" toward Israel, brought EC plans for comprehensive energy policies into disarray. Where solidarity among EC member states should have been the order of the day in the fall of 1973, every member government sought to safeguard its own interests first, presenting a rather contemptible demonstration of naked national egoism. The Netherlands' defiant sympathy with the cause of the Jewish state made it a victim of a complete Arab embargo on oil shipments. Yet its Community partners, who did not display Holland's pugnacious outspokenness to the Arabs, refused to help. This prompted the Dutch to exert pressure on their neighbors, Germany, France, and Belgium to obtain either Community political support against the Arabs and engage in some oil-sharing arrangement or face the cut-off of Dutch supplies of North Sea natural gas.[45] But little immediate support was received as higher gasoline prices, gasless Sundays, and other emergency measures induced individual EC member countries to seek special favors and special oil deals from the Arabs, with France in the forefront of such endeavors.

The apex in fawning at the feet of the Arab leaders came during the Copenhagen summit meeting of heads and chiefs of government of the EC countries in December 1973. This meeting was called to give new impetus to the European union, make progress in the movement toward economic and political union, and work toward a common voice of Europe in world affairs. But things did not quite work out this way despite a charitable face-saving communique at the end of the meeting. On the eve of the opening of the conference, the foreign affairs ministers of six Arab oil producing countries arrived at the Danish capital. These unexpected arrivals replaced Community business as the center of interest of the conference. An editorial in *Agence Europe Bulletin* of December 15, 1973, asked the question:

> Is it a European Summit in which the Arab powers are allowed to participate, or a case of an Arab Summit being held in parallel? We may ask from where this initiative came, which has clearly caused some surprise. In Algiers it had been decided to address a "message" to the European Summit, but it was not known that the "bearers" of this message would be either so numerous or so high-ranking.

The number of words that were written into the Copenhagen communique on energy policy was in diametric opposition to the actions taken by the heads and chiefs of government of the EC member states. The Nine allowed themselves to be divided and ruled by the oil producing countries, which divided them into friendly and not-so-friendly countries. Two of them, France and Britain, sold their dignity for the favors of the Arabs. The most badly affected member of the Community, the Netherlands, was forgotten even though the Dutch had been one of the most vociferous champions of British entry for years. Solidarity in the Community was certainly nothing more than a sham.[46]

Despite the debacle of the Copenhagen conference, the Commission pushed on in seeking a common approach to the problems of energy rather than see bilateral deals develop between the member states and the Arab oil producing countries. The United States was also in favor of a common approach, and wanted it to include Canada, Japan, and Norway. After various delays, the U.S. government succeeded in convening a 13-nation Washington Energy Conference in February 1974. The purpose was to work out a common program for easing the energy crisis. In the end it was agreed to set up a coordinating group, which was to decide how to organize in the most efficient manner the program of coordination. In particular, the Energy Coordinating Group (ECG) was given the missions of:

1) the conservation of energy and restraint of demand

2) setting up a system of allocating oil supplies in times of emergency and severe shortages

3) the acceleration of development of additional energy sources so as to diversify energy supplies

4) the acceleration of energy research and development programs through international cooperative efforts[47]

France declined to participate in this coordinating group, voicing again the old refrain that the United States was trying to establish economic and political hegemony over Europe. Perhaps because of the resistance of France to identify itself with the general aims of the Conference, no agreement was reached on a proposed "code of conduct" to regulate the efforts that several governments were making to work out special deals with Mideastern oil producers in order to assure their own energy supplies. France, for example, was negotiating pacts with Saudi Arabia, Kuwait, and Libya that would guarantee it millions of barrels of oil in return for stepped-up deliveries of French weapons and technology to the producers. These efforts later obtained results and set an example that other members of Washington Conference participants were to follow.

French suspicions that the conference was called to reassert U.S. leadership over disintegrating alliance affairs and to create

285

some new interlocking machinery to tie European energy plans and activities to American resources were not entirely unfounded. American science and technology were not only used as a bait to solve energy problems per se, but they were also to be means to achieve diplomatic purposes. Commercial gains for the supply of American-built nuclear generating equipment and enriched uranium may also have been motivating factors. To reinforce the proposed technological ties in the energy field, former President Nixon reminded European statesmen during a White House dinner held on the occasion of the Washington Conference that they could not be independent of the United States in economic and political affairs and at the same time expect to rely on American support in security areas. Nixon declared that "Security and economic considerations are inevitably linked, and energy cannot be separated from either."[48] As Henry Nau points out, the energy crisis was to supply practical proof to Europeans that they could not do without U.S. leadership in alliance affairs and that such leadership could not be accepted in security areas and rejected in economic areas.[49]

Despite U.S. rejection of bilateral agreements with Arab oil producing countries negotiated by France, Great Britain, Germany, and Japan (because such agreements appeared to signal defection from existing alliance systems), the U.S. government also concluded a series of bilateral accords on trade, investment, and technology with Arab states.[50] The first of the American agreements was signed with Saudi Arabia. U.S. justification for this and other bilateral accords was their link to a Middle East settlement with an eventual moderation of oil prices.[51]

The U.S. government extended a special invitation to the Community to participate in the Washington Conference, an invitation that had also been favored by the member states. In view of the anticipated position of France, participation by the Community as an entity raised the problem of reaching a unified Community position. On the other hand, to decline the invitation could have meant exclusion of Community institutions from the search for energy solutions, which would have further weakened Euratom functions. For this reason, the Commission was represented at the energy conference by the Presidents of the Council of Ministers, and the Commission participated in its sessions.[52]

Following the Washington Conference, the Committee of Permanent Representatives and experts from the Council of Ministers examined the possibility of implementing the common energy proposals made earlier by the Commission itself, hoping that France could be induced to join the other member states in the deliberations of the ECG, also known as the Group of Twelve[53] and so progress toward all objectives could be made. The delegations of the member states working on the policy proposals were confident that acceptance and implementation would result in greater solidarity of the member states. Of course it was not surprising that there were some divergent opinions regarding the Community's stance toward the outside world, France and Italy were especially anxious to see the Community express itself with a single voice concerning energy; the other delegations felt that solidarity had to take into consideration coordination with the positions of other consumer and producer countries. Nevertheless, all delegations were hopeful that the Council of Ministers would be able to approve the broad outlines of a common energy policy with appropriate strategies to implement this policy, including the establishment of a Community Energy Council.

The crucial meeting of the Council of Ministers took place on July 24, 1974, and to the consternation of the Commission, ended in complete failure.[54] Eight member states, including France, appeared to have agreed on voluntary objectives and the establishment of an Energy Council, which would restructure the planning, supply, and demand in the energy field. The British representative, however, refused to go along. Fortunately, the British reversed their position two months later and the Council approved the main guidelines of the energy strategies proposed by the Commission.[55]

Despite this approval, however, the obstacles for full Community participation in solving the energy problems of the Group of Twelve were not removed, because the French continued their refusal to be involved in the work of this group. As a consequence, the Community could not be represented in future sessions of this group or in any other multilateral effort, as, for example, a group under the auspices of the OECD. Full participation of the Community, not simply as an observer but as a decision-making partner, was of the utmost importance, especially since it was planned by the Group of Twelve to set up an international energy agency within the framework of the OECD. One of the problems that could be solved only by full Community action was the assurance that future agency decisions would be compatible with the EEC Treaty and not in contradiction with the common energy policy being evolved within the EC.[56] The International Energy Agency was established in November 1974 with headquarters in Paris. The membership was expanded to 18 countries to include Austria, Spain, Sweden, Switzerland, Turkey, and New Zealand; France declined to join. The IEA took over the functions of the Group of Twelve.

After nearly a year of controversy in the EC Council, a common energy policy was adopted in December 1974. The major goal of this policy is to reduce Community dependence on imported energy by 1985 to a level of at least 50 percent, if not 40 percent. Table 8.1 shows the hoped-for Community supply pattern in 1985 based on 50 or 40 percent dependence. In terms of net figures, the Community energy needs in 1973 were 1005 million tons of oil or its equivalent, and are estimated to rise to 1575 million tons in 1985.[57] To achieve these objectives, the production of soft coal and peat must be increased and the import of coal from third countries expanded; and research on and production of natural gas must be stepped up. Also, it will be necessary to construct new nuclear power stations of at least 160 GW(c) (million watts of electricity), if possible, of 200 GW(c) by 1985; and to develop new sites for hydroelectric and geothermal power plants.[58]

Concurrently with the development of the Community energy objectives the Group of Twelve had been formulating and activating an international action program in the event of future oil supply crises, the essential aspect of which is a scheme of sharing oil resources in such a contingency. The major trigger for international action and the sharing of oil supplies begins when oil deliveries fall below 90 percent of normal supplies.[59]

288

In addition to oil sharing the Twelve obligated themselves to continuing energy-saving measures and to cooperation in the field of research and development of new energy sources.[60]

Table 8.1
Total Primary Energy Requirements[a]
(percent)

	For the record		1985 Objectives (figures rounded off)	
	1973 Estimates	1985 Initial Forecast	50 percent dependence	40 percent dependence
Solid fuels	22.6	10	17	17
Oil	61.4	64	49	41
Natural gas	11.6	15	18	23
Hydroelectric and geothermal power	3.0	2	3	3
Nuclear energy	1.4	9	13	16
Total requirements	100	100	100	100

Source: *Bulletin of the European Communities Commission,* no. 12, (1974):15.

a. Internal consumption + exports + bunkers.

Looking into the future of the international program developed by the Group of Twelve, taken over later by the IEA, it is clear that the implementation of this program will require a minimal institutional framework due to the need for continuous statistical and other kinds of information required for the coordination of the program among the participating countries. It is conceivable that the OECD may provide this framework, since all members of the IEA also belong to the OECD. If this were to be the accepted institutional structure for the coordination and action program, most activities would take place in Paris, where the headquarters of OECD are located. As a consequence, participation by France in the IEA may be encouraged, and if she were to accept, the Commission could also be included in the work of the IEA. In this way, additional common Community policies could also be achieved through an indirect route, and this would constitute considerable progress. The significance for the Community of such a step is further enhanced by the fact that the IEA may concern itself also with other aspects of the energy crisis. Among these are the organization of international cooperation in the field of enriched uranium production; economic and monetary coordination measures to be implemented to cope with the multiple effects of price rises, discussed earlier; and relations with the non-energy producing developing countries hard hit by the oil price increases.[61]

In order to find a solution for the problems facing the petroleum consumers and producers a prepatory meeting for an international energy conference was convened in April 1975. The participants for the consumers were the EC, the United States, and Japan. The producers were represented by Algeria as leaders and by Iran, Venezuela, and Saudi Arabia. Since the Third World would be affected by any conference of this type, India, Brazil, and Zaire were asked to attend. The IEA, OPEC, and the U.N. were represented by observers.

The agenda for the preparatory meeting proved to be troublesome. The United States wanted the conference to be limited to petroleum issues (prices, harmonization between supply and demand, petrodollars), whereas the developing countries wanted to extend it to other raw materials and the relation between the industrialized and developing countries in general. Of the EC member states, Great Britain and the Netherlands did not object to a fairly extensive agenda, but France, leaning toward the U.S. position, favored separate conferences for each product or group of products.[62]

Fruitless disputes on the title, scope, and procedures of the planned conference marked the preparatory meeting from the beginning. The rigid attitude of the oil producing and other developing countries could not be overcome by any of the compromises offered by the consumer states, and the emerging deadlock aborted the meeting.[63]

Despite this failure to initiate a useful dialogue between the oil consumer and producer countries, an IEA ministerial meeting at the end of May 1975 suggested new initiatives for the resumption of the preparatory meeting. Secretary of State

Kissinger suggested that for such a new meeting a number of committees be established to explore the problems of raw materials other than petroleum, but substantive negotiations would have to be conducted in fora other than the energy conference. The communique issued at the end of the IEA session had a distinct optimistic tone, lauding present and future cooperation not only in energy conservation measures, but also in the acceleration of nuclear energy programs and the search for other alternate sources of energy.[64]

Following the IEA meeting a very preliminary "Euro–Arab" dialogue was initiated in Cairo in June 1975 to explore ways of more fruitful cooperation between the Community and its member states with Arab countries in the Middle East and North Africa. Conceivably, these could include the issue of oil deliveries in return for technological and economic assistance. However, no concrete results emerged from this meeting because the Arabs insisted on a general political contest and the Europeans were interested in a few specific projects.[65] Nevertheless, this dialogue may be resumed later and could be seen as part of a broader offensive on the part of the EC and the United States to begin future realistic talks between the oil consumers and producers as envisaged in the May IEA session, and confirmed in the July 1975 summit meeting of EC chiefs of government[66] in order to assure adequate petroleum supplies and the maintenance, if not reduction, of petroleum prices.

In the meantime, the member governments have fully realized that research and development in the generation of electricity from nuclear sources must be accelerated as much as possible. Estimates now indicate that France and Germany will be in the forefront of the production of electrical nuclear power and that two-thirds of electric power thus produced in the European Community by the end of the decade will be done by France and Germany. Both countries are expected to have an estimated nuclear power capacity of 20,000 megawatts by 1980. As Table 8.1 shows, by 1985 the Community should have reduced its dependence on oil and increased its use of electricity from nuclear sources. By the year 2000, 80 percent of the electricity utilized may well be produced from this source, and if this expectation can be realized, the Community will have

291

achieved a considerable level of independence from oil. New developments in the construction of nuclear reactors for peaceful purposes may also make the European Community countries less dependent on U.S. nuclear fuel supplies, on which they must heavily rely at present.[67] In this field, France and Germany have established various cooperative undertakings, both in the areas of basic research as well as in the mining of uranium.[68] Moreover, two European enterprises have entered the uranium-enrichment field. They are URENCO, a British-led consortium with which the Germans and Dutch are associated, and EURODIF, led by France and drawing on Italian, Belgian, and Spanish resources. Both URENCO and EURODIF have aggressively sought customers and URENCO has been able to penetrate the U.S. market. The American reaction to these undertakings has been less than friendly; not only did they signify serious competition to the entrenched American position in the worldwide delivery of enriched uranium, but they also made it more difficult to tie in sales for American generators with guaranteed uranium shipments. Despite American attempts to raise the issue of nuclear proliferation, the European developments may signal the beginning of the end of American superiority in nuclear technology, and the emergence of a new center for scientific and technological excellence in the peaceful use of nuclear energy.

The Commission has been anxious to develop some kind of common policy for enrichment, and has participated in talks under the American proposal to share enriched uranium. If a European enrichment plant cannot be built, the Commission would like to see, as a minimum, existing facilities brought under European management. However, national concerns have precluded even this arrangement, although the Council of Ministers considers URENCO and EURODIF to be part of a European framework for the generation of electricity from nuclear sources.[69] As the various nuclear capabilities are strengthened, the need for purely national solutions to the problems of nuclear energy among the member states may diminish; and hence more comprehensive energy policies and the Commission's greater role in the management of these policies may be encouraged.

STRATEGIC PROBLEMS

Since the late 1950s many Europeans have been doubtful about the resolve of the United States to engage in nuclear warfare with the Soviet Union in the event of a Soviet conventional or nuclear attack on Western Europe, especially if the nuclear attack were carried out with low-yield weapons directed against secondary targets such as Lubeck or Grenoble. Over the years, the U.S. government has made many statements seeking to assure the West Europeans that nuclear aid would come in case of Soviet aggression, but even these repeated declarations have not been able to dispel the doubts in Europe. In fact, during the last few years these doubts have grown as a result of the many direct negotiations that have occurred between the two superpowers.

What can the West Europeans do to increase the assurance of their defense? Are there any alternatives to the nuclear strategic umbrella provided by the United States? What common European policies may provide greater security, and what role could the Community as an institutionalized decision-making framework play in the formulation of these policies?

The first effort to make a distinctly European contribution to the defense of Western Europe and the United States was the abortive plan to establish a European Defense Community with integrated European armed forces. Although a treaty to this effect was signed in 1952, it was not ratified because the French Chamber of Deputies refused to give its approval. During the 1960s a variety of efforts were made by different West European countries to cooperate in the construction of military planes and other hardware. Table 8.2 provides a graphic illustration of these plans and includes a nonmilitary plane called the Airbus. The MRCA 75, a multirole combat aircraft, is in an advanced stage of development and may join the air forces of some of the Community member states by the end of the 1970s. However, the efforts of European technological cooperation in the military field have been affected adversely by the desire of many EC governments to give preference to national producers of materiel and by the tendency of U.S. manufacturers to engage in hard-sell campaigns to furnish American planes, tanks, and guns. The sale of the F–16 combat plane to Belgium and the Nether-

Table 8.2

Multinational Complementary Agreements for Technological Collaboration

Project/Type	Year Started	United Kingdom	German Federal Republic	France	Italy	Belgium	Netherlands	Status
Atlantique maritime patrol aircraft	1959		*	*	*	*	*	In progress
J-79 turbojet for F-104G	1960-65		*		*	*		Concluded
Tyne turboprop for Atlantique and Transall	1961		*	*		*		In progress
RB-162 lift jet	1965	*	*			*		In progress
Fokker F-28 Fellowship	1965	*	*			*		In progress
SA-321 Super Frelon heavy-duty helicopter	1967		*	*				In progress
A-300B Airbus	1969		*	*				Concluded
MRCA 75	1969	*	*		*			In progress
Total		3	8	4	3	5	1	

Source: William E. A. Wulf, "An analysis of European Technological Collaboration and Its Implications for Further European Integration: With an Emphasis on the Collaboration Efforts of the European Aerospace Industries" unpublished M.A. thesis, Louisiana State University in New Orleans, January 1970, pp. 141–142.

lands in 1975 triumphing over the competing French Mirage plane is a case in point.

When it became clear toward the end of the 1960s that Great Britain was likely to become a member of the European Community, voices were heard encouraging the expansion of efforts at military cooperation to the nuclear field. These efforts were stimulated not only by the continuing fear that the United States might withhold assistance with nuclear weapons in the event of a crisis, but also by the increased demands in Congress that the number of American forces in Europe be reduced. All these developments set the stage for serious consideration of the desirability and feasibility of closer collaboration among the European alliance members in the military sector. This collaboration was not conceived of as a competition to NATO but was envisaged as a strengthening of the NATO alliance.

A European Nuclear Force

Proponents of cooperative action in the nuclear field were initially a group of conservative Members of Parliament who anticipated important payoffs for West European unification and greater independence from American nuclear weapons, on whose complete control the U.S. government continued to insist. Although neither the Johnson nor the Nixon administrations had any objection to this plan,[70] the organization of a nuclear force poses some very difficult organizational problems.

As Harold van B. Cleveland points out, a European nuclear force might consist of either simply British or French national contingents, or it might include a jointly owned and fully integrated denationalized force.[71] German participation could take the form of financial and technological contributions and perhaps membership on a control board (whose decisions would have to be unanimous), but would not include a separate or separable national contingent of nuclear weapons. An arrangement of this kind would preclude a potential German nuclear force and would be in keeping with the Nuclear Non-Proliferation Treaty, which was signed by the West German government

295

after Brandt had assumed the Chancellorship. It would also be consistent with British membership in the European Community and could, in fact, cement the relationship between the three major powers in this regional integration experiment. It could provide a new impetus for an integrated European conventional army, whose creation within the framework of the EDC was aborted in 1954. During the 1960s de Gaulle and his ministers had dropped hints from time to time about a European nuclear force, for which the French nuclear weapons—the famous *force de frappe*—would be the core unit, but no concrete suggestions seem to have been made by the de Gaulle government.

Clearly, German participation in such a nuclear force is the most crucial and complex issue in the organization of such a force. German sensitivities with respect to a second-rank position in international politics are well known and are understandable in view of the tremendous economic strength the Federal Republic has been able to amass during the 1960s and 1970s. Therefore, it came somewhat as a surprise when in the spring of 1969 Franz Josef Strauss, former defense and finance minister of the Federal Republic, with a reputation of being strongly nationalistic, declared his approval for an integrated European nuclear force composed of British and French contingents as a desirable step toward a European federation. Strauss suggested that Britain and France would be in full, exclusive control of their nuclear weapons so long as they were stationed on their respective territories. However, if these weapons were deployed on the soil of a third country, a "double-key" system would have to prevail, according to which the government of the third country would have a veto right over the use of these weapons, but would not be able to order their employment without the permission of the respective French or British authorities.[72]

Prime Minister Wilson rejected Strauss' views and, responding to a question in the House of Commons, stated that the British government was opposed to a grouping of nuclear weapons under an integrated European nuclear force.[73] This position of the British government was confirmed in April 1970, when Britain's Defense Minister, Denis Healey, pointed out that the thirteen other European members of NATO would not consider such a force acceptable unless they were allowed some influence over it, and unless the creation of such a force would not lead to a reduction of the American commitment on the European continent. However, the Defense Minister of the Conservative Shadow Cabinet, Geoffrey Rippon, continued to support the thesis that French–British cooperation might be the foundation of an independent European deterrent force and thereby would constitute a significant pillar of NATO.[74]

Whether a nuclear capability for the European Community countries is a viable option remains questionable. In the first place, the Community countries that would be only minimally involved in a nuclear capability especially the smaller countries, might well consider the nuclear option as divisive. It therefore would be a disintegrative rather than an integrative effect on Community aspirations for a policital union.

The Eurogroup

Nuclear option built around French and British capabilities may also disturb the harmony among the Eurogroup, consisting of Belgium, Denmark, the Federal Republic of Germany, Greece, Italy, Luxembourg, the Netherlands, Norway, Turkey, and the United Kingdom. For those countries outside the European Community it would represent a privileged group and would thereby reduce the effectiveness of NATO. During the preparation for the negotiations in the Conference on European Security and Cooperation, the NATO countries outside the European Community expressed concern about the exclusive Community caucus convened to agree on a common Community position. The closer the EC members draw together and consult with each other before engaging in consultation with their NATO allies from outside the Community, the more divisive and even disruptive becomes the influence of political cooperation within the EC on political cohesion and effectiveness within NATO. As a consequence, all European NATO partners outside the EC and the NATO bureaucracy carefully watch EC activities in the fields of foreign and security policies.[75]

Community caucuses on security policies may also disturb the United States and Canada and may be regarded as an "exclusive regionalism," which is counterproductive to the mission of NATO. Although the Community countries, striving to achieve at least economic and monetary union and later perhaps political union, cannot be denied the right to elaborate their own policies in all foreign policy fields, a European nuclear force is likely to be the wrong means to move toward political union. Clearly, the political obstacles for the development of a European nuclear capability are enormous, and most of them arise from the alliance itself. In addition, any meaningful participation of West Germany in such a nuclear force would evoke serious objections in the Communist countries of Europe, and therefore would diminish any chances of attaining a long-term detente, which is desired by large numbers of Europeans.

Another European option would be an integrated conventional force for the Community countries, akin to the plans made for the abortive European Defense Community. While such an endeavor could contribute to the policy cohesion of the Community countries, it would raise the same suspicions among the governments of the non-Community European NATO members described above. Until such time that all Western European NATO countries could become members of the Community—an unlikely prospect for the foreseeable future, especially as far as Portugal and Turkey are concerned—it may be best for the total defense posture of NATO to consider the Eurogroup as the main focus for collaboration within NATO. This group has established the European Defense Improvement Program (EDIP), which obligated itself in 1971 to spend $1 billion in additional defense spending over 5 years. Through this program tanks and artillery pieces, various naval vessels, and some modern combat and transport aircraft have been added to NATO's conventional force in Europe. Indeed, in 1973 and 1974 the European spending was increased above the $1 billion annual figure in order to take care of rising prices and to continue the EDIP momentum.[76]

Most of the initiatives for the activities of the Eurogroup have come from Great Britain and Germany. In addition to EDIP, the Eurogroup deals with general planning, which is car-

carried out in association with the meetings of the NATO Defense Ministers in the Defense Planning Committee. The Eurogroup has also elaborated a common position with respect to the presence of American forces in Europe. The members of this group are anxious to maintain the maximum number of U.S. forces in Europe, forces which in fiscal year 1975 were costing the United States about $5 billion. If the expenditures for the United States-based support for these forces is added to the $5 billion figure, the total is $8 billion. This figure represents most accurately the total cost of the U.S. forces in the European area. The U.S. balance of payments deficit resulting from these expenditures has been offset at least in part by the Federal Republic of Germany's willingness to buy military materiel in the United States and purchase U.S. government bonds. Other European NATO allies have also purchased some of their military equipment in the United States. The Jackson–Nunn amendment to the 1974 Defense Appropriation Authorization Act stipulates that unless the European allies offset balance of payments deficits caused by military expenditures in 1975, the President must reduce the number of U.S. forces in NATO Europe by the percentage of the uncovered gap to the total deficit. In the wake of U.S. withdrawal from Indochina and the American Government's need to assure the NATO allies of the firmness of the U.S. defense commitment, U.S. combat forces are likely to be maintained at previous levels in Western Europe. However, some reduction in American forces can be undertaken without damaging their combat effectiveness. This can be done by reducing the logistical support forces and strengthening the combat units of the U.S. Army, Navy, and Air Force.

The structure of the Eurogroup is very simple. Several subordinate working groups have been formed to deal with training, logistics, armaments, and medical service. No special secretariat exists to administer the work of the Eurogroup and most administrative tasks are carried out by the national ministries, whose ministers provide the chairmanships for the group as a whole as well as the subordinate working groups.[77] In this respect the organizational framework resembles that of the Political Committee, which was discussed in chapter 2.

Detente Policy

In the early 1970s the NATO allies responded affirmatively to the overtures of the East Bloc countries for negotiations and detente, and participated in the Conference on Security and Cooperation in Europe (CSCE). However, the United States did not accept the CSCE proposal until the Soviet Union had agreed to negotiations on the Mutual and Balanced Reduction of Forces (MBRF) proposed by NATO initially in 1968 at its meeting in Reykjavik, Iceland. We have already mentioned in chapter 2 the proposals made by the Nine in the preparatory talks for the CSCE taking place in Helsinki.[78] These proposals emerged from the caucus of the Nine and were elaborated in the framework of the Political Committee and the meetings of the Foreign Ministers. They were of particular interest to the Community institutions since they involved economic and technical facets of cooperation and political, humanitarian, and cultural aspects of improving human and cultural contacts between East and West. For these reasons, the Commission argued that although the CSCE was basically a conference of individual states, it should have a voice in the deliberations.

To tackle the problem of Commission participation, an ad hoc group was set up, consisting of representatives from the Ministries of Foreign Affairs of the Community member states and from the Commission. This group was made responsible to the Political Directors (comparable to Deputy Undersecretaries at the Ministries of Foreign Affairs), who constituted the leadership echelon of the Political Committee. The next higher level of responsibility was that of the Foreign Ministers and the President of the Commission. It was within this framework that Community consultations were coordinated and different obligations of the member states were balanced.

A more difficult problem, partly technical and partly of substantive significance, was the direct representation of the Community in the Conference. Clearly the Commission had the right to represent the Community in international organizations when Community competences were involved. On the other hand, in the CSCE, whose membership consisted of states, representation of even one international organization such as the Community could greatly complicate things. If the Community as a legal unit had been given equal status with the states, other international organizations might well have asked for a similar right. The solution found was to permit representatives of the Commission to take part in the Conference as members of the national delegations of the country exercising the presidency of the Community Council of Ministers. However, these Commission representatives were allowed to speak only when questions of Community competence arose.[79]

During the Helsinki Conference and later during the time that the Conference moved to Geneva, many meetings took place at different levels for the coordination of policy proposals. Additional meetings were called in the capital of the country holding the Council presidency. Although the system worked rather well most of the time, there were also major weaknesses. The foremost weakness was the lack of a secretariat, which meant that in each capital where meetings of the Political Committee or the ad hoc group met, temporary logistical facilities had to be set up for preparing agendas, reproducing proposals and amendments, etc. Information about such meetings arrived late at times, and proper preparation was difficult. The problem of language was also serious at times. In the majority of cases French was spoken, in the minority, English was used. Most participants therefore were working most of the time in a foreign language, which even under the best of conditions makes it difficult to argue finer points.

Another problem has been the fact that the Political Directors running the Political Committee were also busy with other responsibilities, and therefore were unable to prepare themselves for the meetings in the proper way. Tickell reports that for this reason

old issues get re-opened, and those concerned with higher matters of policy get entangled—sometimes I fear with relish—in the snares of drafting or redrafting. Sometimes there is conflict between decisions reached in some cozy capital and the ability of those in a smoke-filled negotiating room far away to put them into effect. Things have often moved too fast for the process of consultation up the hierarchy.

301

There have also been times when moving at the pace of the slowest has led to gnashing of teeth; others when one of the Nine has, perhaps due to a misunderstanding, moved ahead of his colleagues and spoken out too boldly in public or appeared to abandon a common position. Few of us have not done this at one time or another. Such slips are inevitable and thus forgiveable, but obviously they should not take place.[80]

Despite these problems, the achievements in evolving common policies have been considerable. From the beginning of the preparatory consultations in Helsinki, the very effectiveness of the Nine, above all because of the day-to-day consultations, had given them unexpected responsibilities of leadership. In these almost daily consultations, many of the conflicting ideas among the Nine were thrashed out and some kind of consensus was reached on how to organize economic cooperation, what to do about cultural exchange, how to assure freer movement of people, and how to increase confidence in new military measures to promote detente.

With the Americans preoccupied with improving their bilateral relations with the Soviet Union, it appeared that the U.S. government preferred to play a relatively modest role. Therefore, while coordination among the fifteen members of the NATO alliance operated relatively well, it was increasingly the Community members who provided the motor and the direction for many proposals submitted in Helsinki despite the suspicions of the non-Community allies referred to earlier.

Preceded by intensive bargaining, the CSCE negotiations came to a successful conclusion in Helsinki in July 1975. In the economic cooperation field the Community countries especially wanted to stipulate that the advantages and obligations resulting from economic, commercial, scientific, and technical cooperation should be "of equal range." With respect to the application of the most-favored-nation-clause they wanted to specify the "spirit of reciprocity.[81] However, in the final agreement, watered down phraseology was used because the Soviet Union did not accept the terminology of the Nine and other Western countries. In the area of exchange of information, ideas, and cultures, the rather specific concepts of the West did not prevail either, since the Soviet Union insisted on the strict maintenance of the principle of sovereignty, limiting the truly free interchange of information and ideas. Initially, the United States was determined that no CSCE agreement could be reached unless the negotiations on Mutual and Balanced Force Reduction (MBFR) would also be successful. However, perhaps because of the increase in Soviet military forces and armament during the last few years and the concern of the U.S. government following the retreat from Vietnam to reassure its NATO partners of its credibility as an ally, the pursuit of MBFR seemed to make little sense in the summer of 1975 and the earlier precondition for the conclusion of the CSCE agreement could be abandoned. Moreover, for many European leaders MBFR was meaningless because they saw in the Vienna negotiations primarily talks on a bilateral U.S.–Soviet level and, in addition, they had no partiular interest to see the presence of American troops reduced while the Soviet Union was expanding its military capabilities.[82] Probably the main winner in the CSCE agreement was the Soviet Union, inasmuch as her hegemony over Eastern Europe received formal confirmation by the West.

In spite of optimistic Communist statements following the Helsinki agreement, it seems that the East European countries had reservations about the development of the CSCE. They had hoped for a short conference in an atmosphere of cooperation with general conclusions and an agreement on the status quo. Instead of this, over a period of three years the Western delegates concentrated on freer movement of people, ideas and information—a subject that the delegates from the East viewed very critically, because they regard proposals in this area as interference in their internal affairs and against their laws, customs and traditions. In turn, the Western delegates continue to hope that although major results were not achieved, the many proposals on freer East–West movement will have had an impact and will produce gradual changes in Eastern Europe that will be beneficial for political and economic cooperation.

In addition, the cooperation among foreign policy officers and large groups of experts of the Community countries that produced common policies for the Nine may well have been invaluable. Cooperation habits can be learned, and if these habits of cooperation can spill over into other areas, areas more sensitive in terms of national foreign policy than those under consideration in Helsinki and Geneva, the Community may eventually be able to "speak with one voice."

On the other hand, as far as the negotiations of the MBRF were concerned, they were clearly outside the realm of competence of the Community, and therefore the coordination activities in this field of policy did not include Community representation. What the future will hold in this respect is difficult to determine at this point. But the limited progress in military and strategic cooperation shown by the Eurogroup, and the rather modest success in transnational cooperation in the building of military hardware suggest that the Community institutions should concentrate on expanding their competences in the economic areas if they wish to broaden their input into the foreign policies of the Nine. We will return to this subject in the next chapter.

NOTES

1. *European Community* (Washington), no. 131 (February, 1970):4; *Agence Europe Bulletin,* January 26, 27, 1970.

2. For details see Robert W. Russell, *"L'Engrenage,* Collegial Style, and the Crisis Syndrome: Lessons from Monetary policy in the European Community," *Journal of Common Market Studies* 12, no 4 (June 1974).

3. EEEC Treaty art. 105, para. 2.

4. See Russell, op. cit.

5. *Fourth General Report,* 1961, p. 11.

6. *Fifth General Report,* 1962, p. 11.

7. *Fourth General Report,* 1970, p. 72, para. 83.

8. For details see *A Plan for the Phased Establishment of an Economic and Monetary Union,* supplement to bulletin no. 3, 1970, of the European Communities.

9. *Fifth General Report,* 1971, p. 137.

10. *Agence Europe Bulletin,* March 9, 1972.

11. The Italian government set up a two-tier exchange market on January 22, 1973, and let both the "commercial" and "financial" lira float. Later in 1973 it received from other EC countries a line of credit amount-

ing to more than $1.5 billion and additional swap credits from some nonmember states.

12. For details see *Seventh General Report,* 1973, pp. 176-178.

13. See *Bulletin of the European Communities,* no. 1 (1974):23.

14. CF. *Eighth General Report,* 1974, pp. 98-99; and *Agence Europe Bulletin,* September 2/3, 1974.

15. *European Community,* no. 183 (January/February 1975):17.

16. Ibid., no. 187 (June 1975):21.

17. See for example, *Die Zeit,* February 1, 1974, p. 1

18. Commission of the European Communities, *Report of the Study Group "Economic and Monetary Union 1980"* (Brussels, March 1975), p. 1-2.

19. For details see ibid., pp. 29-35.

20. Cf. Robert Triffin, "The International Monetary Chaos and the Way Out," *Journal of Common Market Studies* 12, no. 1 (September 1973):104-117.

21. Composed of Finance Ministers and central bank governors of participating states.

22. Triffin, op. cit., 106.

23. Department of State News Release, *Trade Patterns of the West 1972* (August 1973).

24. IMF Meetings in Washington 1972 and Nairobi 1973. Committee of Twenty meetings are usually in Washington, but also in other capitals, such as Rome in January 1974.

25. *Sixth General Report,* 1972, p. 100, 110.

26. *Seventh General Report,* 1973, p. 190.

27. *New York Times,* July 17, 1975.

28. *Time* (July 21, 1975), p. 44.

29. See *Agence Europe Bulletin,* July 15/16, 17, 1974.

30. Ibid., October 23, 1974.

31. West Germany, Belgium, Canada, France, Italy, Japan, the Netherlands, Great Britain, Sweden, and the United States.

32. Emile van Lennep, "Kurzfristige Auswirkungen der Erdolkrise und die langfristigen Probleme der Welt-Energieversorgung," *Europa Archiv,* no. 6, (1974):167-174.

33. Cf. ibid., p. 171.

34. Werner Feld, "The Competences of the European Communities for the Conduct of External Relations," *Texas Law Review,* July 1965, footnote 111.

35. The French attitude toward Euratom was made evident as early as 1961 when the French government declined to renominate strongly politically-minded and "European" Etienne Hirsch for the presidency of the Euratom Commission. Although Hirsch declared that the French president of Euratom is not in the service of France, this did not prevent his replacement by the much less political-minded and less independent Pierre Chatenet. For further details see Robert H. Beck, et al., *The Changing Structure of Europe* (Minneapolis: University of Minnesota Press, 1970), p. 20.

36. It should be noted that France has not signed the NPT and as of mid-1975, Italy, Belgium, and the Netherlands had not ratified the Treaty.

37. For details of the negotiations on this issue see Frans A. M. Alting von Geusau, *Beyond the European Community* (Leyden: A. W. Sijthoff, 1969), p. 207-214.

38. Paul C. Szasz, "International Atomic Energy Agency Safeguards," in Mason Willrich (ed.), *International Safeguards and the Nuclear Industry* (Johns Hopkins Press, 1973), p. 137. See also pp. 73-141.

39. For additional details see ibid., pp. 136-138.

40. For further details see *Second General Report,* 1968, pp. 251-255.

41. CF. *Fourth General Report,* 1970, p. 208.

42. See *Sixth General Report,* 1972, p. 235.

43. *Seventh General Report,* 1973, p. 327.

44. Ibid., p. 328.

45. See *Time,* December 3, 1973, p. 53.

46. Cf. *Die Zeit,* January 11, 1974.

47. *Bulletin of the European Communities Commission,* no. 2, 1974, p. 21.

48. *Department of State Bulletin,* March 4, 1974, pp. 230-234.

49. Henry R. Nau, "Diplomatic Uses of Technology in U.S. Energy Policy," paper presented at the Convention of the International Studies Association/South, Lexington, Kentucky, October 22-25, 1974, Cf. also his *National Politics and International Technology: Nuclear Reactor Development in Western Europe* (Baltimore: Johns Hopkins University Press, 1974).

50. For a summary review of these agreements, see Treasury Secretary William Simon's testimony before the Subcommittee on Multinational Corporations, Committee on Foreign Relations, U.S. Senate, August 12, 1974 (preprint).

51. Cf. Nau, op. cit., p. 16.

52. *Bulletin of the European Communities,* no. 2, (1974):13-21.

53. Eight EC members plus the United States, Canada, Norway, and Japan.

54. *Agence Europe Bulletin,* July 25, 1974.

55. Ibid., September 18, 1974.

56. Ibid., October 11, 1974. See also October 17, 1974.

57. John McLin, "Oil, Money, and the Common Market," West Europe Series 9, no. 2, American Universities Field Staff Reports (February 1974).

58. *Bulletin of the European Communities Commision,* no. 12 (1974): 15-16.

59. *Agence Europe Bulletin,* July 29-30, 1974.

60. Ibid., July 11, 1974.

61. Ibid.

62. Ibid., April 5, 1975.

63. For an analysis of the reasons for failure see the editorial in ibid., April 17, 1975. See also April 10, 1975 for the Community's compromise proposal.

64. Ibid., May 28, 29, 1975.

65. See ibid., June 9/10, 12, 1975.

66. See *New York Times,* July 18, 1975.

67. The Community was shocked when the United States announced an embargo on enriched uranium shipments to Europe in April 1975. However, the embargo was quickly lifted and Secretary Kissinger promised in the May meeting of IEA that there would be no delays in such shipments (*Agence Europe Bulletin,* April 17, 1975). We should note that the Community also receives enriched uranium supplies from the Soviet Union. For details see *Eighth General Report,* 1974, p. 200.

68. Willrich, *International Safeguards and Nuclear Industry* (Baltimore Johns Hopkins University Press, 1973) op. cit., pp. 49-69.

69. *Agence Europe Bulletin,* March 21, 1974.

70. See Dean Rusk's statement on this subject in December 1967 (*New York Times,* December 3, 1967); and Gerard Smith, Director of the U.S. Disarmament Agency, "The French Temptation," *Interplay* 2, no. 7, (February 1969):48-49.

71. *The Atlantic Idea and Its European Rivals* (New York: McGraw-Hill, 1966), p. 148.

72. *International Herald Tribune,* May 20, 1969.

73. *Le Monde,* May 24, 1969.

74. *Atlantic News,* April 14, 1970.

75. Lothar Ruhl, *The Nine and NATO,* the Atlantic Papers, (Paris: The Atlantic Institute for International Affairs, July 1974), p. 34.

76. *Special Report,* "Economic Interdependence and Common Defense," Washington, D.C., Department of State, October 1974.

77. For details see Thomas Jansen, "Die Institutionen," and Karl Carstens "Zusammenfassung und Ausblick" in Karl Carstens und Dieter Mahncke (eds.), *Westeuropaische Verteidigungskooperation* (Munich: R. Oldenbourg Verlag, 1972), pp. 215-235, 236-256 respectively.

78. Cf. *Le Monde,* January 17, 1973, p. 5.

79. For details see Crispin Tickell, "Enlarged Community and Security Conference," *Aussenpolitik* 25, 1(1974):13-22.

80. Ibid., 20.

81. See *Agence Europe Bulletin,* July 4, 1975.

82. Cf. Gerald L. Steibel, *Detente: Promises and Pitfalls* New York: Crane, Russak, 1975), pp. 62-66.

9

How Close to "One Voice"?

In chapter 1 we pointed out the desire of the governments and many people of the Community's member states to see Western Europe speak with one voice in world affairs. In this concluding chapter we will address ourselves to the questions of how far this aspiration has been fulfilled and what the prospects may be for the future. To what extent has the Commission succeeded in having external relations transferred to the competences of the Community institutions in accordance with the EC Treaties? How far has the intergovernmental policy coordination mechanism been able to evolve a "European" foreign policy? What has been the effect of formal and informal Community external relations activities on the process of political integration? To what degree have the EC external policies been able to translate the Community's economic power into political influence in the international arena? Finally, how have the Community's external policy actions affected the international position of the United States, and what are the future relations between the United States and the enlarged Community likely to be?

THE SIGNIFICANCE OF "EXTERNALIZATION"

For the answer to some of the above questions the concept of "externalization," developed by Philippe Schmitter in connection with neofunctionalist integration theory is relevant. Referring to a regional integration scheme such as that represented by the Community, Schmitter advanced the hypothesis that:

Once agreement is reached and made operative on a policy or set of policies pertaining to intermember or intraregional relations, participants will find themselves compelled—regardless

311

of their original intentions—to adopt common policies vis-à-vis nonparticipant third parties. Members will be forced to hammer out a collective external position (and in the process are likely to have to rely increasingly on the new central institutions to do it).[1]

Schmitter later revised and refined his hypothesis by taking into account more systematically the role of external conditions with respect to intreregional changes. He stated:

External conditions begin . . . as "givens." While the changes in national structures and values become at least partially predictable as consequences of regional decisions, the global dependence . . . of member states and the region as a whole continue to be exogenously determined for a longer time. Nevertheless, [by policy externalization, these conditions] . . . will become less exogenously determined, if integrative rather than disintegrative strategies are commonly adopted. The "independent" role of these conditions should decline as integration proceeds until joint negotiation vis-à-vis outsiders has become such an integral part of the decisional process that the [global] international system accords the new unit full participant status.[2]

Schmitter suggests that the achievement of international status of the regional unit—in our case the European Community—depends on the comparative performance of regional institutions and on the degree to which the officialdom of these institutions, that is, the Commission and its staff in particular, engage actively and deliberately in the promotion of new policies that may be acceptable to or indeed desired by national political elites.[3]

The promotion of such policies has been a major part of the struggle of the Commission to implement the provisions of the three treaties, and in particular those of the EEC Treaty dealing with external relations competences. Especially during the last years there seem to have been strong efforts made to propose common commercial policies that took into account existing national policies or that would meet national policy aspirations. Examples are the Commission's policy proposals toward Japan and the Communist countries. The successful reduction in the number of bilateral trade agreements of the member states testifies to the transfer of competences to the Community, as does the fact that many of the bilateral trade accords that remain in force are often devoid of significant substantive content. However, we must also take note of the increasing use of comprehensive economic cooperation agreements concluded by the member states with third countries. These agreements circumvent competences transferred to the Community institutions in the trade field and permit national foreign policy elites (administrative and political) to maintain maximum control over economic foreign policy matters. The motivation for the desire to maintain this control may be twofold. Economic policy action is considered an effective bargaining tool for the attainment of important national foreign policy goals. Moreover, massive control over economic matters may serve bureaucratic objectives of the national foreign service bureaucracies in retaining the strongest possible influence and power in all phases of the foreign policy decision-making process.

The formal transfer of external relations competences to the Community institutions has also been undermined by the foreign policy coordinating mechanism vested in the Political Committee and the extra-Community meetings of the Foreign Ministers of the Nine. While Commission representatives participate in meetings of these bodies when matters of concern to the Community itself are deliberated, this mechanism competes with the external relations activities of the Community in a number of areas. It reflects the need for externalization as a force toward integration in the sense of Schmitter's definition, but demonstrates that common policies can be adopted outside the Community framework with, initially at least, little benefit for the unification process. Indeed, foreign policy coordination through the Political Committee may have a disintegrative effect by achieving the same results as externalization with no cost or threat to the aspirations and objectives of national administrations and political elites. In fact, the latter may emerge strengthened from the policy coordinating mechanism since they can claim to have achieved the aim of the EC member states to speak with one voice without surrendering any meaningful layer of national sovereignty. In other words, the Political Committee and its procedures provide for many elites the best of two worlds—the image of Community power and the retention of effective control over foreign policy by the national governments.

Only when specific Community provisions (such as the tool of association) add to the arsenal of foreign policy instruments available to national policy makers; or when a provision such as the Common External Tariff necessitates the use of the Community mechanism, does it seem likely that the prospects for an effective externalization process to contribute to integration are fairly good. Clearly the instrument of association has been utilized increasingly to extend the economic sphere of influence of the Community in Africa, the Mediterranean, the Caribbean, and the Pacific and has thereby achieved added political penetration as well. Although some of the member states had various reservations at different times about the Community's association policy, all basically supported it when some of their criticisms were met. The preferential arrangements (corollaries to the associations) in the Mediterranean and with the remaining EFTA countries were also approved as sound Community policy by the governments and public in the member states, regardless of the discrimination to trade with "outsiders" caused by these agreements. Indeed, it seems that those agreements were seen as a natural consequence of the growing power of the Community, which had the "responsibility" to offer to the countries involved the special relations often sought very eagerly by their governments.

While the conclusion of association and other preferential agreements may well have produced externalization effects conducive to further integration, and continues to do so, the negotiation of trade agreements, multilaterally and with individual countries, may have been less effective in this respect. As we have seen in chapter 5 the control over the Kennedy Round negotiations by the member governments was pervasive, and new positions by these governments had to be agreed upon at every turn before the Commission representative could make new offers or accept offers by third countries. Although at times the Commission cut the Gordian knot by advancing compromises that were acceptable to all parties, the governments of the member states remained the final arbiters. The same was true also when preliminary talks about the new Round of tariff-cutting negotiations were held.[4] Close supervision and inter-EC bargaining occur also in Community negotiations on trade agreements with individual countries. The potential externalization impact has been further weakened by the recent tendency of EC member states to conclude economic cooperation accords; although we should note that the Commission is seeking to include cooperation clauses in its latest agreements with certain Latin American and Asian countries following its success with the Indian trade cooperation accord.[5] The talks with Canadian Prime Minister Trudeau in the fall of 1974 also referred to cooperation on investments and natural resources, and it seems that the inclusion of various kinds of cooperation in new trade agreements or in the renewal of such agreements has become a preferred Commission strategy. Whether this will result in a tug of war with member governments about what kind of cooperation is reserved to national agreements and what may be allowed for Community discretion is difficult to predict at this time. Clearly, access to raw materials has become so important for the economies of the member states that it will be accepted by the national governments in whatever form it can be achieved. New Community association agreements clearly will be concerned about this point as well.

The Generalized Preference System is an outgrowth of the provision on the CET and therefore requires uniform management. Changes in this system can be made only after agreement by the member governments, and thus need the adoption of common positions. However, externalization effects upon integration flowing from changes in the preference system are likely to be very minor because the bargaining involved among member governments usually relates to their jockeying for better relations with individual Third World countries and pertains to particular products on a case-to-case basis.

As we have seen, the right to active diplomatic representation has been granted to the Community by the member states only grudgingly and with limitations. The breakthrough was the authorization for the Commission to appoint a diplomatic representative with ambassadorial rank to Washington in 1972.

Additional diplomatic missions are being authorized gradually, with Tokyo and Ottawa the next sites. We should stress that these missions represent the Commission and not the Community as a collective unit. The diplomatic prerogatives of the member states *qua* nation–states remain, and are guarded jealously; the Community's ambassador in Washington, while fully accredited to the U.S. government, is not really regarded as an equal by the ambassadors of most of the member states. Policy coordination and consultation among the member state embassies in Washington and other capitals of the world are nothing more than a reflection of such activities in the Political Committee, and therefore no externalization consequences flow from the establishment of the Commission's rights for diplomatic representation.

Similar conclusions must be drawn from the grant of observer status to the Commission by the United Nations. Some policy coordination between EC member states in the U.N. has always taken place; in fact, analysts of General Assembly voting behavior have always considered the member states as a subgroup among the Western groups of U.N. members. With the Federal Republic of Germany finally joining the United Nations as a full member, granting the Community's observer status was a natural consequence. However, it is doubtful that this status will enhance the cohesion of the Community or produce any measurable prointegrative effect. The divergences of opinion and positions expressed by EC member governments participating in international conferences such as UNCTAD, where the Community was also represented by observers from the Commission and sometimes from the Council of Ministers,[6] and the frequent inability of these observers to reach consensus of all Community participants, appear to confirm this judgment.

EXTERNAL CONDITIONS AND EXTERNALIZATION

Regional units such as the Community or countries within a region for which appropriate conditions exist to embark on an economic or perhaps political integration scheme may be forced

HOW CLOSE TO "ONE VOICE"?

into policy externalization by actions or perceived intentions of extraregional governments and interests.[7] The strong desire for European unification that was manifest during the 1950s was stimulated by the perception of an outside threat—namely feared Soviet expansion toward Western Europe. It was in part this perceived threat that motivated the governments of the original Six to establish the ECSC and these motives may also have had a subtle minor influence in the decision to set up the EEC and Euratom.

The discrimination against "outsiders" inherent in regional integration schemes based on customs unions or free trade areas is apt to generate reactions by third country governments and nongovernmental entities such as large business corporations to overcome the discriminating features through various means, and perhaps to participate in the benefits "insiders" derive from this scheme. The strategies of American multinational corporations to surmount Community discrimination have been the establishment or expansion of subsidiaries in the Common Market or the acquisition of existing European companies. This raised the threat of domination of Community industries by American multinational enterprises (MNEs)—a threat that might force policy externalization and thereby provide impetus to political integration. Jean-Jacques Servan-Schreiber's book, *The American Challenge*[8] sounded the trumpet for West European industry to close ranks and to meet the challenge of American business giants by promoting the creation of large European companies through mergers and transnational joint enterprises. Without such developments, which would perhaps result in a Community-wide industrial division of labor under European auspices, it was argued that European independence might be impaired. However, despite widespread condemnation of American domination of the European economy and the acknowledgments of the need for large transnational European enterprises to combat superior American technology and managerial skill, most elites and the bulk of the public in the Community countries did not perceive that European independence in general was seriously threatened. In this connection, a poll conducted in France during February and March 1970, is interesting. According to this poll, the majority of Frenchmen were in favor of American investments in France. Only one person in four declared that American investments in France were positively harmful to French interests, although the proportion rose to one in three among farmers and one in two among members of the Communist Party. The strongest support came from people in the 20–34 age group and from industrial executives and members of the liberal professions.[9]

Although in March 1970 France proposed a common position on investments from third countries that would contain subtle provisions against U.S. interests, the Commission rejected such a strategy, which would erect barriers against such investments or impose restrictions on the activities of foreign MNEs in the Community. However, it advocated minor advantages to European firms when bidding on public contracts for the delivery of goods and services. Thus, on the whole, American MNE operations in Europe have not lead to policy externalization of consequence to the process of political integration.[10] Whether the beginning wave of large-scale investments in Community firms by Arab oil producing countries (e.g., Iran in the German firm of Krupp) will produce a different externalization effect in the future cannot be judged at present.[11] In the meantime, European multinational firms and large national companies aspiring to multinational status increasingly have established subsidiaries outside the Community and especially in the United States. In fact, investments by EC companies in America have risen much more rapidly during the last few years than during the 1950s and 1960s, rising nearly 20 percent from 1973 to 1974. This increase in establishing subsidiaries abroad by Community firms can be regarded as an indirect kind of externalization response, although its immediate effect on integration is likely to be minimal.

The decision announced by President Nixon in August 1971 to terminate convertibility of dollars into gold, and impose a 10 percent import surcharge was, at least in part, a reaction to Community discrimination toward outsiders and an exertion of outside pressure on the Community. The prospects of the first American trade deficit combined with the continuing outflow of dollars and the increasingly unsettled exchange markets were the

318

major reasons for this decision, which materially affected trans-atlantic relations. The announcement shocked the Community leadership, Great Britain, and Japan, whose governments had not been consulted in advance. The American measures were meant in part (and seen by the Six and others) as tactics to gain unilateral trade concessions and force favorable realignment in exchange rates. In response, the Community leaders adopted a rapidly hardening common position strongly condemning these measures, In cooperation with other West European countries and Japan they succeeded in compelling the United States to drop the surcharge after a little more than three months. At the same time French President Pompidou accepted a compromise regarding the revaluation of the franc in exchange for dollar devaluation during a meeting with President Nixon in the Azores in December 1971. Policy externalization was achieved as the result of American pressures, but the effect upon political integration was minor and not lasting.

The best means to overcome the trade discrimination of the Community toward outsiders caused by the Common Market and the various preferential arrangements would be pressures toward the full elimination of tariffs and quantitative restrictions among all of the EC's trading partners. Although the Trade Expansion Act of 1962 contained authority for tariff elimination on certain products traded between the United States and the Community; and although the trade legislation of 1974 gives the President even more far-reaching authority in this respect, the full abandonment of tariffs is a political impossibility almost anywhere at the present time.[12] Nevertheless, as we have seen in chapters 4, 5, and 7, pressures have been exerted by both developed countries—especially the United States—and developing countries to reduce the discrimination against the exports of their products caused by special and reverse preferences granted to affiliated states. Indeed, these pressures have shown some success, especially as far as broadening the generalized preference system is concerned. But apart from internal bargaining among the member states on the details of the concessions, they have not intensified policy externalization among the EC member governments beyond the common position taken in support of the maintenance of the Common Market in general and of the association and preferential arrangements policies in particular.

As discussed in chapter 5, during prenegotiations for another round of reductions of tariffs and nontariff barriers, the United States attempted to link trade, monetary, and security matters, hoping that the final outcome of the overall bargaining would be a package deal of benefits and concessions in all three areas. The Community countries were more or less unanimous in rejecting this strategy, although parallel negotiations on trade and monetary matters appeared to be inevitable, a fact that was recognized in Brussels. No particular gains for the integration process were derived from this common stand by the Community countries, which really was nothing more than a continuation of the negotiating system begun with the Dillon and Kennedy Rounds.

We have discussed in the preceding chapter the "European" option in the defense field within or outside NATO, especially the desirability and feasibility of a European nuclear force, and the activities and aims of the Eurogroup. Although with the exception of Ireland, all EC member states also belong to NATO (France adheres to the NATO Treaty but does not participate in the organizational tasks), NATO actions, procedures, and objectives constitute an external element as far as the Community is concerned. Indeed the security of the Community and its member states depends on what NATO decides, and this includes the decision as to whether American tactical and strategic nuclear weapons are to be employed in case of aggression from the Soviet bloc. These weapons are completely under the control of the U.S. government.

With a number of Europeans being doubtful about American resolve to employ nuclear weapons if only minor targets were attacked by East Bloc forces with atomic arms, this situation is perceived by some officials in the EC member states as near-intolerable dependence of the Community on outside forces.[13] If such sentiments of dependence on NATO and the American strategic deterrent were to spread widely and generate discussions in the Community countries about the need of true and dependable European defense systems with all decisions made by nationals of the member states, would this not lead to some degree of policy externalization in the defense sector and thereby give new impetus to the creation of political union? Perhaps the European Council (formerly known as the summit meetings of the heads of government) could be given the additional function of deciding about security and defense matters. While affirmative answers to these questions may conjure up pleasing vistas for staunch prointegrationists, in the real world of domestic and international politics little policy externalization and even less impetus for political integration can be expected from this scenario in the foreseeable future. Such developments would diminish the defensive value of NATO because of divisions and frictions among its members. Even if the Community countries were to assume jointly the enormous expenditures necessary to build an independent, viable, conventional and nuclear force (a dubious assumption, considering domestic political priorities), it is very unlikely that their security could be assured against the great military power of the Soviet bloc. The other six NATO members, and of course especially the United States, would still be needed for an essential security guarantee. Nor does it make much sense to argue that the "European" force could serve as a complement to a reduced NATO or act as its "deputy" because simply by being a separate unit with its own command structure, it would adversely affect the total combat effectiveness. Finally, any plans for an independent Community armed force would arouse the suspicion of the Soviet Union, as French President Giscard d'Estaing has correctly prognosticated,[14] because it would introduce an uncertain element of asymmetry into the existing strategic balance, and would reduce the predictability of action in the Western camp. In fact, it may be precisely a unified NATO with strong support by all member states that could provide the proper security umbrella under which externalization of most foreign policy fields by the Community might make progress, and thereby contribute to the construction of a political union.

The greatest extraregional challenge (and at the same time the greatest opportunity for policy externalization with a powerful effect on the progress of integration) has been the energy crisis. We have seen in chapter 8 that in the face of the overall reduction of oil production by the Arab oil producers, coupled with the steep price rise, the imposition of an embargo on one of the member states (the Netherlands), initially not only did not strengthen solidarity within the Community, but in fact led to its erosion. Indeed, Belgium, Britain, and Italy imposed restrictions on the export of petroleum products to other EC member states. The spectacle of the foreign ministers of the Arab oil producing countries invading and mesmerizing the Copenhagen summit meeting of 1973 demonstrated the impotence of the Community and its surrender to outside challenges. Despite the Commission's efforts to induce all member states to adopt a common position, various member governments found convenient reasons, dictated by selfish national interests, to dissociate themselves from cooperation and a coordinated stand. Although dependencies of the member states on Arab oil producers vary, with Italy relying on imported oil for 74 percent of its energy needs and Britain for only 48 percent, it does not necessarily follow that independent action is the proper course; in fact, it is self-defeating in the long run. Because of the advanced stage of interdependence among the economies of the EC countries, individual policies of demand restrictions and import curbs as well as controls on capital movements cannot work. Indeed, such policies are likely to disintegrate and destroy the Community.

As we have pointed out in the preceding chapter, the Commission has attempted to play a role in various international groups that have been set up to coordinate policy of the major consumer countries vis-à-vis the oil producers. It participated as a full member in the Euro–Arab dialogue, which brought together representatives of the Commission, the Council of Ministers, the nine member states, and twenty countries of the Arab League. It assisted in working parties in Europe and the Middle East to study concrete problems of development in poor Arab countries, technical assistance, investment, etc.[15] But despite these activities and repeated policy proposals on the use and conservation of energy in Europe in order to scale down the burgeoning deficits in the Community's balance of payments, no *effective* policy externalization has taken place in the energy field. The root cause for this failure may not only be divergent national interests and foreign policy goals of the member states, but also (as suggested by former Chancellor Willy Brandt) the existence of wide gaps between the economic situations in the member states.[16] In fact, Brandt was fearful that the danger of the collapse of the Community was real, echoing a statement by Jean Sauvagnargues, French Foreign Minister, that "the priority of priorities is to avoid the disintegration of the Common Market . . . Europe today needs masons more than architects."[17] Perhaps Jon McLin of the American Universities Field Staff is right when he says that the main task before the Commission and the Community will be "to prevent the unravelling of past achievements. Instances where the challenge will be particularly acute are the customs union, threatened with ever more [national] import restrictions, and the liberalized regime for capital movements, which is already infringed by Italy and Britain."[18] Progress in integration will come again only after the process of disintegration has been halted completely.

On balance, then, external conditions have not produced much policy externalization that could pave the way for further unification progress. Common positions have been adopted by member states on a number of foreign policy issues in the trade and monetary fields, but their common positions were more often reached on the basis of intergovernmental contacts and relations than within the Community framework of decision making. Perhaps the most potent device of the Community system to achieve uniform approaches to foreign economic policy problems has been the imperative of the Common External Tariff; but beyond this, some of the external challenges were met only through the intergovernmental instrument of the Political Committee,[19] which produced the necessary coordination to evolve common positions of the Six and later Nine.

It has always been an interesting question whether transnational cooperation as manifested in the Political Committee constitutes a learning process for the participating officials, and whether learned habits acquired through such transnational cooperation could favorably affect the integrative progress of the Community. EC civil servants attend some of the Political Committee meetings and working party sessions, suggesting that

323

cooperation in these bodies brings together not only national bureaucrats but also a number of Eurocrats. Could the fact of these two groups of officials working together on shared problems of foreign policy, combined with the repeatedly expressed desire of Europe's need to speak with one voice produce tendencies on the part of the national officials to transfer at least all economic and monetary foreign policy competences to the Community institutional framework, thereby aiding political integration? While it seems recognized that cooperation habits can indeed be learned, several arguments are sufficiently persuasive to answer this question largely in the negative. We have already pointed out in chapter 2 that getting to know the Community and integration as experienced by thousands of national civil servants in their involvement in many EC countries did not produce automatic love affairs.[20] In addition, bureaucratic traditions and considerations of power and prestige are likely to prompt the national foreign office officials to seek the full retention of their foreign policy control and prerogatives whenever possible. Moreover, the national officials tend to hold the administrative capabilities of the Eurocracy in low esteem, a view that reaches the ministerial level in some states such as Germany.[21] Finally, full national sovereignty and sentiments of nationalism continue to hold their fatal attraction for the member governments and will not be abandoned unless immediate economic benefits such as greater business opportunities from an enlarged and unified market or higher incomes for farmers can be gained. As a consequence, it seems doubtful that in the foreseeable future Community competences will be broadened in the foreign policy field as the result of the Political Committee's activities or that political unification will gain new impetus.

In summary, while the Commission has succeeded in fleshing out the competences for external relations assigned to it by the EC Treaties, the struggle has not been won completely. In particular, the Community's commercial policy toward Communist countries and with Japan lacks full control by the Community institutions; and the continued conclusion of bilateral economic cooperation agreements by some of the member states impairs the Commission's assigned authority in external relations. On the other hand, the Political Committee's policy coordinating activities have contributed materially to the formulation of "European" foreign policies in the economic and political spheres; and coordination has reached into the security field, as demonstrated particularly by the joint approach of the EC states toward the negotiations on the European Security Conference. However, the successful coordination mechanism has not resulted in a "spillover," whereby new external competences were transferred by the member states to the Community institutions. Learned habits of cooperation between national foreign service officials and Eurocrats are unlikely to have a favorable effect in initiating such a spillover, at least in the foreseeable future.

THE FUTURE OF COMMUNITY–U.S. RELATIONS

We have discussed in some detail various aspects of the Community–U.S. relationship: problems and conflicting attitudes on trade and monetary matters; American displeasure with EC preferential arrangements and their political implications; European displeasure with high-handed American monetary policies and nonfulfillment of the ASP pledge; misunderstandings and only limited collaboration in the energy crisis; and how to deal with security matters and "burden-sharing." Part of the American malaise stems from the not surprising, but seemingly not really anticipated, expansion of the Community's economic power, looked upon with a combination of jealousy and mistrust. Part of the European malaise stems from the understandable unwillingness to accept any longer the continuing treatment as the junior partner in the Atlantic relationship nearly thirty years after the creation of NATO. The Europeans want full recognition from Washington of their political independence and of their global, not only "regional," interests in world affairs. They don't want to be considered an economic giant and a political dwarf. They want to be consulted on American policies and actions vis-à-vis the Soviet Union and China, and have a paranoiac fear of any U.S. agreement with these two powers being concluded at Western Europe's expense.

Despite the Community's economic muscle, the realities of security and energy compel an appreciable level of dependency of the EC countries on the United States, regardless of what European aspirations may be. Eurogroup cooperation and even a European nuclear force (if the many problems discussed in the preceding chapter could be overcome) does not guarantee Western Europe's independence, no matter how appealing this objective may be. West European power alone cannot insure its security vis-à-vis the Soviet Union, which, if it chooses, is the only country that in the foreseeable future is likely to threaten Western Europe's independence by means of war or overwhelming military pressure. Even if Western Europe or the Community had achieved political unity, it would still have to rely on the United States to manage any crisis with the Soviet Union, and it would depend on the Middle East for oil. If the delivery of oil were to be subjected again to an embargo, and this embargo would be more intense than that of the fall of 1973, only the United States could aid in alleviating the resulting crisis by sharing its resources with the Community countries. As for security and military defense, there cannot be any uncoupling of Western Europe from the global deterrence of American strategic power. Thus, the Community and the United States are condemned to continued alliance and solidarity. As Lothar Ruehl states correctly:

> Solidarity with the United States in time of major crisis is not a matter of choice for its European allies. . . . It is a physical fact and must be regarded as such by all, and particularly by a potential enemy, who would have to reckon with the whole NATO war potential whatever the European governments or a supranational European government might publicly declare. This is the essence of "strategic solidarity" in an alliance between "non-equals." . . . The political status of Western Europe would not essentially change this situation.

Moreover,

> ... if a conflict of such importance took place on an East–
> West axis of confrontation and the United States were forced
> to intervene militarily, there could be no neutrality and no
> restriction to the use of American troops and American
> arms stationed in allied countries even if they wished to re-
> main uninvolved.[22]

The policy implications flowing from these analyses are
loud and clear. The United States and the European Community must cooperate to the greatest extent possible in the
years to come. Policies must be developed that provide mutual strength, and the continuing squabbles about lack of consultation and the desire for independence, especially on the
part of the Europeans must be subdued. Cooperation requires
some kind of burden sharing on the part of the Europeans,
and greater willingness of the U.S. government to see Europe
as an equal partner in the defense of the Atlantic Community.
In the face of mounting inflation, defense expenditures must
be rationalized by the American and European contingents
of NATO—otherwise, a declining economy in the industrialized
countries could make a shambles of the defense structure built
up since 1948.

The strategic interdependence of America and Western
Europe has been strengthened by the bleak energy picture. The
outlook for lower prices for crude oil is poor, and unless the
consuming countries can bury their search for national advantages in dealing with the Arab producing countries, the custom-
ary way of life in the Atlantic countries is likely to suffer
severely. During the first 10 months of 1974 the OPEC countries received $75 billion, of which $30 billion was used for
importing goods and services.[23] The remainder was invested in
various capital markets, with the United States receiving the
lion's share. However, for the industrialized countries these
investments provide few reasons for satisfaction, since many of
them are only of short-term duration. A large share of the goods
imported by the OPEC countries is military hardware, which
may give rise to concern over a shift of power not only in terms

of money but also in terms of strategic advantages. It does not matter whether the European Community or the United States obtains a larger proportion of the orders placed for these goods, because, in the long run, only concerted action by the consumer countries to influence a reduction in the price of crude oil will provide a satisfactory solution to the economic problems. Thus there is an equally strong imperative for economic cooperation and concerted action between America and Western Europe as there is in the strategic field.

Although domestic political forces will work powerfully against the adoption of rational coordinated policies in both the military and economic fields, perhaps the stark necessity for such policies as a matter of survival will gradually be recognized by the policy makers on both sides of the Atlantic. Only by following this pattern will it be possible for the EC countries as well as the United States and Canada to retain the international political leverage necessary to assure the security and well-being of their citizens and the integrity of their way of life.

In their relations with the Third World, more emphasis on cooperation rather than competition between the European Community and the United States would also be healthy. Clearly, the EC association policy, with its web of personal relationships between high officials and politicians of the Community and affiliated countries has had a significant political impact throughout the whole Third World. While the resulting discrimination of outsiders has been painful to many developing countries, it has also served as a powerful magnet, prompting many governments to seek privileged relations with the Community. The limited generalized preference system and the commitment to commodity price stabilization schemes have been used actively by the EC institutions as means to respond favorably to loud complaints of individual Third World countries and at the same time to present itself as the champion of some of the general UNCTAD demands. Yet, if concrete actions on the part of the EC in this field produce benefits for particular Third World countries, all economically advanced countries including the United States will profit. In fact, such actions may induce the U.S. government to speed up the introduction of a generalized preference system of its own, and could furnish practical experience that would make it possible for the U.S. wait-and-see attitude regarding commodity stabilization agreements to be translated into either active support or perhaps complete rejection.

In the field of raw materials cooperation between the Community and the United States is especially imperative. Practices of any kind of preemption should be renounced, and cooperative mechanisms within the framework of the OECD, similar to the International Energy Agency's procedures for sharing oil under emergency conditions, should be instituted. Although the United States has been historically opposed to commodity agreements, and has not found its limited experience in such accords very satisfactory, it needs to take a second look. Perhaps approaches such as joint ventures involving private enterprises and government agencies in developed and developing countries, similar to those the Community is likely to use,[24] might be useful vehicles for the United States as well. America has great expertise, management skills, and marketing knowledge in this field, acquired in large part by its multinational corporations over many years of intensive extraction activities of many natural resources. Of course, use of joint ventures also carries with it the danger of severe competition, and therefore requires coordination between the EC and the United States through the OECD or any other specialized caucus. The last thing the Community and the United States could afford would be the world's slipping into competing blocs, one led by Western Europe, and comprised of Africa, and perhaps part of Asia; and the other under the leadership of the United States, including Latin America, perhaps Japan, Australia, and New Zealand.[25] The strategies developed to deal with access to raw materials must be carefully attuned by all Western industrialized countries— this includes Japan—on a global basis and with due consideration of the constraints of economic interdependence. In these coordination efforts essential defense needs must not be overlooked.

To achieve greater harmony across the Atlantic it may be necessary to have periodic summit meetings of heads of governments from the Community countries, the United States, and Canada.[26] The growing complexity of transatlantic relations makes such meetings necessary, and they should be held at least once a year. While the various summit meetings of the EC countries have not always met the expectations of all parties concerned, they have become a valuable instrument for reaching a consensus on some salient issues. If regular Atlantic summit meetings could achieve at least this goal they would fulfill an important purpose essential for the security and economic well-being of the Western world. This is all the more important now since the Community has become involved in a triangular relationship with the Soviet Union and the People's Republic of China, in which China is becoming an advocate of the Community as a legal entity and a very desirable trading partner, while the Soviet Union retains its basic opposition to the Community system and its procedures. This relationship, added to the pervasive impact of the Community on Third World affairs, reflects the growing political influence that the Community is likely to exert on the international system as a whole.

NOTES

1. Philippe C. Schmitter, "Three Neo-Functional Hypotheses about Regional Integration," *International Organization* 23 (Winter 1969):165.

2. "A Revised Theory of Regional Integration," *International Organization* 24 (Autumn 1970):848.

3. Philippe C. Schmitter, *Autonomy or Dependence as Regional Integration Outcomes: Central America*, Research Series, no. 17, Institute of International Studies, University of California, Berkeley, 1972, p. 7.

4. In Europe these negotiations are often called the "Tokyo" Round because it is in that city that the preliminary talks opened.

5. See chapter 7.

6. See chapter 7 for details.

7. Cf. Schmitter, *Autonomy or Dependency as Regional Integration Outcomes: Central America*, p. 8.

8. (New York: Atheneum, 1968).

9. *Journal of Commerce* (March 10, 1970).

10. Cf. Werner J. Feld, *Transnational Business Collaboration Among Common Market Countries* (New York: Praeger, 1970), p. 112–114 for details.

11. See *Times Picayune* (New Orleans) November 30, 1974, for further details.

12. Cf. William Diebold, Jr., "U.S. Trade Policy: The New Political Dimensions," *Foreign Affairs*, 52, no. 3 (April 1974):474–496.

13. See editorial in *Agence Europe Bulletin*, May 30, 1975.

14. Ibid.

15. Ibid., November 20, 1974.

16. Ibid., November 21, 1974.

17. Quoted in Jon McLin, *Oil, Money, and the Common Market* (American Universities Field Staff: West Europe Series, vol. 9 no. 2) 1974, p. 5.

18. Ibid., p. 12.

19. See chapter 2; sometimes still called the Davignon Committee.

20. See p. 51.

21. See Werner Feld, "The National Bureaucracies of the EEC Member States and Political Integration: A Preliminary Inquiry," in Robert S. Jordan (ed.), *International Administration: Its Evolution and Contemporary Applications* (New York: Oxford University Press, 1971), pp. 228–244, especially 237–240; and McLin, op. cit., p. 10.

22. Lothar Ruehl, "The Nine and NATO," *The Atlantic Papers*, 2 (1974):43.

23. *Agence Europe*, November 27, 29, 1974.

24. pp. 244, 245, 246 and *Agence Europe Bulletin*, June 6, 1975.

25. Cf. Ernest H. Pregg, *Economic Blocs and U.S. Foreign Policy* (Washington, D.C.: National Planning Association, 1974), especially p. 11.

26. Curt Gasteyger, "Europe and America at the Crossroads," *The Atlantic Papers* 4 (1971) (Paris: The Atlantic Institute), pp. 49–50.

INDEX

Note: The lower-case n following page numbers refers to information contained in end-of chapter Notes.

336